Studies in International, Transnational and Global Communications

Um angesichts zunehmender Globalisierung Kommunikationsprozesse und Medienentwicklungen zu verstehen, ist eine Perspektiverweiterung über staatliche und kulturelle Grenzen hinweg unerlässlich. Eine Vielzahl von medienvermittelter Kommunikation entwickelt sich jenseits von oder quer zu nationalstaatlichen Grenzen. Gleichzeitig gilt es, die Beharrungskräfte von Nationalstaaten nicht zu vernachlässigen und in vergleichenden Perspektiven Unterschiede und Gemeinsamkeiten bei Medienentwicklungen in verschiedenen Ländern und Regionen herauszuarbeiten und zu erklären. Studien zu Formen medienvermittelter Kommunikation in allen Weltregionen sollen helfen, den Blick für Phänomene der Globalisierung und ihrer Auswirkungen auf Medien und Kommunikation zu erweitern.

Die Reihe ist offen für eine Bandbreite an Feldern der Kommunikationswissenschaft, für die internationale und transnationale Ansätze konstitutiv sind oder fruchtbar gemacht werden können, wie zum Beispiel Auslands- und Kriegsberichterstattung, Journalismusforschung, Public Diplomacy, Medien und Transformation, politische Kommunikation, Mediensystemforschung (Medienpolitik, Medienökonomie), Nutzungsforschung, Medien und Migration. Genauso sind unterschiedliche theoretische und methodische Zugänge der sozialwissenschaftlichen Forschung willkommen. Die Reihe soll dabei sowohl aktuelle Fall- und Länderstudien als auch Überblicksdarstellungen beinhalten.

In the face of increasing globalization, understanding communication processes and media developments requires a widening of perspective beyond national and cultural boundaries. A multitude of mediated communications is developing beyond or across national borders. At the same time, it is important not to neglect the enduring force of nation-states, and to identify and explain differences and similarities in media developments in various countries and regions using comparative perspectives. Studies on forms of mediated communication in all regions of the world should help to broaden the view on the phenomena of globalization and their impact on media and communication.

The series is open for a variety of topics related to international and transnational communication, such as foreign and war reporting, comparative journalism research and political communications, public diplomacy, media and transformation, media systems research (media policy, media economics), audience research, media and migration. Theoretical and methodological approaches from different social sciences are welcome. The series intends to include current case studies and country-specific studies as well as broader overviews.

More information about this series at http://www.springer.com/series/15233

Carola Richter · Anna Antonakis
Cilja Harders
Editors

Digital Media and the Politics of Transformation in the Arab World and Asia

Springer VS

Editors
Carola Richter
Institute for Media and Communication Studies
Freie Universität Berlin
Berlin, Germany

Cilja Harders
Otto Suhr Institute of Political Science
Freie Universität Berlin
Berlin, Germany

Anna Antonakis
Freie Universität Berlin
Berlin, Germany

Studies in International, Transnational and Global Communications
ISBN 978-3-658-20699-4 ISBN 978-3-658-20700-7 (eBook)
https://doi.org/10.1007/978-3-658-20700-7

Library of Congress Control Number: 2018936520

Springer VS

Printed on acid-free paper

This Springer VS imprint is published by the registered company Springer Fachmedien Wiesbaden GmbH part of Springer Nature
The registered company address is: Abraham-Lincoln-Str. 46, 65189 Wiesbaden, Germany

Table of Contents

Introduction: Digital Media and the Politics of Transformation – a Dialectical and Multi-Scalar Reading

Carola Richter, Anna Antonakis and Cilja Harders

Indisputably, media cannot be ignored when analyzing political and societal transformation processes. Historically, media have always played a role in reshaping public debates and reorganizing social and political hierarchies (see, e.g. Armbrust, 2012 or Fahmy, 2011 for a historical perspective on the role of media in the Middle East). In recent times of digitalization, the process of mediatization, i.e. of incorporating media into everyday life communication, has increased tremendously (Hepp & Krotz, 2014). Thus, since the beginning of the century, hopes rose that with decentralized digital means of communication literally everybody would get a say in shaping our social and political life (Shirky, 2008; Castells, 2011). While "ordinary people" (Bayat, 2009) incorporated new media technologies into their quotidian life, other actors strategically used them to disseminate their agenda, while established rulers had to adapt to the challenges and opportunities of these technologies as well. In communication studies as well as in political sciences, the seminal uprisings in the Arab world in 2010/2011 have inspired a lot of rather techno-euphoric research that emphasized the transformative role of digital media, in particular in authoritarian countries (Richter & Badr, 2016). Meanwhile, however, other scholars have highlighted the new possibilities of authoritarian regimes to actually better control the public sphere through digital media (Morozov, 2011). Zeynep Tufekci refers to authoritarian learning when she notes that governments "have developed methods to respond to this new information environment" (Tufekci, 2014, p. 2). Moreover, Kranzberg's famous dictum of technology as not being neutral seems to be more relevant than ever – algorithms developed by corporate companies increasingly determine what can be seen and said via digital media (Fuchs, 2014). Thus, "algorithmic harms" influence new digital public spheres and shape attention economies (Tufekci, 2015; 2017).

Against this background, this book takes a deeper look at how digital media relate to social and political transformations and emphasizes that they can only be

C. Richter et al. (Hrsg.), *Digital Media and the Politics of Transformation in the Arab World and Asia*, Studies in International, Transnational and Global Communications, https://doi.org/10.1007/978-3-658-20700-7_1

understood while analyzing interlocking political and technological developments. These developments happen on different scales ranging from the global to the local, including nation states' regulatory efforts, global corporate policies and regional or local actors' strategies in coping with, adapting to or resisting such policies.

Much political science literature on the uprisings of 2010/11 has been focusing on the question whether political change in the sense of regime change happened and if so, to what degree. *Transition* in this sense implies more than a change of government and is thought to describe the transition from authoritarian to democratic rule, often in stages such as liberalization, democratization and finally consolidation (Merkel, 2010). *Transformation*, in contrast, encompasses a broader notion of mid-term to long-term political and social change, below and beyond the regime elites in power. Transformation and transition are linked, but not in a purely functionalist way in the sense that any socio-political or economic transformation necessarily leads to a change in power structures. Rather, as Harders (2013) among others has argued, the widening gap between young, dynamic, and globally connected societies and ossified regime elites was a major source of a deep crisis of legitimacy, which has fed into the mass uprisings in the Maghreb, Mashriq and the Gulf 2010/11 and in Iran already in 2009. Meanwhile, it became aptly clear that through practicing street and virtual politics, people claimed to be part of the public sphere and themselves created new publics, while at the same time, a dynamic process was set in motion, in which oppositional forces and the regime forces alike learned from their respective practices. The "Politics of Transformation" thus includes both (media) strategies and tactics that societal actors use to push for social and/or political changes *and* strategies and measures that institutionalized or governmental actors use to control, prevent or hijack these actions. Transformation in this sense refers to the changes in practices that result from building new competencies and negotiating meanings via media technologies. The contributors to the present volume discuss several types of such interaction dynamics, ranging from building a group's identity as in the case of Iranian women's rights groups or Arab anarchists, to creating public forums for deliberation as in the case of Egypt's constitutional debates or Tunisia's feminist activists, to, finally, creating spaces of support for authoritarian governance as in China's Weibo services. This also includes the creation of new networks and enabling "scale shifts" in coordinated protest actions, leading to a "broader contention involving a wider range of actors and bridging their claims and identities" as social movement scholars McAdam, Tarrow and Tilly hold (2001, p. 331). At the same time, the contributors stress the fragility of these mediatized identities, their volatility and the constraints that actors live through or perceive. (Self-)censorship, as the case of the Palestinian blogosphere illustrates, limits the possibilities of imagining change within the online communities and in relation to the wider society.

The contributions in this volume all emphasize the dialectical relations of digital media and transformation because new opportunities come with new constraints (see also Cammaerts, 2015; Radloff, 2013; Youmans & York, 2012; Deibert, 2008). Each author uses an actor-centered perspective to shed light on the current cases of political and social transformation in the Arab world and Asian countries. By choosing a country-based approach this book seeks to inquire into the ways digital media are employed in the context of restricted media systems and state-dominated public spheres. It features original research about various social and political actors that can be seen as active challengers of the status quo in their respective countries, such as women's rights activists, public intellectuals, anarchists, youth movements and Islamists. The authors apply different theoretical lenses to make sense of the politics of transformation, such as social movement theory, actor-network theory, Bourdieu's field theory or a public sphere approach. At the same time, different qualitative and quantitative methods, such as network analysis, content analysis and discourse analysis as well as interviews, are used to find out more about the actors' intentions, tactics and valuations as well as their structural embeddedness. This broadness in theory and methodology highlights the diversity of approaches to the politics of transformation and also mirrors the interdisciplinarity of our approach.

We would like to stress three aspects that emerge from such an analysis of the manifold links between socio-economic contexts, communication infrastructures, and political contexts and that are highlighted by the authors of this volume:

1. Analyzing *power relations on different levels and scales* is key to understanding the multifaceted role of media in the politics of transformation. Anna Antonakis reminds us that international power relations and the unequal distribution of resources as well as national structural constraints must be taken into consideration. Using a case study in Egypt, Hanan Badr, for example, points to a specific local political culture in which pressures from powerful political actors are at work that cannot be neglected in the analysis. Reviewing the case of Weibo-communication in China, Zihao Lin, Andrea Hamm and Susanne Reinhardt show that through the joint power of the state and companies, grassroots empowerment can effectively be curbed. Almut Woller and Anna Antonakis point to the algorithms of Facebook and other social media that do not necessarily support the politics of transformation because they censor content that does not seem appropriate aligned with the company guidelines. Thus, it seems too simplistic to speak of "liberation technologies" as Larry Diamond has done (Diamond, 2010). Actually, the analysis of power relations is not only important for authoritarian

states but also goes even beyond the authoritarianism-democracy distinction or the issue of what regime type we investigate. The main questions that need to be explored are: Who has power over which technologies – visibly and invisibly – and how is this power implemented? We need a concerted effort to answer these questions by focusing on different levels of analysis. As other authors have put it, "[s]tudying the technical operation of information controls and the political and social context behind them is an inherently multidisciplinary exercise" (Crete-Nishihata, Deibert & Senft, 2013, p. 34).

2. By emphasizing the strong impacts of multi-scale and intersecting power relations at work, all of the contributors *warn us against overestimating the often hoped-for democratizing effects of digital media* on the national level. Lin, Hamm and Reinhardt emphasize with regard to China that the "beautiful world of the Internet" does not simply change everything – in particular when looking at the hierarchies of who gets to speak and who can be heard. This approach is echoed by Abir Kopty, who analyzes the connectivity among activists in Palestine. She, similarly to Mina Naeli, focuses on the problems related to the competition between activists. Naeli concludes that the fragmentation and individualization pushed by social media can overrule a sense of community among the activists that is actually needed to fight for a common cause. Antonakis takes up the idea of a "forced reliance" (Kazansky, 2016, p. 192) of activists on social media and highlights, similarly to Naeli, the skepticism activists now tend to raise about Facebook and other social media networks because the actors' output on those networks seems to privilege self-promotion over the actual cause. Antonakis in Tunisia and Badr in Egypt show the pitfalls of deliberation via social media during what was claimed to be a democratic transition process. There are still dominant national and international actors rebuilding offline hierarchies online – but also new hierarchies are being built among the actors themselves. These findings feed the observation that the right to talk is not equal to the power to be heard.
3. What can be noted on a more positive side is that *digital media enables a greater visibility of actors* and their issues to like-minded people and allows ideas to circulate. Merlyna Lim puts it this way: "Imagination allows the collectives to envision a more desirable future". The effects of the visibility of the "self" and the "other" are also highlighted by Naeli with regard to the women's rights movement in Iran and in Woller's description of Arab anarchists. Both show that digital media help to diffuse materials regionally and globally that can be incorporated into one's own local tactics. At the same time, the feeling of belonging to a broader community is emphasized through the vis-à-vis visibility. This does not necessarily lead to community-building and networking – in both the virtual and the physical way. In a more critical perspective, Antonakis points

to "multifaceted visibilities" with regards to the different resources of actors impacting the new constraints and opportunities of "being visible". Thus, the authors of this volume do not necessarily comply with the impression of the early literature on the "Arab Spring" that digital media can actually mobilize people at the drop of a hat to take to the streets. Lim instead explores the short- and long-term causes that had helped to motivate people to search for like-minded individuals and sometimes found them online. In short, both technological and social seeds of change need to be explored (Rambukkana, 2015, p. 4).

Chapter Overview

Merlyna Lim, in her comprehensive study on protest movements worldwide, shows the complexities of the politics of transformation. Her contribution presents the perfect opening by calling to go "beyond the revolutionary moment" and instead study social change that underlies the unfolding transformational projects. Drawing on a rich empirical body, she shows how digital media are part of different stages in protest movements. Taking into consideration the global-local nexus, she traces similar characteristics and mechanisms in digital media activism in Arab and Asian countries while at the same time presenting regional differences entailing regional contagion effects, the urban middle class population and digital connectivity.

Almut Woller, who investigates Arab anarchists through the lens of diaspora, proposes another transregional perspective. Starting with an emphasis on the long history of anarchism in the Arab region, she shows how digital media have increased regional and transregional visibility of actors that feel part of an anarchist community. Shedding light on the anarchist discourse, she demonstrates how symbols and ideas are spread, appropriated and negotiated, creating a specific mode of permanent resistance against the state.

Abir Kopty's contribution focuses on the specific case of Palestine. The research combines network analysis and qualitative interviews with Palestinian online activists that are geographically separated due to the politics in the region. The author explores the dynamics between and within the international and local online communities that emerge. In her theoretical discussion, she applies Bourdieu's field theory to shed light on power relations, trust, competition, conflicts, censorship and modes of domination in this online sphere.

The state's influences in determining the digital social field are exhibited in *Zihao Lin, Andrea Hamm and Susanne Reinhardt's* contribution on China. The authors build on a similar Bourdieusian theoretical framework to look at the reproduction of offline power structures in the digital field and introduce and define digital capital within their case study. The authors conduct a network analysis on the Chinese Twitter-like Sina Weibo services and expose elite clusters that dominate the political discourse. They conclude that state-critical public intellectuals that are often cited in Western literature are massively outweighed by powerful company actors that pursue a state-political agenda.

Mina Naeli's contribution empirically explores the impacts of Internet usage on internal relations of women's rights activists in Iran. In her study, she finds that more conventional forms of Internet-mediated communication, mainly e-mail groups and websites, strengthen the activists' collective identity and stimulate collaboration among and within the activist groups. At the same time usage of social media by individual activists raise tensions within the women's rights activism network. Her study supports the argument that individual social media representations give rise to "slacktivism" by fostering narcissism and distracting activists from participation in actions on the ground.

Anna Antonakis distinguishes digitalization and globalization as two different dimensions that need to be taken into account when studying transformations in a specific country. It is obviously not the nation state alone that shapes the communication infrastructure but also transnationally operating social media companies and service providers. She develops a critical view on media and the politics of transformation from a feminist perspective and applies this perspective to the example of feminist activism and the renegotiation of gender in Tunisia. She argues for the integration of an intersectional lens into studies of digital divides and representations.

Hanan Badr delves into the deliberation potential of social media in Egypt of 2012, investigating the online debates about the constitutional drafting process. She selected four social movement actors for her case study, ranging from Revolutionary Socialists to Salafists. Drawing on theories of the public sphere and political culture, she argues that in Egypt during this particular period of time, the political culture was radically polarized along ideological lines that were also reflected online. Deliberation was thus curbed and substituted by a particularistic agenda-setting.

Acknowledgements

The book is the material outcome of an international workshop organized by the editors in December 2015 at Freie Universität Berlin.

First and foremost, we would like to thank all contributors for their insightful analysis. It was our pleasure to compile their work. In addition, the editors of this book are very thankful to those senior scholars who commented on the presentations by the authors during the workshop in 2015 and consequently helped to improve the papers and made them speak to each other: Natalie Fenton, Donatella della Ratta, Eid Mohamed and Deva Woodly. Thanks also to Martin Schiller for his support in organizing the workshop and bringing all these interesting scholars together. We would also like to thank the Department of Political and Social Sciences at Freie Universität Berlin for its kind support that made the workshop and the publication possible. Finally, we are very grateful to Marta Misiulaityte for copy-editing and Jutta Brennauer for formatting this manuscript.

References

Armbrust, W. (2012). A History of New Media in the Arab Middle East. *Journal for Cultural Research, 16*(2-3), 155-174.

Bayat, A. (2009). *Life as Politics. How Ordinary People Change the Middle East*. Stanford: Stanford University Press.

Cammaerts, B. (2015). Technologies of Self-Mediation: Affordances and Constraints of Social Media for Protest Movements. In J. Uldam & A. Vestergaard (Eds.), *Civic Engagement and Social Media – Political Participation Beyond the Protest* (p. 97-110). Basingstoke.

Castells, M. (2011). A Network Theory of Power. *International Journal of Communication*, 5, 773–787.

Crete-Nishihata, M., Deibert, R. J., & Senft, A. (2013). Not By Technical Means Alone: The Multidisciplinary Challenge of Studying Information Controls. *EEE Internet Computing, 17*(3), 34-41.

Deibert, R. (2008). Black Code Redux: Censorship, Surveillance, and the Militarization of Cyberspace. In M. Boler (Ed.), *Digital Media and Democracy – Tactics in Hard Times* (p. 137-163). Cambridge: MIT Press.

Diamond, L. (2010). Liberation Technology. *Journal of Democracy, 21*(3), 69-83.

Fahmy, Z. (2011). *Ordinary Egyptians: Creating the Modern Nation through Popular Culture*. Stanford: Stanford University Press.

Fuchs, C. (2014). *Social Media: A Critical Introduction*. London: Sage.

Harders, C. (2013). Bringing the Local back in: Local Politics Between Informalization and Mobilization in the Age of Transformation in Egypt. In M. Bouziane, C. Harders, & A.

Hoffmann (Eds.), *Local Politics and Contemporary Transformations in the Arab World. Governance Beyond the Center* (p. 113-136). New York: Palgrave Macmillan.
Hepp, A. & Krotz, F. (Eds.) (2014). *Mediatized Worlds.* Houndsmills: Palgrave.
Kazansky, B. (2016). Privacy, Responsibility, and Human Rights Activism. *FCJ-195 fibreculturejournal.org,* (26), 189-207.
McAdam, D., Tarrow, S. & Tilly, C. (2001). *Dynamics of Contestation.* Cambridge University Press: Cambridge.
Merkel, W. (2010). *Systemtransformation. Eine Einführung in Theorie und Empirie der Transformationsforschung.* Wiesbaden: Springer VS.
Morozov, E. (2011). *The Net Delusion: The Dark Side of Internet Freedom.* New York: Public Affairs.
Radloff, J. (2013). Digital security as feminist practice. *Feminist Africa,* (18), 145-155.
Rambukkana, N. (2015). *Hashtags as technosocial Events. In: Hashtag Publics: The Power and Politics of Discursive Networks.* Peter Lang: New York, 1-10.
Richter, C. & Badr, H. (2016). Communication Studies in Transformation – Self-reflections on an Evolving Discipline in Times of Change. Arab-German Young Academy – *Transformation Group Working Paper* No. 2/2016.
Shirky, C. (2008). *Here Comes Everybody: The Power of Organizing Without Organizations.* London: Penguin Press.
Tufekci, Z. (2014). Social Mouvements and Governments in the Digial Age: Evaluating a complex Landscape. *Journal of Intrenational Affairs, 68*(1), 1-18
Tufekci, Z. (2015). Algorithmic Harms beyond Facebook and Google: Emergent Challenges of Computational Agency. *Journal on Telecommunications and High Technology Law, 13*(2), 203-218.
Tufekci, Z. (2017). *Twitter and Tear Gas – The Power and Fragility of Networked Protest.* New Haven and London: Yale University Press.
Youmans, W. L., & York, J. C. (2012). Social Media and the Activist Toolkit: User Agreements, Corporate Interests, and the Information Infrastructure of Modern Social Movements. *Journal of Communication, 62*(2), 315–329.

Sticks and Stones, Clicks and Phones: Contextualizing the Role of Digital Media in the Politics of Transformation[1]

Merlyna Lim

In the last decade, we have seen major protests occurring around the world. The frequency of these protests has increased dramatically since the so-called Arab Spring started in Tunisia in December 2010. Since then, there have been thousands of protests emerging in various places in the world. Visual depictions of the protesters occupying public spaces made it to the headlines of international media such as the New York Times, The Guardian, and Der Spiegel, and were broadcasted in news hours by major satellite television channels such as CNN, BBC and Al Jazeera. Thousands, hundreds of thousands, and even millions of bodies flooded the streets and the squares in massive sit-ins. During their peak moments, these protests were packaged, promoted, and displayed as "media spectacles" – "technologically mediated events, in which media forms like broadcasting, print media, or the Internet process events in a spectacular form" (Kellner, 2010, p. 76). The media were mostly preoccupied with symbols and icons emerging from these protests as well as with the technologies of protests, and some were even quick to label these uprisings Facebook, Twitter, and Instagram 'revolutions'. The media attention, however, generally focuses on selected moments, which fade as the spectacle wanes.

Admittedly, academic analyses of these events are more nuanced, and some demonstrate an attempt to reveal a more complex relationship between digital media and political changes. And yet, as pointed out by Rodriguez, Ferron, and Shamas (2014, p. 3), "many of these studies, with their focus on the 'newness' of ICTs, reduce the richly contextual human relations that surround media use into a flat and unrevealing technological determinism". Over the years, the technological

1 This article is based on a public keynote lecture I delivered at the international conference on "Media and the Politics of Transformation in the Arab world and Asia" held at Freie Universität Berlin, 10 December 2015. Special thanks go to James for making my Berlin visit unforgettable and the writing process smoother.

C. Richter et al. (Hrsg.), *Digital Media and the Politics of Transformation in the Arab World and Asia*, Studies in International, Transnational and Global Communications, https://doi.org/10.1007/978-3-658-20700-7_2

utopianism that dominated earlier research has been tempered by more nuanced research on the limitations as well as the potential of digital activism (see Hirzalla & van Zoonen, 2011; Juris, 2012; Enjolras et al., 2013; Lim, 2013a). However, the volume of writing implicitly proposing that revolutions can occur principally, if not solely, through digital activism is still very large (see Almazan & Garcia, 2013; Bhuiyan, 2011; Chebib & Solail, 2011; Johnson, 2012; Khamis & Vaughn, 2011; Mansour, 2012; Shirky, 2011; Stepanova, 2011). Distancing myself from technological utopianism, in this article I attempt to contextualize the role(s) of digital media in the political transformation processes. I argue that it is necessary to step back in order to view complexities of the events that unraveled in various places, to go beyond the individual moments, and start looking at the various processes preceding them. Drawing on empirical analysis from the Middle East, North Africa (MENA) and Asia, I will identify regional patterns and constellations of digital media as an instrument for protest and mobilization, and examine how regional and national contexts may define and/or shape mobilizations and social movements.

1 'Revolutionary Moments' vs. 'Social Change'

Before going further, it is important to provide clarification that 'revolutionary moments' we have seen in Egypt, Tunisia, Hong Kong, and elsewhere are neither the end result of social movements nor the culmination of 'social change'. Echoing Lakey (2012), I view social change and transformation as a long process involving complex trajectories. The mass uprisings such as those that unraveled in Tahrir Square and Central Hong Kong were the culmination of mass confrontations resulting from a rapid growth of the movement itself as it reached the point where enough people had become involved. As exemplified in the cases of Egypt and Tunisia, mass confrontation can open a power vacuum and, therefore, is crucial as it is a moment of opportunity for the revolutionary movement to step into the vacuum and create, step by step, a new society, to perform a bottom-up restructuring and begin a transformational project (Lakey, 2012).[2]

In its life cycle, a social movement goes through various phases. Blumer (1969) and Tilly (1978) outline four phases, which begin with the *preliminary* stage where people become aware of an issue and leaders emerge. Mass uprisings are part of the second stage, the *coalescence* stage, where people collectivize, mobilize, and

2 For a perspective on transformation that does not necessarily target structural change see the contribution of Almut Woller on Arab anarchists in this volume.

publicly display their resistance. The third phase is the *institutionalization* stage, where the movement no longer relies on grassroots volunteerism but an established organization. The latest phase is the *decline* stage that happens when participants of the movement fall away, the movement successfully brings about the change it sought, or the public no longer takes the issue seriously.

Out of these four stages, the institutionalization stage, or what della Porta and Diani (2006) term a *bureaucratization* or *formalization* phase, is the most crucial one to social movements' pursuit for societal reform and transformation for social change. This stage is characterized by higher levels of organization and coalition-based strategies. It includes institutional building to prepare and construct a parallel institution needed when reforming or transforming the system or, in a more extreme case, replacing the 'old' system/regime with a new one. Accordingly, we will need to keep in mind that a social movement is an ongoing process, and the transformation that comes with it will always take time. In many places of the world, we see ongoing, unfinished processes that may or may not progress towards societal change and transformation.

2 The Global Wave of Protests: Commonalities and Complexities

To provide a broader context of the politics of transformation in MENA and Asia, it is useful to review a large number of large-scale national protests, namely those involving more than 1,000 protesters and covered by mainstream media between 2010 and 2015, and identify their commonalities and complexities. In my examination, I built and expanded on Carothers and Youngs' (2015) dataset and analysis, which covers 103 protests in 60 countries from May 2010 to August 2015, and combined their dataset with the database of protests (only 2010-2013) from the Initiative for Policy Dialogue and Friedrich-Ebert-Stiftung Working Paper (Ortiz et al., 2013). Further, I also added more protests that happened in September-November 2015 by filtering the search for protest related news articles on Google within an associated time range. In total, my dataset includes 145 protests occurring in 76 countries. In reviewing these protests, I identify a number of factors that demonstrate commonalities as well as revealing complexities of the contemporary activism globally, with emphasis on the MENA region and Asia.

2.1 Spread Globally: The Pre-Eminence of the Local and the National

As accurately observed by Carothers and Youngs (2015), the recent wave of protests differs from the last major wave of protests in the late 1980s and early 1990s. Unlike the previous era, protests are occurring in every region, including the Middle East, affecting every major regime category, from authoritarian countries to semi-authoritarian states and democracies (Carothers & Youngs, 2015, p. 4). As demonstrated by 1999's 'Battle in Seattle', the incorporation of the Internet in global activism was one of the most significant innovations in protest practices in the 1990s (Kahn & Kellner, 2004). The Internet-based communication networks allowed organizers to reach vast and dispersed constituencies and audiences (Smith, 2001), making it easier to establish a network of resistance beyond national boundaries. In addition, the digital networks helped to rapidly disseminate information about resistance, not only in the Global North but also in the Global South, and allowed coordinated action across borders, brokered by experienced activists across the globe (Reitan, 2007, p. 11). The transnational and global nature of the digital networks in the late 1990s was thus compatible with transnational issues that dominated the wave of protests in the early 1990s.

In the latest wave after 2010, while the protests had similarly expanded territorially and were trans-local in their character, the scope of activism has been scaled back to local and national levels. Recent protests often developed from similar issues, such as corruption and economic injustice, but most were "rooted in local and national political debates and concerns" (Carothers & Youngs, 2015, p. 5). In the last decade, the Internet itself has become increasingly local. The technology, especially with the popularity of social media, has become an integral part of everyday life and is more reflective of the sociality, as well as the resistance, that emerges from everyday social spheres. Social media, "first and foremost, is social" and social media activities "mostly revolve around fun, self-expression and social gain" (Lim, 2013a, p. 653). It can, however, allow individuals and groups to converse over political debates and concerns and potentially transform these conversations into collective resistance.

Protesters are generally motivated by short-term causes, but the conditions that enable the development of protests are longer-term in nature (Carothers & Youngs, 2015). Most protests, especially large-scale ones, are complex in nature involving multiple short-term causes where protesters are motivated by several concerns. The Tunisian uprisings, for example, reflected the Tunisians' quest for dignity, anger over corruption, high unemployment, and desire for democracy.

2.2 Short-Term and Long-Term Causes

As can be seen in Figure 1, short-term causes extracted from the dataset are wide-ranging, covering issues as diverse as fuel prices, corruption, women's rights, and a number of other issues. These short-term causes, however, can be clustered into three categories, namely: socio-economic, political (system and governance), and citizen rights. In MENA, for example in Tunisia and Egypt, the combination of socio-economic (e.g., high unemployment, widening income gap, food prices) and political factors (e.g., corruption, police brutality, authoritarianism) appears to have been the main cause for the majority of the population to rise up. Meanwhile, large-scale protests in Hong Kong and Malaysia have been driven primarily by political conditions (e.g., lack of/poor democracy, lack of transparency) and citizen rights (e.g., freedom of speech, freedom of expression, voting rights).

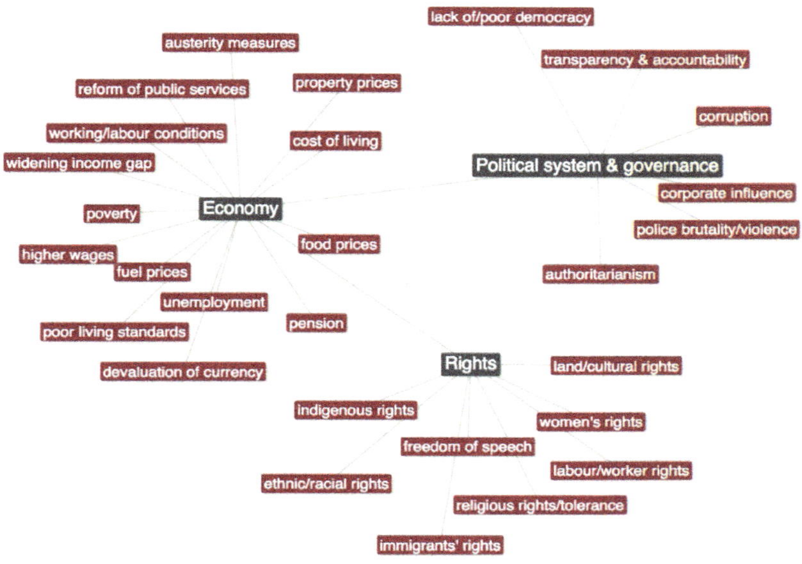

Fig. 1 Short-term causes of protests (Source: author)

While short-term causes stipulate immediate milieus for protests to emerge, they only contribute a partial understanding. To "fully understand the protest wave, it is also necessary to consider the longer term enabling factors at work, which encompass various elements of change – technological, economic, and political" (Carothers & Youngs, 2015, p. 6). The long-term causes usually brew for many years and eventually create the conditions for collective resistance to arise.

The first long-term cause is the rise of new educated middle classes globally, especially in the MENA region and Asia, brought about by considerable economic growth in the past ten to twenty years. Protest movements across the globe, from Tunisia to Malaysia, while they might have been sparked by an event in poor areas (such as Sidi Bouzid), have generally been concentrated among the middle and upper-middle classes in urban areas. The new middle classes "develop expectations beyond material goals and gain access to education, travel, communication technologies, and other resources that give them new perspectives and capabilities" (Carothers & Youngs, 2015, p. 6). In some countries, such as Tunisia and Egypt, economic growth had also resulted in stark new inequalities between sub-groups within the middle classes. For a large number of middle-class individuals, the increasing gap between expectations and realities has created a fertile ground for potential support for protests.

The second long-term cause is the mushrooming of non-governmental and civil society organizations around the globe in the last two decades, especially in developing parts of the world where civil society had previously been weak (Carothers & Youngs, 2015). By 2006, Egypt had more than 23,000 NGOs, over 10,000 in Tunisia, and over 26,000 in Morocco (Anheier & Toepler, 2009, p. 269). In Asia, there was a tremendous growth of NGOs and CSOs in 1990s and 2000s. In 2000, there were more than 20,000 registered NGOs in China and several thousand at district and community level in Vietnam (Yamamoto, 2000, p. 43). In 2009, Thailand had 19,878 registered NGOs, Malaysia 14,000, the Philippines 70,200 (Nesadurai, 2012, p. 223). Furthermore, the youths, who were among those on the front line of the uprisings in 2011 in the MENA countries and Asia, have been central to the formation of this growth. In fact, over the past decade, many civil society organizations have been established by youth groups who came together around youth-related issues. Examples include the Al-Thoria Studies Center in Jordan, which was established by youths and has a young staff base; the April 6 Youth Movement in Egypt, which was founded by the youth members of Kifaya (the movement that engineered the first oppositional protests against Mubarak in 2003) (Lim, 2012); and the Scholarism, a Hong Kong-based secondary school student activist group formed in May 2011, which initiated a mass protest against the Moral and National Education, a new curriculum endorsed by the Chinese central government in July 2012 (SCMP, 2012). While not always democratic and sometimes even characterized by elements subversive to democratization, civil society may assist the emergence of democratic forces in a given society.

The third long-term cause is the failed reform and/or, in some semi-authoritarian countries, problematic democratic transition. The previous cycles of global political changes in the 1980s and 1990s had contributed to reform, economically and/or politically, in dozens of countries, yet many of those states faced difficulty and/or failed to bring their transitions to fruition. The so-called third wave of democracy that swept through the globe and especially Asia in the 1990s has increased citizen awareness and expectations that the government should be accountable to its people. However, most countries struggle to make democracy and reform work, leaving citizens dissatisfied with the way democracy and reform function in practice, and making these countries fertile soil for protests (Carothers & Youngs, 2015).

Digital media is neither a revolutionary driver nor a cause of the protests. However, the rapid change in communication technologies make information more widely available to people, giving them "a greater awareness of how others are asserting themselves against entrenched power holders in other countries and of how their own political and economic conditions compare with those of others" (Carothers & Youngs, 2015, p. 9). Digital media, especially social media, facilitate exchanges among citizens, enabling them to collectivize around shared grievances rooted in long-term conditions as well as short-term causes.

2.3 Triggered by Local Events

Long-term causes create necessary conditions for collective awareness (of shared dissatisfactions and contentions) and short-term causes provide an immediate environment for collective networks of resistance to emerge. For protests to break out in certain places at certain moments, they need triggers that are usually manifested in the form of local events, most of which are highly symbolic and visually dramatic. For example, the dramatic self-immolation of Muhammed Bouazizi in Tunisia and the high-profile police brutality case of Khaled Said in Egypt.

Such local events, however, would not trigger widespread protests if not publicized widely. In other words, the event needs to be viral in order to trigger protests. Here digital media can potentially play an important role in making a local event viral. However, such a process is not easy or natural. As exemplified in my detailed analysis of the Tunisian uprisings (Lim, 2013b, p. 937-938), the virality of Bouazizi's self-immolation was possible through the employment of three key mechanisms:

> "First, the availability of the archetypal image that had iconic value – Bouazizi's burning body – elevated the non-event of the poor to the public spectacle. ... Second, frame alignment with a master frame that culturally and politically resonated with the entire society successfully fostered a sense of injustice and identity that united the people of Tunisia. ... Third, the activation of a hybrid network ... to facilitate connective structures that became a platform to generate collective action among Tunisians who shared collective identities and collective frames, and *connective action* [Bennett & Segerberg, 2013] among individuals who sought more personalized paths to contribute to the movement through digital media."

2.4 Not Spontaneous but with Historical Roots

My analysis reveals that most protests are not spontaneous but involve a longer-term mobilization and are rooted in a long history of resistance and struggles. The major mass protests that took place globally, including those in Tunisia, Egypt, Malaysia, and Hong Kong which were comfortably framed as 'spontaneous and sudden' by Western observers, should be seen as the result of long processes of the transformation of politics. If Occupy Hong Kong, which is more popularly called the Umbrella Movement, suddenly made it onto our radar, it was not because the uprising suddenly emerged from social media, but because many observers, especially Western media, had not been paying attention to various events preceding it. As a matter of fact, just months prior to the Occupy Hong Kong protests in September 2014, there was a big protest on the first of July. This was one of the annual rallies that have decorated the streets of Hong Kong since July 1, 2003, where half a million Hong Kongers rallied to successfully overturn Article 23 of the Basic Law, which would have prohibited any act of treason, sedition and subversion against the People's Government of Central China.

Similarly, the failure of international mainstream media to cover expressions of dissent in the Arab world, Asia and elsewhere has contributed to the collective imprint that these uprisings are 'sudden and spontaneous'. The Tunisian and Egyptian uprisings were more than a decade in the making (Lim, 2012; 2013b), while the seed of the Malaysian Bersih movement was planted in 1998 through the emergence of the reform (*reformasi*) movement and various political protests afterwards (e.g., Hindraf, anti-ISA, and anti-Lynas) (Lim, 2016; 2017).

In the Egyptian case, raw data from the protests demonstrated a remarkable escalation in the decade before the uprising. The Solidarity Center (2010) recorded 2,623 protests taking place between 1998 and 2008 and a total of 284 worker protests in the first half of 2009 alone. The 2011 Tahrir uprising cannot be detached from the historical landscape of protests and resistance spanning more than one decade, involving various activist groups and organizations such as the Kifaya movement, the April 6 Youth Movement, the activism of textile factory workers, and the 'We are all Khaled Said' Facebook-facilitated group (Lim, 2012). Every historic moment has history and some moments are anchored in long, deep, and complex histories.

2.5 The Chief Role of 'Hybrid Media/Communication Networks'

As pointed out by many scholars, and suggested in earlier parts of this article, social media have been vital in the mobilization of contemporary protests. However, it is important to note that in most cases, social media were not the primary tool for mobilizing and organizing protests. Rather, we witnessed an extensive utilization of cellular phones in all of these protests, with an incorporation of social media in some of them, and, most importantly, the chief role of 'hybrid media/communication networks' beyond cellular and social media. The more detailed analysis of the roles of digital media, including social media, will be provided in the next section.

3 The Specific Roles of Digital Media

Observably, there are similar characteristics and mechanisms in digital media activism and mobilization across the regions. Digital media is not only incorporated immediately before and during the protests, but is also embedded in various processes of the politics of transformation through popular protest movements. In the following sections, I analyze the roles of digital media by tracing how the media is embedded in various stages of the making of social movement and ground my analysis in the empirical stories from Tunisia, Egypt, Hong Kong, and Malaysia. I outline a social movement's development from its genesis, as it emerges in multiple spheres of imaginaries and resistance, through its successive trajectories, as it engages and mobilizes diverse publics, to its unfolding as interconnected events, as it displays collective power through public performances (Lim, 2015).

3.1 Multiple Spheres of Imaginaries and Resistance

The role of digital media can be traced to the origin or the onset of the movement, namely the spheres of imaginaries. Social movements begin with the ability to imagine. Imagination allows the collectives to envision a more desirable future, different from the present. Radical imagination is fundamental to any collective attempt to ascertain resistance and solidarity in the form of a counter-hegemonic movement (Khasnabish & Haiven, 2014).

Multiple spheres are required for a collective radical imagination to emerge and sustain itself. Indeed, social movements rarely originate in one imaginary sphere. From my research, I learned that for each and every social movement, there were multiple spaces of origin that emerged separately and then gradually came to constitute one larger, denser network. The 2010-2011 Tunisian revolutionary uprising originated in the radical imagination that emerged both in the long tradition of labor activism as well as in more than one decade of digital activism against state censorship (Lim, 2013b, p. 923-26). The capacity to imagine a different, more desirable future among Egyptians that culminated with the 2011 Tahrir uprising did not simply start with the 'We are all Khaled Said' Facebook page. Its genesis can rather be traced back to the Kifaya oppositional movement against Mubarak in 2003-2007, the labor activism of textile factory workers in 2006-2009, and the activism of the April 6 Youth Movement—the main organization behind the 2011 Tahrir protests (Lim, 2012). These spheres of resistance were online, offline, and in-between spaces (the April 6 Youth Movement used cyber-cafés as one of the main activism sites).[3]

The 2014 Occupy Hong Kong movement also originated in multiple different spheres, such as through the establishment of the OCLPHK (Occupy Central with Love and Peace Hong Kong) group by the university law professor Benny Tai a year prior to the big protest in September 2014. It additionally emerged through the legacy of Hong Kong urban street march culture, student activism, and labor unionism that has a long history of public civic engagement (Butenhoff, 1999; Chiu & Lui, 2000). Occupy Hong Kong was also rooted in more recently formed student activist groups, most notably Scholarism, a Hong Kong-based secondary school student activist group. The spheres of imagination in the Occupy Hong Kong movement can be traced to numerous classrooms of secondary schools and universities, where students, teachers, and professors mingled and immersed in frequent communication and interactions, as well as heavy online interchanges and conversations on various political blogs, Facebook groups (every single school and university student activist group maintains an active presence on Facebook), Twitter, and Instagram.

Power is exercised through the propagation of dominant socio-political imaginaries. The dominant imaginaries, such as that of the state, tend to express and

---

3 For an analysis of the performance of the April 6 movement after the uprisings in 2011 see the contribution of Hanan Badr in this volume.

re-inscribe power. The radical departure from the dominant imaginaries is crucial to the creation of sites in which alternative and radical imagination can emerge, grow, and spread; sites in which narratives of resistance can be created, communicated, and practiced (Lim, 2014; 2015). Digital media add to the possibility of multiple spheres of radical imagination emerging. In these spheres, everyday practices of resistance are communicated and exchanged, in *repetition* and *routine*, through *interactivity* and regular *flows* and *exchanges*.[4]

3.2 Mobilizing Diverse Publics

Beyond the imaginaries, social movements are ultimately about establishing and expanding networks of resistance involving diverse publics. In the process, social movements go through various mechanisms, from brokering and bridging to the mobilization processes marked by framing and diffusing.

Brokerage or *brokering*, the "production of a new connection between previously disconnected sites" (Tilly & Tarrow, 2006, p. 31), is one of the most important mechanisms in social movements. Brokering is a mechanism needed to allow small circle conversations, usually formed among disaffected elites, to traverse various representational channels and interest group distinctions and reach diverse publics. In the network dynamics, brokerage is a process that happens when a certain node acts as a broker that connects two nodes that are otherwise separated (in the absence of ties). When there are no or limited physical spaces available to do so, blogging and other types of networking in the digital space may facilitate these brokering and bridging processes. Prior to the 2011 Egyptian uprisings, circles of oppositional actors were isolated from each other, polarized along political and religious orientations, such as right-wing Islamism (e.g. the Muslim Brotherhood), liberal secularism (e.g. Wafd and Al-Ghad activists), and left-wing secularism (e.g. activists of the Egyptian Communist Party) (Lim, 2012, p. 237). As physical spaces were controlled, the brokerage could not happen in an offline setting. In the Egyptian blogosphere, however, the brokerage occurred when bloggers who belonged to diverse ideologies were linked to each other to form a plural and diverse oppositional network (Lim, 2012, p. 237; Radsch, 2008). Similarly, in the Malaysian electoral reform movement, the brokerage occurred as previously disconnected Malaysian activists and concerned individuals belonging to various ideologies

4 Abir Kopty's contribution in this volume discusses the somewhat clashing utopian and dystopian perspectives on the envisaged impacts of digital media on movement formations.

(e.g. Islamist, secular and liberal) and backgrounds (e.g. Malay, Chinese and Tamil/Indian) networked in the blogosphere, and this mechanism contributed to the formation and expansion of the reformist network (Lim, 2016; 2017). The brokerage, as exemplified in the Egyptian and Malaysian blogospheres, allowed disconnected activists and proto-activists (concerned individuals who seek to join activism networks) to assimilate their experiences and to deliberate beyond their own existing ideological boundaries.

The brokerage can extend to a process known in the resource mobilization theory as 'linkages', namely *bridging* two disparate networks to expand resources (McCarthy & Zald, 1977) by allowing resources to be mutually shared. *Bridging* allows small groups with limited resources to expand and grow within an interconnected collaborative network (Yuce et al., 2014). Brokering and bridging, exemplified in the Egyptian and Malaysian blogospheres, can also be seen as a necessary step towards transforming multiple ideologically bound and resource-poor groups into a relatively resourceful networked movement that has access to various social groups and representational channels.

Beyond brokering and bridging, to mobilize diverse publics, social movements need to apply a mechanism called *framing*, a process that is central to mobilization as it can foster collective identity across geographically dispersed individuals (Garrett, 2006) by allowing them to identify shared grievances through framing processes (Aday et al., 2012). Here, framing processes refer to the way that meaning is constructed to legitimize collective activities and actions (Gamson, 1992). The role of frames is to organize and guide action by rendering events meaningful (Snow et al., 1986), mostly by clarifying and simplifying the reasons and rationales of participation. Since it is affordable and ubiquitous (in urban areas), digital media can be used to disseminate the resistance vastly and rapidly.

Digital and especially social media, however, are not inherently friendly to the narrative of injustice central to social movements. Social media comprise the world of memes dominated by sensational narratives around celebrated personalities. In this landscape, it is unlikely for complex narratives of injustice to be virally disseminated (Lim, 2013a). Activists, therefore, have no choice but to simplify and even oversimplify the narratives, generating symbols and icons that resonate with the larger public in order to increase the possibility of successful mobilization (Lim, 2013a). The simplification practices are inherent to the creation of an injustice frame (Gamson, 1992) that emboldens the sense of injustice, evokes shared emotion and rage, incites public outcry, and mobilizes antagonism against the common enemy.

This framing process was evident in Tunisia as activists transformed Muhammed Bouazizi, a street vendor who never graduated from high school, into a symbolic figure of the Tunisian uprisings. Bouazizi was 'framed' as an unemployed university graduate who self-immolated himself after being publicly humiliated by a female police officer, thus crafting a story that culturally and politically resonated with the entire population, particularly the highly educated urban middle class youth, which ultimately galvanized public outrage against President Ben Ali (Lim, 2013b). Similarly, in the Egyptian uprisings, activists transformed Khaled Said, a young man killed by Alexandrian police in a drug-related scene, into a unifying poster-child of Egypt's disparate reform movement. Not only did activists elevate Said into "a figure with saint-like qualities", but they also simplified "the dynamics of his life that led up to his death" (Ali, 2012). Through the activists' frame of injustice, the story of Said as "young, social media savvy, urbanized, and anti-authoritarian" successfully ignited the rage and evoked the motion of urban educated middle class youths in Cairo and Alexandria as they rallied against Mubarak (Ali, 2012; Lim, 2012). Another commonly used framing method is establishing an image of a targeted opponent as the incarnation of evil and a universally certified enemy, such as Adolf Hitler. Visually depicting Ben Ali, Mubarak, and Chief Leung of Hong Kong with a Hitler mustache is a conspicuous attempt to paint them as a certified enemy – a reincarnation of Hitler, an evil, and a common enemy of the people.

To engage diverse publics, social movements need to expand socially, demographically, and geographically (Tilly & Tarrow, 2006). In the Tunisian and Egyptian uprisings, digital media were limited in their capacity to reach across geographical boundaries because of low Internet penetration rates and because of the deep divide between urban and rural areas. In Tunisia, 85 percent of the population had access to a cellular phone but only 20 percent were Facebook users in 2010; while the broadband connection was robust in coastal areas, the poorer interior areas were mostly disconnected and did not even have reliable mobile phone coverage (Brisson & Kontiris, 2012, p. 97). A hybrid network consisting of social media, big media (e. g. Al Jazeera), and small media (e. g. cellular phones, laptops, pocket cameras, and memory cards) contributed to a successful mobilization. In this context, *intermodality*, namely the linkages from the Internet and social media to other networks, is a crucial process. An example from Tunisia below illustrates the importance of *intermodality*:

> "When massive protests broke out in these two border towns near Algeria, police blocked the roads, isolated the towns and squashed the protests with brutal massacres … [but] could not prevent the information from going out. People took videos with their mobile phones and pocket cameras documenting police brutality and passed them to activists who transferred them to memory cards. Activists put memory cards inside sneakers and threw the sneakers over the border to Algeria. From here, these cards were transported to Tunis to be uploaded online by activists in the capital and some eventually got to Al Jazeera's news desks" (Lim, 2013b, p. 934).

Malaysia, where 60 percent of the population is online, tells a different story. The Bersih movement, which took place in urban areas such as Kuala Lumpur, Johor Baru, and Penang where the Internet penetration rates are between 70 to 85 percent, relied heavily on social media (Lim, 2016; 2017). Yet, Bersih activists still had to employ low-tech communication networks, such as flyers and SMS (Short Messaging Services), to reach rural areas, and hold traditional *ceramah* (lectures/speeches) in mosques and community centers (Khoo, 2014; Lim, 2017). Activists also commenced a *Balik Kampung Bawa Berita* (bring the news back to your village) initiative which encouraged Malaysians who had online access to bring Bersih messages to the offline communities in their home towns/villages in the form of hard copies (printouts) and CDs (of blog postings, websites, and YouTube videos) (Ibrahim, 2012). The *intermodality* of various media helped the Bersih movement to diffuse its message across diverse publics (Lim, 2017). In Tunisia and Malaysia, activists utilized digital media to break the government's control and monopoly over the production of knowledge and the information flows. However, to further diffuse the movement and reach diverse audiences, activists needed to incorporate the practices of *intermodality*.

3.3 Public Performance of Social Movements

Social movements claim their power through the public performance of resistance by occupying public spaces. By marching on the Habib Borguiba street (Tunis), the Tahrir Square (Cairo), the Central Hong Kong, and the Independence Square (Kuala Lumpur), social movements demonstrated people's capacity to act collectively and to appear simultaneously in the political "space of appearance" (Arendt, 1958, p. 200). With the incorporation of digital media, connected individuals can publicly perform their resistance in online space by promoting, among other things, hashtag activism.[5] However, as "[b]odies and their visibility to public are central in the struggles for power", the practice of protest and symbolism still necessitates physical sites for corporeal assemblies and "[b]y occupying public spaces with visible bodies, social movement presents itself vis-à-vis the power it seeks to challenge, symbolically and corporeally" (Lim, 2015, p. 121).

5 A hashtag is a type of metadata, consisting of a word or an un-spaced phrase prefixed with the hash character (#), used to cluster conversations around certain topics in social networking sites. Hashtag activism refers to an effort to collectively curate a massive number of short statements by using certain hashtags.

In their public display of resistance, movements need to sustain their presence beyond the initial protest amidst possible government shutdowns and physical attacks. In the Egyptian uprisings, protesters needed to anticipate physical violence around Tahrir square and its adjacent downtown streets. These downtown streets, unlike those in other parts of Cairo, are wide and spacious, and welcoming to large vehicles such as riot vans, armored vehicles, and water cannons (Al Saleh & Arefin, 2011). It was therefore valuable that knowledge about the physical surroundings and how to survive and react to the physical encounters with police forces was disseminated online and offline in the form of a 26-page manual prior to January 25th, 2011. While calls for protests were posted on social media, the protests themselves began in a number of key mosques and churches. These sites were located in densely populated working-class districts such as Shubra and El-Dakrour. While marching toward the square, protesters urged Egyptians watching them from balconies and windows to join them, leading to the growth of masses (El-Ghobashy, 2011). At various junctures leading to the square, protesters encountered security forces. The security forces, however, were disoriented as the protests had begun from multiple locations involving various protest groups (El-Ghobashy, 2011). In such a situation, Twitter was not contextually useful. The knowledge to maneuver the physicality of the battleground thus became more significant than Twitter.

By comparison, in the historic 2012 Bersih 3.0 protest in Kuala Lumpur, protestors utilized smart phones while marching and used Twitter not only to coordinate, but also to support and assist each other in maneuvering the riot police's physical coercion. Prior to the protest, activists made marching routes downloadable in GPS format (see Figure 2). Twitter usage in this case was more embedded in the physical space. Twitter exchanges were marked by frequent occurrences of the place names where the masses were gathering, such as Dataran Merdeka, Masjid Jamek, Pasar Seni and Jalan Tun Perak. In Figure 3, we can see the relationships between various words used in Bersih related tweets, illuminating visual overviews of place-related and atmospheric/situational words. Protesters reported using Twitter to assist each other in physically navigating around tear gas and water cannons and in finding alternative routes out of police barricades.

Fig. 2 Figure 2: An example of Bersih 3.0 rally marching routes, downloadable in GPS format (Source: author)

Fig. 3 Phrase nets of the most frequently used words in Bersih 3.0 related tweets[6] (Source: author)

Similarly, Occupy Hong Kong was marked with a heavy utilization of social media during the protests. Most exchanges on Instagram took place in the sites of protest such as Admiralty, Soho, and Central Hong Kong (Johnson, 2014). Social media was predominantly utilized by protesters to communicate, coordinate, and physically survive the protests. Information about physical safety and survival, such as an electronic safety guide for tear gas exposure, a manual of civil disobedience, and legal helpline numbers (in case of arrest), was disseminated online mainly using social media platforms.

The sustainability of a protest is also supported by its visibility beyond local sites, to national and global audiences. By reaching global audiences via the utilization of digital media and transnational/international broadcast media, the movement expands beyond the boundary of state control and authority, and it opens new opportunities for international support and pressure. In the uprisings in Egypt, Tunisia, Malaysia and Hong Kong, global audiences were a world away from the squares, parks, and streets where the protesters were gathering. They did, however, help to globalize the movement and to amplify local voices and narratives. The linkages between collective bodies in the squares and connective bodies in digital media can help the sustenance of social movements.

6 The graph was created using PhraseNet from Many Eyes, a data analytics platform from IBM (Viegas, 2015).

4 Regional Differences

While there are similar mechanisms and patterns in the roles of digital media pertaining to activism and mobilization across the regions, regional and national contexts differentiate these practices in the MENA countries and Asia. In my analysis, I identify differences based on three categories, specifically: regional contagion effects, urban middle class population, and digital connectivity.

4.1 Regional Contagion Effects

A contagion effect was evident in the emerging Arab World protests of 2011. Within a month of the downfall of the Tunisian dictator Ben Ali in January 2011, the protests spread like wildfire to Egypt and almost every Arab country. Protesters copied and borrowed the methods and tactics of the revolts, with varying intensity and outcomes. The strong contagion effect, however, is not apparent in Asia. Arguably, there are a number of factors contributing to this dissimilarity, which I will explain in the following paragraphs.

Spatial contagion of protests, whether it is national, regional, or transnational, fundamentally relies on information transmission; that is, the actions and messages of the protests must become known so they can spread. Media and communication networks are vital to this process. In the context of MENA, the role of Al Jazeera cannot be minimized. Since its establishment in 1996, the Qatar-based satellite news network has redefined journalism and has become a force in Arab politics (Sakr, 2007, p. 113). By working closely with locally based journalists, correspondents, and informants, Al Jazeera also established the practice of networked journalism[7] that was vital to the dissemination of information in repressive media landscapes. By providing the infrastructure of transnational networks for information transmission, Al Jazeera contributed to the regional contagion effect in the MENA region. The hybrid network formed by the linkages between Al Jazeera, other regional media (e.g. Al-Arabiya and BBC Arabic Television), and social media networks further strengthened the contagion effect in the region.

The fundamental underlying factor contributing to the effect is the cultural proximity of the MENA countries. Cultural proximity refers to "nationally or locally

7 Networked journalism can be defined as "journalism that sees publics acting as creators, investigators, reactors, (re)makers, and (re)distributors of news and where all variety of media, amateurs and professionals, corporate and independent products and interests intersect at a new level" (Russell, 2011:1).

produced material that is closer to and more reinforcing of traditional identities, based on regional, ethnic, dialect/language, religious, and other elements" (Straubhaar, 1991, p. 51). This is not to say that the Arab world is culturally homogenous. Rather, it is to recognize the importance of shared language and cultural attributes as a unifying force in the region, particularly the prominence of Arabic as a unifying language despite the existing other cultural-linguistic groups in MENA, such as the Amazigh (or Berber) populations in North Africa. Meanwhile, unlike in Asia, at the time of the uprisings there was no fragmentation of the social media landscape in the MENA region. Social media platforms such as Facebook and Twitter were commonly used in the MENA countries. With the cultural proximity and the commonality of social media platforms among nation-states, Al Jazeera and digital media facilitated the materialization of overlapped and networked transnational spheres of resistance in the 2011 uprisings.

Asian countries do not share comparable cultural proximity. While some Asian countries may share a certain degree of proximity in political ideology, economic liberalization, or socio-cultural modernity, the information transmission across borders needs a translational process that does not automatically transpire. The lack of a unifying language and transnational news networks in the region are among the dominant barriers to the translational process. In Asia, social media landscapes come in diverse forms and operate in multiple socio-political contexts, including multiple language and political systems. Chinese social media users, for example, adopt Weibo and WeChat that are distinctively Chinese and are not widely used anywhere else.[8] Blog posts, Facebook posts, and tweets produced in Asia demonstrate a variety of languages and cultural codes that are unique to each country. In my examination of the Occupy Hong Kong and the Malaysian Bersih movements I did not find any cross-country information flow. While both movements scaled up from the national to the global to include diasporic communities, each was still anchored in the boundary of the nation-state. With the pre-eminence of national contexts, while protests in one country may inspire activists in other countries, the contagion effect is less likely to take place in Asia, especially when compared to that of the MENA region.

8 For a more detailed analysis of Weibo and its implications for society, see the contribution of Zihao Lin, Andrea Hamm and Susanne Reinhardt in this volume.

4.2 Urban Middle Class Population

Asia has undergone rapid growth and urbanization as well as significant economic transformation. As its economies expand, its middle class grows and its population moves to the cities. As of 2017, 49 percent of the population live in urban areas (2.2 billion) (World Bank, 2017). In 2013, it was estimated that 1.8 billion of the total world population were in the middle class and this number will grow to 3.2 billion by 2020 (Kharas & Geertz, 2010). Asia is almost entirely responsible for this growth as its middle class is forecast to triple to 1.7 billion by 2020 (Kharas & Geertz, 2010).

Asia is also highly digital. With 1.8 billion Internet users, it is the region with the fastest growth and accounts for half of the world's total Internet users (We are social, 2017). Over 90 percent of this online population live in urban areas, predominantly in mega-cities such as Shanghai, Beijing, Bangkok, Manila, and Jakarta. Such demographic, large-scale protests in the region, as exemplified by the Occupy Hong Kong and the Malaysian Bersih movements, are highly urbanized and predominantly rooted in middle-class driven causes, revolving around issues such as political rights, freedom of speech, transparency, and accountability. This is not to say that lower classes and/or urban population do not participate in any protests. In fact, in the last five years, countries such as Indonesia and the Philippines have witnessed numerous worker and labor strikes. In China, in 2010 alone there were over 180,000 small-scale protest events (Carothers & Youngs, 2015). These protests, however, are either routinized and contained within a certain social group (among workers or laborers only) or focused on micro-level issues (e. g., an unfair ruling by a village council) and rarely escalate to a national level. Social media usages in the region mainly revolve around urban middle class concerns, issues, and consumer cultures, and are generally disconnected from the lives and experiences of the poor.[9]

The urban middle class population is also witnessing substantial growth in the rest of the emerging world, including in the MENA region. While countries are at varied levels of urbanization, the majority of the region's inhabitants, 64 percent of the total population of 361 million, now reside in urban areas. The growth of the urban population in the MENA region, however, is not accompanied by economic growth. Compared to the economic performance of Asian countries, notably East Asian countries, the performance of the Arab world is remarkably poor. The impressive growth Arab countries enjoyed during the 2000s did not reach much of the urban middle class; rather, it created a new class of economic and political elites

9 For a discussion of different experiences with social media usage according to class and/ or gender and the intersection of digital divides, see the contribution of Anna Antonakis in this volume.

supported by the rise of capitalism (Alaoui, 2016). In the last three decades, most Arab economies experienced less than one percent annual growth of real GDP per capita contributing to "one of the highest income inequality and unemployment rates globally" as well as "the lowest rates of investments of all regions" (Kadri, 2013). To exacerbate this condition, the region also experiences the highest rate of armed conflict. At over 30 percent, the level of unemployment "is most acute among Arab youths, the precise demographic that mobilized during the Arab spring" (Alaoui, 2016). Consequently, for the urban middle class population in the MENA countries, it was the accumulation of economic and social grievances that led to growing discontent in the 2011 uprisings. These grievances were also shared by the lower class populations across the regions. As they voiced their grievances and concerns through social media conversations, the urban middle class, especially the educated youths, engaged themselves with issues that overlapped with concerns and grievances of the larger population, including the poor. In comparison to MENA, the inter-class gap in Asia runs deeper. As the digital population of Asian countries grows, so does the gap between the lives and experiences of the urban middle class and the poor.

4.3 Digital Connectivity

Scholarly analysis of the Arab uprisings in 2010-2012 indeed shows that activists had incorporated digital media, especially social media, in the development of protest movements. However, social media was not the chief tool in mobilizing protest movements, mostly due to the lower penetration of mobile social media in the region. As mentioned earlier, social media users only comprised less than 20 percent of the population in Tunisia in 2011 (Lim, 2013b). Meanwhile, with only 6.5 percent of the population on Facebook (in February 2012, the number was lower prior to the uprisings), the majority of Egyptians were also not on social media (Digital Republic, 2012). With this reality, *intermodality* between social media and the more traditional networks was vital to the mobilizing process of the Arab uprisings.

While not equally distributed across the region, the digitally connected urban middle class population in some Asian countries plays an increasing role in igniting protest movements. Examples from Malaysia and Hong Kong presented in this article demonstrate that digital media are more seamlessly incorporated into the making and the sustenance of protest movements when compared to those in the MENA region. Evidently, social media activism has become a feature of almost every protest movement in Asia, from the anti-corruption movements in Indonesia and India to the anti-extra-judicial killing in the Philippines. By utilizing digital technologies, especially mobile social media (social media platforms accessed through mobile devices), contemporary movements in Asia have helped to expand the communication spheres for citizen democratic discourses in urban areas. However, the urban-digital characteristic of these movements has made them more exclusive, and less connected to rural areas[10] and members of the population who have no access to the Internet. In other words, the digital-ness and the urban-ness of these movements have further amplified their middle-class tendency.

5 Conclusions

As digital media becomes more embedded in everyday routines, especially through social media facilitated perpetual connectedness, political conversations and actions, too, have become more and more entangled with the digital world. It is, therefore, not surprising that the roles of digital media have become more apparent in any political undertakings, including protests and social movements. By anchoring my analysis in the empirical contexts of the MENA region and Asia, in this article I have identified analogous characteristics and mechanisms in digital media activism and mobilization across the region. Digital media's roles are embedded in various stages of the development of social movements. At the onset of movements, digital media augments the formation of multiple spheres of *radical imaginaries* and resistance. As social movements develop and expand to mobilize diverse publics, digital media's roles are embedded in the *brokering, bridging, framing,* as well as *diffusing* processes. As social movements continue mobilizing and claiming its power through public performances, digital media connects to other media – traditional/old and new, big and small, mainstream and alternative – through the *intermodality* mechanism.

However, the impact of digital media on the practices of protests and social movements has complex and unexpected outcomes. Moreover, regional and national contexts differentiate not only the practices but also the results of the incorporation of digital media in protest movements. Regional contagion effects, urban middle class population, and digital connectivity are among dominant factors that shape and influence regionally contextualized roles of digital media. My analysis of the roles of digital media in the politics of transformation in MENA and Asia suggests that technologies indeed have diverse, complex effects in different socio-political

10 For a perspective on an increased connectivity between the capital and other cities in Iran in women's rights activism, see Mina Naeli's contribution in this volume.

and cultural contexts, many, but certainly not all of them affirmative. Digital media are increasingly intertwined in the socio-political spheres. Digital media does not create collective actions, protests, or social movements, but instead enables different ways to participate in any collectivized social activities. Its roles and practices, however, are always shaped, constructed, reconstructed by diverse social, cultural, and historical contexts in which they are situated. In conclusion, I contend that the understanding of the role of digital media in the politics of transformation should be anchored not only in the exploration of *clicks* and *phones* – the socio-political usage of the technology, but also in the inquiry of *sticks and stones* – the stories and histories of resilience, agency, and resistance of people, and the context in which the usage is embedded.

References

Aday, S., Farrell, H., Lynch, M., Sides, J. & Freelon, D. (2012). *New media and conflict after the Arab Spring*. Retrieved from http://www.usip.org/sites/default/files/PW80.pdf

Al Saleh, D. & Arefin, M.R. (2011). *Five days of anger: Revolt in the modern metropolis*. Retrieved from http://www.thepolisblog.org/2011/01/five-days-of-anger-revolting-in modern.html

Alaoui, H. (2016). *Is the Arab world better off, five years after the Arab Spring?* Retrieved from http://macmillan.yale.edu/news/arab-world-better-five-years-after-arab-spring

Ali, A. (2012). Seeds of revolution: De-mythologizing Khaled Saeed. *Jadaliyya*, June 5. Retrieved from http://www.jadaliyya.com/pages/index/5845/saeeds-of-revolution_de-mythologizing-khaled-saeed

Almazan, R. S. & Garcia, J. R. G. (2013). Cyberactivism through Social Media: Twitter, YouTube, and the Mexican Political Movement "I'm Number 132", HCSS '13, *Proceedings of the 2013 46th Hawaii International Conference on System Sciences* (p. 1704-1713).

Anheier, H. K. & Toepler, S. (Eds.) (2009). *International encyclopedia of civil society*. Heidelberg: Springer.

Arendt, H. (1958). *The Human Condition*. Chicago, IL: University of Chicago Press.

Bennett, W. L. & Segerberg, A. (2013). *The Logic of Connective Action*. Cambridge: Cambridge University Press.

Bhuiyan, S. I. (2011). Social media and its effectiveness in the political reform movement in Egypt. *Middle East Media Educator, 1(1)*, 14-20.

Blumer, H. (1969). Collective behavior. In A. M. Lee (Ed.), *Principles of sociology* (p. 65-122). New York, NY: Barnes and Noble Books.

Brisson, Z. & Kontiris, K. (2012). *Tunisia: From revolutions to institutions*. Retrieved from: http://www.infodev.org/en/Document.1141.pdf

Butenhoff, L. (1999). *Social Movements and Political Reform in Hong Kong*. Westport, CT: Praeger Publishers.

Carothers, T. & Youngs, R. (2015). *The complexities of global protests.* Washington, DC: Carnegie Endowment for International Peace.
Chebib, N. K. & Sohail, R. M. (2011) The reasons social media contributed to the 2011 Egyptian Revolution, *International Journal of Business Research and Management, 2*(3). Retrieved from http://www.cscjournals.org/csc/manuscript/Journals/IJBRM/volume2/Issue3/IJBRM-52.pdf
Chiu, S. W. K. & Lui, T. L. (2000). *The dynamics of social movements in Hong Kong.* Hong Kong: Hong Kong University Press.
della Porta, D. & Diani, M. (2006). *Social movements: An introduction* (2nd Ed). Malden, MA: Blackwell Publishing.
Digital Republic (2012). *The Egyptian Facebook (R)evolution.* Retrieved from http://jeffesposito.com/wp-content/uploads/2011/02/Digital-Republic_Facebook_Twitter-Revolution.pdf
El-Ghobashy, M. (2011). The Praxis of the Egyptian Revolution. *Middle East Report, 258.*
Enjolras, B, Steen-Johnsen, K. & Wollebæk, D. (2013). Social media and mobilization to offline demonstrations: Transcending participatory divides? *New Media & Society, 15*(6), 890-908.
Gamson, W. A. (1992). *Talking Politics.* New York, NY: Cambridge University Press.
Garrett, R. K. (2006). Protest in an information society: A review of literature on social movements and new ICTs. *Information, Communication and Society, 9*(2), 202-224.
Hirzalla, F. & van Zoonen, L (2011). Beyond the Online/Offline Divide: How Youth's Online and Offline Civic Activities Converge. *Social Science Computer Review, 29*(4), 481-498.
Ibrahim, H. M. (2012). Balik kampong bawa berita benar: Malaysia perlukan perubahan. Retrieved from https://harismibrahim.wordpress.com/2012/10/22/balik-kampung-bawa-berita-benar-malaysia-perlukan-perubahan/
Johnson, P. (2014). *Prevalence of #occupycentral in Hong Kong Instagrams.* Retrieved from http://letstalkdata.com/2014/10/prevalence-of-occupycentral-in-hong-kong-instagrams/
Johnson, S. (2012). *Future Perfect: The Case for Progress in a Networked Age.* New York, NY: Riverhead.
Juris, J. (2012). Reflections on #occupy everywhere: social media, public space, and emerging logics of aggregation. *American Ethnologist, 39*(2), 259-279.
Kadri, A. (2013). *Arab world vs. East Asia: Economic development?* Retrieved from http://blogs.lse.ac.uk/mec/2013/02/01/arab-world-vs-east-asia-economic-development/
Kahn, R. & Kellner, D. (2004). New media and internet activism: From the 'Battle of Seattle' to blogging. *New Media & Society, 6*(1), 87-95.
Kellner, D. (2010). Media spectacle and media events. In N. Couldry, A. Hepp, & F. Krotz (Eds.), *Media events in a global age* (p.76-86). New York, NY: Routledge.
Khamis, S. & Vaughn, K. (2011). Cyberactivism in the Egyptian Revolution: How Civic Engagement and Citizen Journalism Tilted the Balance. *Arab Media & Society, 14.* Retrieved from http://www.arabmediasociety.com/articles/downloads/20120313094800_Khamis_Cyberactivism_updated.pdf
Kharas, H. & Gertz, G. (2010). *The new global middle class.* Retrieved from https://www.brookings.edu/wp-content/uploads/2016/06/03_china_middle_class_kharas.pdf
Khasnabish, A. & Haiven, M. (2014). Why social movements need the radical imagination? *Transformation.* Retrieved from https://www.opendemocracy.net/transformation/alex-khasnabish-max-haiven/why-social-movements-need-radical-imagination
Khoo, Y. H. (2014). Mobilization potential and democratization processes of the Coalition for Clean and Fair Elections (Bersih) in Malaysia: An interview with Hishamuddin Rais. *Austrian Journal of South-East Asian Studies, 7*(1), 111-120.

Lakey, G. (2012). *Strategizing for a living revolution*. Retrieved from http://turning-the-tide.org/files/living%20revolution%20strategy.pdf

Lim, M. (2012). Clicks, Cabs, Coffee Houses: Social Media and the Oppositional Movements in Egypt (2004-2011). *Journal of Communication, 62*(2), 231-248.

Lim, M. (2013a). Many Clicks but Little Sticks: Social Media Activism in Indonesia. *Journal of Contemporary Asia, 43*(4), 636-655.

Lim, M. (2013b). Framing Bouazizi: White Lies, Hybrid Network, and Collective/Connective Action in the 2010-2011 Tunisian Uprising. *Journalism: Theory, practice and criticism, 14*(7), 921-941.

Lim, M. (2014). Seeing Spatially: People, Networks and Movements in Digital and Urban Spaces. *International Development and Planning Review, 36*(1), 51-72.

Lim, M. (2015). A Cyber-Urban Space Odyssey: The Spatiality of Contemporary Social Movements. *New Geography, 07,* 117-123.

Lim, M. (2016). Sweeping the Unclean: Social Media and the Bersih Electoral Reform in Malaysia. *Global Media Journal, 14*(27), 1-10.

Lim, M. (2017). Digital Media and Malaysia's Electoral Reform Movement. In W. Berenschot, H. Schulte Nordholt & L. Bakker (Eds.), *Citizenship and Democratization in Southeast Asia* (p. 213-239). Leiden: Brill Academic Publisher.

Mansour, E. (2012). The role of social networking sites (SNSs) in the January 25th Revolution of Egypt. *Library Review, 61*(2), 128-159.

McCarthy, J. D. & Zald, M. N. (1977). Resource mobilization and social movements: A partial theory. *The American Journal of Sociology, 82*(6), 1212-1241.

Nesadurai, H. (2012). *Globalisation and economic security in East Asia*. New York: Routledge.

Ortiz, I., Burke, S., Berrada, M. & Cortés, H. (2013). *World Protest 2006-2013*. New York, NY: The Initiative for Policy Dialogue and Friedrich-Ebert-Stiftung.

Radsch, C. (2008). Core to commonplace: The evolution of Egypt's blogosphere. *Arab Media & Society*, 6. Retrieved from http://www.arabmediasociety.com/UserFiles/AMS6%20Courtney%20Radsch.pdf

Reitan, R. (2007). *Global activism*. New York, NY: Routledge.

Russell, A. (2011). *Networked: A Contemporary History of News in Transition* (1st Ed.). Cambridge, UK and Malden, MA: Polity Press.

Rodriguez, C., Ferron, B. & Shamas, K. (2014). Four challenges in the field of alternative, radical and citizens' media research. *Media, Culture & Society, 36*(2), 150–166.

Sakr, N. (2007). Al-Jazeera: Challenger or Lackey? The Politics of News on Al-Jazeera. In D. K. Thussu (ed.), *Media on the Move: Global Flow and Contra-Flow* (p. 116-32). New York: Routledge.

SCMP (South China Morning Post) (2012). *Protest against national education to end after government climbdown*. Retrieved from http://www.scmp.com/news/hong-kong/article/1032535/protest-against-national-education-end-after-government-climbdown

Shirky, C. (2011). The political power of social media. *Foreign Affairs*. Retrieved from https://www.foreignaffairs.com/articles/2010-12-20/political-power-social-media

Smith, J. (2001). Globalizing Resistance: The Battle of Seattle and the Future of Social Movements. *Mobilization, 6*(1), 1-19.

Snow, D. A., Rochford, E. B., Worden, S. K. & Benford, R. D. (1986). Frame alignment processes, micromoblization, and movement participation. *American Sociological Review, 51*(4), 464-481.

Solidarity Center. (2010). *The struggle for worker rights in Egypt*. Retrieved from http://www.solidaritycenter.org/wp-content/uploads/2015/02/pubs_egypt_wr1.pdf
Stepanova, E. (2011). The role of information communication technologies in the "Arab Spring", *PONARS Eurasia Policy Memo, No. 159*, May.
Straubhaar, J. D. (1991). Beyond Media Imperialism: Asymmetrical Interdependence and Cultural Proximity. *Critical Studies in Mass Communication, 8*(1), 39-59.
Tilly, C. (1978). *From mobilization to revolution*. Reading, MA: Addison Wesley.
Tilly, C. & Tarrow, S.G. (2006). *Contentious politics*. Boulder, CO: Paradigm Publishers.
Viegas, F. (2015). *What happens when just about anyone has access to sophisticated visualization tools?* Retrieved from http://fernandaviegas.com/democratizing_viz.html
We are social (2017). *Digital in 2017: Global overview*. Retrieved from http://wearesocial.com/uk/blog/2017/01/digital-in-2017-global-overview
World Bank (2017). *World Bank Open Data*. Retrieved from http://data.worldbank.org
Yamamoto, T. (2000). The future of civil society in Asia. In M. Caballero-Anthony & J. Hassan (Eds.), *Beyond the crisis: Challenges and opportunities*. Kuala Lumpur: ISIS.
Yuce, S., Agarwal, N., Lim, M., Robinson, R.S. & Wigand, R. (2014). Blogging, bridging, and brokering. *Journal of Global Information Management, 22*(4), 1-20.

Self-Mediation Practices of Arab Anarchists

Almut Woller

1 Introduction

Anarchist ideas have witnessed a renaissance in the last two decades not only in social movement practices and tactics. Usually, the 'Battle of Seattle' at the WTO summit in 1999, with hundreds of black-clad activists raging through the streets and disrupting the WTO-business-as-usual, is referenced as a marking event that put anarchist tactics and anarchists back on the global protest scene. But also more recent events bear witness to the strong presence of both *anarchist principles within* social movements, such as in the Occupy movement or the French Nuit Debout protests, and to *anarchists as actors* within movements (Gordon, 2007b, p. 29). Examples are the actions by the 'Destroika' group and other factions within the Blockupy movement in Frankfurt (Germany) in 2015 on the occasion of the opening of the new building of the European Central Bank: a large crowd attacked a police station, burning several police cars and setting barricades on fire, others flowed through lines of police in order to block the access roads to the ECB building (Spiegel Online, 2015); take as another example the violent protests by anarchists on the occasion of Donald Trump's presidential inauguration (Stockman, 2017). Moreover, the feuilletons from New York to Frankfurt have discussed the radical and militant Invisible Committee's publications "The coming insurrection" (2008) and even more so "To our friends" (2014) – surprisingly not only in pejorative ways.[1] Intriguing examples of more large scale projects of social change heavily influenced by anarchism are the notorious Zapatistas in Mexico, but also the anarchist turn "[f]rom Lenin to Bookchin" (de Jong, 2016) within the Kurdish movement. Influenced by the ideas of anarchist academic and philosopher Murray Bookchin, among others, whilst in prison, PKK-leader Abdullah Öcalan pushed the PKK's strategy

1 The Invisible Committee is a collective and anonymous pen name; their original publications are in French.

C. Richter et al. (Hrsg.), *Digital Media and the Politics of Transformation in the Arab World and Asia*, Studies in International, Transnational and Global Communications, https://doi.org/10.1007/978-3-658-20700-7_3

away from national liberation towards democratic autonomy (Öcalan, 2013). The rise in anarchists' presence and in the presence of anarchist ideas is reflected also in academia: take David Graeber in the field of anthropological studies (2009), Richard Day in social movement theory (2004, 2005), or John Holloway's critique of taking over power as transformative strategy (2002). Moreover, journals have been founded throughout the last decade to move anarchist perspectives forward in academia (e.g., Anarchist Developments in Cultural studies, Perspectives on Anarchist Theory). What these eclectic examples and references suggest is that anarchism as political philosophy and movement matters – and it is worth considering it when discussing the politics of transformation after the 2010/2011 uprisings. For those readers less familiar with anarchism (or rather, more familiar with the stereotypes of anarchists as vandals and 'slobs'), I will provide some orientation to understanding "anarchism and its aspirations" (Milstein, 2010) in the section further below on approaches to defining anarchism.

Far from featuring vibrant anarchist 'scenes' such as exist in European or North American countries, Arab countries have nevertheless witnessed the presence of anarchist ideas, activities and tactics well before the uprisings (Kalicha & Kuhn, 2010). In Egypt, Tunisia and Morocco, for example, the "affordance structure" (Cammaerts, 2015) or the "mediation opportunity structure" (Cammaerts, 2012) of digital media coupled with the uprisings from 2011 onwards have enabled the visibility of anarchist discourses and activities. Not only did rebellious actors employ typical anarchist tactics – such was the case in the Black Bloc activities in Egypt in 2013 (El Guindy, 2013) – but collectives that referenced anarchism explicitly as their political leaning also became more visible, such as in the case of Mouvement Désobéissance or Feminism Attack in Tunisia. During and in the aftermath of the so-called Arab Spring, these actors made themselves heard and seen both on the streets and on digital media. Violent direct actions of which videos are uploaded and circulated are only a small part of the bigger picture of self-mediation practices, which comprises, for example, discussions within the anarchist community about practices or techniques to remember the history of own struggles or of the ones of anarchists across time. It is these media practices that I will discuss in the present article. I treat digital media as an affordance structure in which "technologies of a collective self" (Cammaerts, 2015) can unfold.

In order to elaborate this approach I have structured the article in the following way: First, I will attempt to guide the reader in a cursory way through the debate on what anarchism is and what it is not. On the basis of understanding anarchism as political movement I will, secondly, go on to suggest that we think of anarchists as a special kind of political community: a diasporic community. Thirdly, I will explore how anarchists treat each other and anarchism on and through digital media, i.e., how they deal with anarchism and how they establish connections transnationally. In the last section preceding the conclusion, I will illustrate my theses through empirical examples from digital media.

2 Approaches to Defining Anarchism

What distinguishes anarchism from classical social protest movements? Anarchist politics are oftentimes not granted the status of being 'real' politics due to a very narrow understanding of 'the political'. The commonly acknowledged form of democratic politics refers to representative, parliamentary procedures. The mode at the basis of this model of democracy is a "politics of demand" in which actors such as social movements protest within the given structures and articulate demands towards institutions, the parties, and the government. Actions of a politics of demand are "oriented to ameliorating the practices of states, corporations and everyday life, through either influencing or using state power to achieve irradiation effects" (Day, 2004, p. 733). The logic of political transformation that underlies this mode of politics is a "logic of hegemony" (ibid., p. 719) and social movements "tend to advocate only for *counter*-hegemonic struggles against various modes of subordination" (ibid., p. 727, italics in original). 'Hegemonic struggles' means that only by prevailing over others (i.e., by becoming hegemonic) – through successful campaigning, protests, elections, legislation etc. – actors will ultimately be able to shape the course of political and social development. The perspective on transformation is thus fundamentally informed by "the commonsensical assumption that meaningful social change – and social order itself – can only be achieved through the deployment of universalizing hierarchical forms, epitomized by the nation-state" (ibid., p. 717). However, within the politics of demand and its underlying logic of hegemony only the *content* of structures of domination and exploitation is alterable, whereas as the form of given structures and categories are not susceptible of change (ibid., p. 233). As opposed to this, anarchism puts forward a 'categorical' critique of given political institutions, structures and categories such as the state, authority and representation, instead aiming at overcoming all forms of domination and hierarchy in favor of a self-organized, needs- rather than profit-oriented society (Gordon, 2007b, p. 30). Pursuing "non-hegemonic forms of radical social change" anarchist politics follow a mode of "politics of the act" by "actions oriented neither to achieving state power nor to ameliorating its effects" (Day, 2004, p. 717, 723). It is based on "direct action as a primary mode of political engagement, both destructive and constructive" (Gordon, 2007b, p. 29f.). Day clarifies against simplifying interpretations that practicing "a politics of the act does not mean simply 'doing as you please', just as direct action does not mean simply 'blowing things up'" (Day, 2004, p. 734; see Graeber 2009). The logic attached to the politics of the act is the "logic of affinity" which emerges "out of an anarchist tradition of theory and practice which rejects the struggle for hegemony in its dual (Gramscian) nature as domination over others via the state form and 'consensual' direction of others via ideological sway over 'civil society'" (Day, 2004, p. 740). Its key elements are

> "a desire to create alternatives to state and corporate forms of social organization (…) via disengagements and reconstruction rather than by reform or revolution; with the end of creating not a new knowable totality (counter-hegemony), but of enabling experiments and the emergence of new forms of subjectivity; and finally, focusing on relations between these subjects, in the name of inventing new forms of community" (Day, 2004, p. 740).

Against this background, again, transformation is not measured by the establishment of rule-of-law procedures or fair, democratic elections, but rather is a (never-ending) process in which people follow their political aspirations against and outside the given political structures. The "methodology for social change" is shaped by "prefigurative politics" which does not postpone meaningful change to a time after a political revolution but anticipates ('prefigures') the desired society within the current struggle. Anarchism's strength in societal transformations is to draw attention to mechanisms of domination and to developments where means and ends diverge, based on the assumption "that the character of a transformation will have strong effect on its outcome" (Day, 2004, p. 138). It may be considered as a weakness that anarchism's "strongly open-ended conception of politics (…) is detached from any notion of a post-revolutionary resting point" (Gordon, 2007b, p. 30, 42), however, "considerations of efficiency or unity" have no priority per se (ibid., p. 41). Furthermore, the notion of transformation does not only aim at changing the society, for example through labor struggles, but also at the level of micro politics or "politics of the first person" (Katsiaficas, 1998, p. 197; Day, 2004, p. 723) that stresses the transformation of human beings and their subjectivity.[2] As the U.S. based anarchist group CrimethInc. states:

2 The notion of the "politics of the first person" refers to the individual (to the pronoun 'I'). The strategy to put oneself into the center instead of a 'third person' (the proletariat etc.) was characteristic for the movement of the Autonomen (autonomous movement) from the 1970s onwards in Europe (ibid.). It has become central within many anarchist currents around the world.

> "It is crucial that we seek change not in the name of some doctrine or grand cause, but on behalf of ourselves, so that we will be able to live more meaningful lives. Similarly we must seek first and foremost to alter the contents of our lives in a revolutionary manner, rather than direct our struggle towards world-historical changes which we will not live to witness" (CrimethInc., 2000).

Some further remarks on the definition of anarchism are necessary for several reasons: firstly, in some circles, there exists a pejorative misconception of anarchism as chaos, violence, and absence of order, in which the term 'anarchist' is synonymous with 'vandal', and secondly, I want to avoid confusion about what and whom we actually mean when we speak of anarchists. Let me first point to the difference between 'anarchy' and 'anarchism.' Whereas the first denotes the absence of domination (and not the absence of order), the second denotes a *political program* which aims at the abolishment of domination. The choice of the circled letter A as an anarchist symbol disclaims the commonsensical confusion of anarchy or anarchism with chaos, which is not only crooked in terms of the Greek origin of the word[3]: The A is placed within the O as an abbreviation of "Anarchy is Order".[4] To clarify what is meant with 'anarchism', I suggest to speak of it as a political movement and philosophy that was articulated first in the 19th century, that has been transforming ever since, and that embraces a wide range of orientations, from syndicalist labor struggles to more 'lifestyle' oriented practices. This is not compatible with the ontological approach that identifies all movements or struggles throughout history as anarchist that have been organized on the basis of (later-to-be) anarchist principles – or principles that have become central to anarchism as political movement and philosophy (for the ontological approach see e.g. Marshall, 2008 and Veneuse, 2009). For example, direct action – a category central to the anarchist politics of the act – as a principle of political practices has existed long before anarchism as a political movement occurred (e.g. Graeber, 2009). However, not everything that is a direct action is anarchist. Finally, anarchist principles of organization or practices, such as direct action and flattening of hierarchies, may shape a struggle or protest movement, but this is not enough to denote the movement itself as 'anarchist'. For

3 The Greek term 'arche' means authority, domination, rule and the prefix 'a-' is the alpha privativum, the negating alpha. Thus anarchy literally means 'without domination'.

4 Accounts of the origin of the symbol vary: according to Marshall, it was the French group Jeunesse Libertaire that created it in 1964 (Marshall, 2008, p. 445), whereas Wikipedia suggests the Federal Council of Spain of the International Workers Association as the creator of the symbol in 1868 (Anarchist symbolism, n.d.); another source plausibly points the use of the symbol in the Spanish Civil War (afaq, 2008). In either case, it is acknowledged that it refers to a quote by anarchist thinker Joseph Proudhon (Marshall, 2008, p. 445).

example, the Occupy movement was strongly shaped by anarchist principles – no specific demands, no leaders, self-organization, direct action – and so are the Nuit Debout protests in France with their programmatic slogan that defies any politics of demand: "Nos rêves ne rentrent pas dans vos urnes" (Our dreams do not fit into your ballot boxes). In his seminal article, Mohamed Bamyeh rightly points to the "Anarchist Method, Liberal Intention, Authoritarian Lesson" (2013) of the uprisings in Egypt – anarchist principles were a shaping factor in 2011. However, whereas it is necessary to point to the prevalence of typically anarchist practices and tactics, I fear it would be a distortion to call Occupy, Nuit Debout and the "Arab Spring" straightaway an anarchist movements/revolution. I think it is legitimate to subsume the various tactics such as the ones just mentioned under a label of "anarchistic" where they "partake of a logic that can be found within certain self-identified strains of anarchist theory and practice" (Day, 2004, p. 731), but I suggest that at least some sort of qualification has to be made. My approach to defining anarchism, at least for the purpose of my current research, thus aligns roughly with Uri Gordon's who addresses anarchism "as a political culture, with distinct forms of organization, campaigning and direct action repertoires, and political discourse and ideology" (2007a, p. 5).[5] This narrower, non-ontological definition should help sharpen the analysis of anarchism in the Arab region.

3 Anarchism in the Arab Region

In my study, I use the term 'anarchists' for the groups and individuals that I want to research, but this is meant to include the broadest possible spectrum of anarchists who self-identify as such. It includes anti-authoritarian, libertarian and autonomous radical left actors as long as they – metaphorically speaking – spray a circle around the letter A and do so with political intention. The names chosen by groups to describe their leanings or to self-identify depend largely on the colonial history and

5 I do not, however, share the usage of the term ideology in this context. Whenever talking about political goals, programs or convictions, they should be named as such. The use of 'ideology' as a 'neutral' term to describe *any* political thought or practice (feminism as much as chauvinism, racism as much as anti-capitalism, etc.) goes back to Lenin's revision, analytical flattening, and finally, reversion of an analytically rich Marxian approach – which, alas, Stuart Hall, on the basis of Althusser, has made popular in Cultural Studies and social sciences, by defining ideology as "mental frameworks" of any social group (Hall, 1986, p. 30; overview see Rehmann, 2013; further critique from the perspective of the Marxian Value Criticism see Kurz, 2007, esp. para. 4).

thus on the non-Arabic languages dominant in the respective countries. Whereas in the Maghreb countries we mostly encounter the French 'libertaire', 'anarchiste', or 'anti-autoritaire', the Egyptian way of calling themselves anarchists is mostly through the noun 'anarkiyyoun', as well as through the adjective 'taharrouri', i.e., 'libertarian', or 'la-sultawi', i.e., 'anti-authoritarian'. The choice of name also depends on where a person would position herself within the anarchist spectrum: those oriented towards workers' struggles and in favor of syndicalist (workers' unions') strategies for social transformation would rather refer to 'ishtirakiyya taharrouri-yya', i.e., libertarian socialism, whereas autonomous groups who are more inclined toward strategies of social and cultural transformation of society and of their lives would mostly refer to 'la-sultawi'. 'Fawdawiyyoun', however, would be the Arabic equivalent of 'slobs' or 'vandals', typically a pejorative term imposed by others that refers to the misconception of anarchism as chaos, violence and absence of order.[6]

Fig. 1 Graffiti reading "A's Back" (Circle-A). Tunis 2014. (Source: author)

6 For an introduction to anarchism from within anarchist academia, see Milstein, 2010, or Gordon, 2007a. For an outstanding two-part documentary on the global history of anarchism see the Arte documentary "Ni Dieu ni maître – Une histoire de l'anarchisme" by Ramonet (2013).

Fig. 2 Graffiti reading "The Union of Anarchists in Lebanon" (Circle-A in the center). Beirut (quarter of Hamra) 2017 (Source: author)

In order to avoid misunderstandings I should note that I do not include in my analysis the famous soccer ultras (Heck, 2015; Jerzak, 2013). It is by now widely acknowledged that ultras played a tremendous role for protecting protesters during the Arab uprisings, thus enabling the squatting of Tahrir square in Egypt and literally safeguarding the revolution (Gibril, 2015). In Tunisia as well, ultras significantly helped to clear public spaces from police and can claim their share in setting in motion a fundamental political transformation process. What, then, is the relation between ultras and anarchism? Whereas ultras certainly play a role in circulating and appropriating anarchist repertoires in their respective countries (black bloc tactics, confrontation with police and state, rudimentary criticism of capitalist commodification of soccer, spreading Circle-A graffiti and other anarchist codes), their practices are primarily bound to soccer and not to the political transformation of society at large (Heck, 2015). This can be well illustrated with ultras from a Tunis soccer club who call themselves "Zapatistas" and spread Zapatista graffiti. Of course, it is possible that an ultra can at the same time be an anarchist – and indeed, the Egyptian ultras have politicized their movement at different stages since 2011 (Gibril, 2015) – but ultras are not anarchists *per se*, in the definition I suggest, merely on the basis of anarchist practices (direct action) and symbols that they have included.

Fig. 3 Graffiti by ultra group of a Tunis soccer club reading "Zapatista". Photo taken in suburbs of Tunis 2014. (Source: author)

Most of the scholarship on anarchism is produced from within the movements and deals with the Global North, including Russia and anarchism's role in the Russian revolutions and uprisings (1905, 1917, Kronstadt 1921) and in the Spanish Civil War. But there are also works that turn their attention to the Global South, of which one outstanding example are van der Walt's and Schmidt's (2013) studies on the anarcho-syndicalist movements globally and Kalicha and Kuhn's (2010) collection of interviews with anarchists from all over the world. It would be a mistake to think that anarchism is alien to the Arab world or that the spread of anarchism has been a one-way street from colonial 'center' to 'periphery'. The seminal work of Ilham Khuri-Makdisi (2010) about radical networks in the Mediterranean bears witness to the historical presence of anarchists and radical, anarchist discourses especially in Egypt and Lebanon, but also in the transnational connections between the Mediterranean and South America. Being marginal, but far from being irrelevant, anarchists found means to network with peers transnationally using print publications and personal mobility. Khuri-Makdisi sketches in detail how, through print media, anarchists at the turn of the 19th century spread radical, socialist and anarchist ideas and maintained connections across far distances:

> "The periodicals were central to the establishment and maintenance of this global community and sense of solidarity, a feeling that was also consolidated by the constant circulation of members of this network, who brought with them letters, news, books, and periodicals by fellow anarchists" (p. 119f.; see also p. 94f.).

Situationists[7] around Guy Debord, such as Mustapha Khayati, were active in Algeria in the 1960s, their manifesto was translated into Arabic and they have left traces that have as of yet been little researched (NOT BORED! a and b)[8]; in Jordan as well, radical currents in art (here Dadaism) have interrelated with anarchism (Kalicha & Kuhn, 2010, p. 195). Not much can be said about anarchism for the period from the 1920s until the "reemergence of anarchism in Egypt" in the 21st century so far, both for "historical and (…) historiographical" reasons (Galián, 2015, p. 351, 357). Possibly, anarchist activists were absorbed into sharpening the anti-colonial struggle (Gorman, 2011) and repression of leftist dissidents under Nasser. Just like Galián, who has conducted empirical research on one anarchist group in Egypt and who speaks of a *re*-emergence of anarchism, I am not suggesting a historical continuity between anarchism in the Mediterranean region then and now. In fact, Gordon claims (for the Global North) "that contemporary anarchism is only ephemerally related to the nineteenth- and early twentieth-century thread of libertarian-socialist movements and ideas, which was effectively repressed out of existence in the first half of the last century by Fascism, Bolshevism and the American Red Scare" (2007b, p. 30; Ramonet, 2013, part two).

Hence, I mean to take the historical case described by Khouri-Makdisi as a peg on which to hang the idea that today it would be easier than ever for marginal(ized) actors to become visible and connect with peers transnationally simply because digital media are easily accessible and can spread content across large distances with comparatively little effort. Unlike television as a mass media tool that potentially

---

7 The Situationist Internationale, influential in the 1950s and 60s, started "in an artistic milieu, [but] finally developed a more overtly political position from which its members gave full expression to their hostility to every aspect of existing society" (Plant, 2000, p. 1). Situationism influenced Marxist thought, but "the movement also stands in a less distinct line of pleasure-seeking libertarianism, popular resistance, and autonomous struggle" (ibid.).

8 Laura Galián's dissertation on Situationism in the Arab World is forthcoming in 2018.

circulates protest practices and discourses transnationally, the distinct quality of digital media lies in their potential not only to make visible, but also to facilitate connectivity. Transnational connectivity is an important notion for a political community that rejects nation states as a category of belonging and whose members strive for a social and political transformation without domination. Digital media constitute an affordance structure (Cammaerts, 2015) because they are a potential resource for the imagined anarchist community to see each other, know of each other, engage in discussions together, and archive history from their own perspective. This has already been pointed out in other contexts, for example, with regards to mediated networks of Muslim communities for which "the technologies of the Internet and the advent of the blogosphere offer a decisively innovative set of interconnected pathways toward a public sphere that reaches far below and rises high above the territorial level of the nation-state" (Lim, 2009, p. 179). The question thus arises: how does this affordance structure matter to anarchists as a community with a necessarily (but not always explicit) transnational orientation? The fact that digital media enable, on the one hand, transnational circulation of anarchist discourses in the form of text, images, videos, etc. and that, on the other hand, they enable contact between anarchists through various tools such as Facebook, blogs, Twitter and email invites the question how exactly digital media are used and integrated into practices that establish, maintain and reinforce this transnational, 'diasporic' community.

4 Anarchists as Diasporic Group

I conceptualize anarchists as a diasporic community in a way that is detached from ethnicity and instead aligns itself with an open paradigm within diaspora studies (e. g. Clifford, 1994; Cohen, 2008; critical: Tölölyan, 1996). I am not the first to apply the concept of diaspora to a non-ethnic community. Especially the research on 'queer diasporas' informs my understanding of anarchists as diasporic community: Fortier finds in "diaspora […] a rich heuristic device to think about questions of belonging, continuity, and solidarity in the context of dispersal and transnational networks of connection" (2002, p. 184). Based on Howard Rheingold's foundational work "The Virtual Community" (1993), which shaped early Internet studies in the field (Wakeford, 2002, p. 128), researchers in queer studies have been treating digital media as spaces where "community-making" can take place, especially in contexts of isolation and marginalization (ibid.). In the context of, for example, lesbian Chinese women, Martin's research analyzes "how […] people in different locations imagine transnational units" (2009, p. 286). Based on qualitative interviews with those women about their media practices, the author sketches the development of different, overlapping feelings of belonging to both geographic and cultural spaces. Martin identifies a "globalist lesbian discourse" that transcends the territorial location (p. 299) as a result of a translocal connectivity that is being experienced in chats und forums. I assume that the case of anarchists is quite similar to the one of queer diaspora described by the authors for three reasons: anarchists share a marginal position in society due to them being at odds with social and political norms; they are an imagined, transnational or deterritorial community; and they both have a vision of a better place, which does not (yet) exist (a utopia in the literal meaning; Fortier, 2002, p. 189, see also Clifford, 1994, p. 328). Unlike queer people, anarchists might not face lifelong discrimination, but are certainly confronted with incomprehension and rejection of their convictions, not to mention repression by the state. Digital media potentially serve these kinds of communities by allowing them to overcome feelings of isolation, to see peers, share their experiences and eventually connect with them. Whereas the Internet has not always initiated connectivity among the diasporic group, it certainly facilitates it and allows for contact that would otherwise be impossible: "Yes, we have met with anarchists from Egypt, and via the Internet I know a few anarchists in Syria. We have obtained the translation of Daniel Guérin's book[9] from Lebanese anarchists […]. I have also come across a manifesto from the Moroccan art scene which refers to anarchism, but I don't know the authors personally" (Kalicha & Kuhn, 2010, p. 195; my translation). The task of research in this field is also to understand more systematically how digital media add to, replace or change non-digital modes of connectivity, such as non-digital media but also in-person meetings, within the diaspora.

---

9 The book referred to was originally published in French by anarchist thinker and activist Daniel Guérin in 1965 with the title "L'anarchisme. De la doctrine à l'action". It was translated by Lebanese anarchist Georges Saad with the help of his French comrades of L'Alternative Liber-taire and published in 2008 as: التحررية: من العقيدة إلى الممارسة (al-taharrouriyya: min al-'aqida ila al-mumarasa). Interestingly Guérin's book was translated again into Arabic in 2012 by Hassan Dabbouq with the title الأناركية من النظرية إلى الممارسة (Al-anarkiyya min al-nazariyya ila al-mumarasa; Guérin, 2012).

5 Interpreting Self-Mediation Practices as Technologies of a Collective, Diasporic Self

Apart from the diaspora lens, the theoretical framework of my analysis of what Arab anarchists actually do with digital media, and with what consequences, is based on Bart Cammaerts' idea of conceiving of social movements as a collective self. This is inspired by Michel Foucault's genealogy of how the subject, the individual self, has constructed itself in different epochs in history – namely through different *technologies* of the self that the self learned to master throughout his or her life. The construction of self aimed, for example, at submission under religious authority (God, the Church) in medieval Christianity: What does an individual have to do in order to lead a good life according to Christian morals? (Foucault, 1997, p. 242ff.). Alternatively, it aimed at knowing yourself, caring for the self, or reflecting upon the self in certain philosophical currents in Greco-Roman philosophy (p. 234ff.). Thus, technologies are means through which the self creates an "ethical relation to the self" (Burkitt, 2002, p. 221), but also through which it internalizes coercive social structures with the overarching aim of leading a good life (ibid., p. 222), "to attain a certain state of happiness, purity, wisdom, perfection or immortality" (Foucault, 1997, p. 225). It should be clear then, that the term 'technology' in this context does not refer to digital media technologies and electronics, but to *practices* as "means through which humans produce not only products and works, but also themselves as human selves" (Burkitt, 2002, p. 224).

Cammaerts transfers the technologies that Foucault identifies for the Stoic philosophical tradition from the formation of an *individual* self to the formation of a *collective* self (2015, p. 89). It is important to understand that he does not imply that we live in an era of Stoic philosophical tradition, but uses three distinct technologies metaphorically as a heuristic framework "to make sense of the roles that social media play for protest movements" (ibid., p. 87). These three technologies are called *disclosure, examination,* and *remembrance*. Against this backdrop he can interpret dissemination of movement discourses as a technique of disclosure; internal organizing, reflection upon and coordination of action as a technique of examination; and archiving, memorizing 'movement deeds', and self-recording as techniques of remembrance (ibid., p. 92). What is compelling about the threefold heuristic of disclosure, examination and remembrance, is that it forces us to draw a more holistic picture of how collectives communicate because the very broad array of diverse communication matters, including posting content to debating on email lists to memorizing actions.

Like Cammaerts, I do not ask from a media-centered perspective what digital media can do for a social movement or group, but rather from the opposite, practice-oriented perspective, "what, quite simply, are people doing in relation to media across a whole range of situations and contexts?" (Couldry, 2004, p. 119). However, my approach differs from Cammaerts's in that I do not analyze a social movement during phases of acute protest and mobilization, but rather a political, transnationally dispersed community in times of absence of acute protest. Thus, I follow the assumption that anarchists use digital media not (primarily) as a means for an end (mobilization, political campaigning, convincing people of a message, etc.), but because they recognize what they do as worthwhile (cf. Burkitt, 2002, p. 222). Conceiving of this community as diasporic, I am interested in how they "cultivate" their collective, diasporic self through self-mediation practices ("cultivation of the self", Foucault, 1997, e.g. p. 234). In other words, what are the mediated social techniques that constitute the anarchist diasporic community? If "technology is a means through which humans produce not only products and works, but also themselves", then self-mediation practices are techniques through which an anarchist diaspora produces not only images, videos and texts, but also themselves as an imagined community or as a collective self (Burkitt 2002, p. 224). Digital media appear as the affordance structure in which technologies of the self can unfold.

6 Open Letters, 'Likes', and Profile Pictures

In the following section, I will illustrate the three categories of disclosure, examination and remembrance by giving examples of the self-mediation practices within the anarchist diasporic community. Each of the three (deduced) 'lead categories' contains several aspects or subcategories which are (inductively) derived from the material. The diaspora lens, again, serves as a heuristic to identify communicative acts as self-mediation practices.

There are two aspects of *disclosure*: One is how anarchists make themselves visible. Visibility has to be acknowledged as a key category for research on digital media, especially for political activism[10] (Ballenthien et al., 2015), but also for communities such as diasporas: Visibility "is not only the precondition for successful political engagement online in many cases, but appears as a shaping factor of contemporary digital culture [...]: Through their visibility individuals can be found and contacted online, and as such it acts as elementary precondition for agile communication and networking" (ibid., p. 4, my translation). In the context of transnational or

10 On the gendered effects of "multi-layered visibilities" in feminist activism see Anna Antonakis' contribution in this volume.

diasporic communities, the assumption that visibility "breeds identification and makes it possible" is very central (Brighenti, 2007, p. 333). When it comes to visibility on digital media, however, research tends to stress surveillance, whereas the aspect of connectivity with peers is less emphasized (see Forschungsjournal Soziale Bewegungen, 2015). For example, through Facebook, collectives become findable and available for contact. This can be well illustrated by the simple presence on Facebook with a group profile. Despite the fact that surveillance and repression on Facebook are a serious issue, especially for political actors with a radical outlook (Cammaerts, 2015; Youmans & York, 2012), it nevertheless appears to be a suitable tool. Clearly, anarchist groups use the social media tool to connect to other groups by 'liking' them and thus to somehow integrate these other, distant groups into their diasporic horizon. And vice versa, they are 'liked' by others, and are thus seen by their diasporic peers.

The second aspect of disclosure is how the groups make anarchist discourses visible and diffuse them. Clearly, digital media potentially make content available that is otherwise simply not accessible due to scarcity or marginalization in local libraries (Kalicha & Kuhn, 2010, p. 195) – it is important to keep in mind the background that the Leninist-Stalinist orientation of socialism in Arab countries was not exactly favorable of radical, libertarian opposition (Bustani, 2014, p. 35). The only book on anarchism available in bookstores in larger cities such as Beirut and Tunis is usually Noam Chomsky's *On Anarchism* (as of 2017 in Beirut and 2014 in Tunis). The only hard copy of an anarchist book in Arabic (to the best of my knowledge) is Daniel Guérin's above-mentioned "Anarchism: From theory to practice". In 2012, an anthology of Mikhail Bakunin's writings was translated to Arabic as a digital version, uploaded on the Internet as a PDF file, and posted on Facebook by the group Arab Anarchists (Arab Anarchists, 2012). The largest blog on anarchism in the Arabic language, الأناركية بالعربية (al-anarkiyya bi-l-arabiyya; i. e., Anarchism in Arabic), was launched by Egyptian anarchists from the milieu of the Libertarian Socialist Movement. They have been posting translations of texts on the Spanish Civil War, of classical anarchist thinkers such as Pjotr Alexejewitsch Kropotkin, translations of contemporary thinkers such as David Graeber, and their own pieces on free love, literature, or on the Egyptian uprising.

In order to illustrate *examination* with two supposed aspects of a) organizing diasporic activities and b) reflecting upon practices within the diaspora, I will give examples from the Tahrir International Collective Network (ICN) website and other blogs. Tahrir-ICN is a wordpress blog (they also have a Facebook page and a Twitter account). It was jointly founded by activist and author Leila Al-Shami together with around five other individuals from different countries; the blog was very active throughout 2012 and 2013, though parallel to the abatement of protest waves in the region the blog activity decreased. In their "manifesto" Tahrir-ICN states that "through this network we want to create a platform for discussions, for presenting the issues of struggle and their local conditions and differences, for presenting and explaining undertaken actions and planning joint activities in future" (Tahrir-ICN, n.d.). They express the need "to get to know each other, to see points of contact and to understand respective local conditions" (ibid.). The blog constitutes a valuable collection of interviews, opinion pieces, news, solidarity notes, calls for meeting and other texts, mostly in English, written by external authors and collected and reposted by the blog admins, mentioning the source. Not everything is concerned explicitly with anarchism, but nine of the about 70 tags feature "anarch*" and search categories include "history of anarchism" and "theory of anarchism". Tahrir-ICN posted a "Call for a first Mediterranean anarchist meeting", thus not only making visible the Tunisian anarchist collective Le Commun Libertaire, but more specifically helping to mobilize for the meeting held in Tunis in March 2015 (Tahrir-ICN, 2015).

An interesting example of the aspect of reflecting on practices is the open letter of the US-based collective CrimethInc. Ex-Workers' Collective. In early 2013, they addressed actors who had formed the 'black bloc' during the anti-Muslim Brotherhood protests in Egypt which gained notoriety in national and international press (LeVine, 2013) and in social media (Moynihan, 2013).[11] Personal profiles and group pages that referred to black blocs mushroomed on Facebook, and there was some hype about this phenomenon that gained a lot of attention from anarchist circles in the West. CrimethInc. then posted an open letter in both English and Arabic on their blog (CrimethInc., 2013), which was subsequently circulated digitally and linked or reposted on other European anarchist blogs, e.g., on the German speaking linksunten (Magazinredaktion, 2013) and on the transnational libcom.org (ASyndicalist, 2013). The letter articulates the aim of 'examining' the practices of those who appear as members of the diasporic community: "We have already been in a kind of dialogue with you, exchanging signals of revolt across the ocean. We've circulated reports of your struggle here, and now we are seeing photos and videos of our actions appear in youtube collages from Egypt. But we want more dialogue than youtube collages allow. We want to be able to discuss strategy as well as tactics, and goals as well as strategy" (CrimethInc., 2013, para. 3). The letter probably never reached the Egyptian addressee[12], but provoked "A Letter to

11 See the contribution of Hanan Badr in this volume on a detailed description of the situation in Egypt after 2011.

12 This has to do with the fact that the Black Bloc was most likely formed by the ultra communities around two of the most prominent Cairo soccer clubs, Al-Ahly and Zamalek,

North American Anarchists" from the Beirut-based collective Radical Beirut who engaged in a meta-discussion about the relationship between anarchists from the post-colonial periphery and the West, best summed up by the following quote:

> "We appreciate the feedback and the exchange, and we think it's desired and needed, but we feel that there are a lot of subtle expectations that we should become another version of you. And we don't want to. Being on the other end of the equation, the one that has been getting drone missiles, uranium depleted shells, and imperialism for decades, we can honestly tell you that whatever you tried, it didn't work well for us, and it seems it didn't work for you as well" (Radical Beirut, 2013).

It was initially posted on their Facebook page where it stirred many comments, afterwards it was again circulated on blogs.

The remaining point to be illustrated is that of *remembrance* with its aspects of archiving own struggles and remembering those of the anarchist diaspora across time. The latter can take forms as subtle as posting a photo of anarchist troops in the Spanish Civil War as one's Facebook profile picture (Libertarian Socialist Movement Egypt, n.d.); or as straightforward as a Youtube video of a public coffee house lecture in Alexandria on the historical presence of anarchism and anarchists in this city (Hassan, 2013); or as elaborate as Tahrir-ICN's translation of a 1950 magazine article about an Algerian anarchist who fought both in Algeria and in the Spanish Civil War in the Durruti Column, the troops led by famous anarchist Buenaventura Durruti (Tahrir-ICN, n.y.). By referring to these past struggles and personalities in their self-mediation practices, anarchists position themselves within this larger history and also appropriate it as their own history. Through this, anarchist discourses become accessible more easily than was the case before the spread of the Internet. A Jordanian anarchist explains how he became acquainted with anarchist thought through the Internet, whereas in public libraries anarchist works are close to non-existent: "We knew about anarchism from the Internet. (...) Back then, there were only a few Arabic texts about anarchism on the Internet, now we find more and more. (...) In Amman's university library you'll find a few Arabic books about anarchism (...) – hidden in a large collection about Marxism" (Kalicha & Kuhn, 2010, p. 194f.; my translation).

Anarchism as a political movement has played an important role in revolutionary periods and in important historical moments. In the case of the Spanish Civil War from 1936-1939 (to which the Egyptian Libertarian Socialist Movement refers on

---

which are both experienced in radical tactics to confront police forces. As mentioned above, soccer ultras are primarily concerned with soccer and probably do not follow the news or debates within the anarchist community.

Facebook), anarchists were a crucial faction on the Republican side that fought the rightist Nationalist side led by Franco (Esenwein, 2005). Today's strength of anarcho-syndicalism in Spain and literary works such as George Orwell's *Homage to Catalonia* (1938), however, remind us of the power of the anarchist movement and that a society oriented towards anarchist principles indeed was a realistic alternative to both authoritarian regimes and representative democracy. Another case that is referenced on Facebook by Arab anarchists through photos and short texts is the Makhnovist movement from 1918-1921 in Ukraine. Up to 80,000 anarchists fought under Makhno's black flag against the tsarist counterrevolution and the German occupation, redistributed land, and helped build local self-governance structures. They strongly opposed the Bolsheviks' bureaucratization of the Russian Revolution, which ultimately led to their killing and persecution under Lenin and Trotsky (Arshinov, 1974; Zak, 2017) and to the crushing of the Kronstadt insurrection 1921 (Avrich, 1991; Voline, 1990). It is remarkable that Arab anarchists today refer to this anarchist history in Central and Eastern Europe and Russia as well as Spain on Facebook, and doing so, I would argue, is a form of asserting one's place within a greater diasporic community and its history.

Besides *diachronic* remembrance there is the aspect of archiving struggles *synchronically*, by activists themselves or by their contemporaries. Certainly, the task of remembering and representing anarchist visions, struggles, and actors in history writing has never been adopted by 'the winners', be it in the European and South American dictatorships, the West's liberal democratic societies, or in the Stalinist Soviet Union. Even within leftist historiography globally, anarchism is far underrepresented.[13] Coming back to the Arab region, Khuri-Makdisi makes a compelling argument that her discoveries "serve to challenge the dominant historiographical narrative of absence, namely, the absence of radical, socialist, and leftist movements" (2010, p. 111). An anti-authoritarian American-Syrian blogger expressed his fear that, in the case of writing Syria's history, "perhaps it's too late, and the hegemonic narratives are too powerful in the present to overcome. But if people start now, maybe the history books can at least be fair" (Atassi, 2013). Where more radical and marginal actors such as anarchists become re-marginalized in the writing of history, the accessibility of digital media tools becomes all the more crucial for the remembrance of radical imaginaries and anarchists' presence in struggles such as

13 A conference on "The left and the Arab revolutions" had nothing to say about anarchism (Jarrar, 2013), and Hilal and Hermann's (2014) otherwise meritorious work, "Mapping the Arab Left", has no mention of anarchism at all. For a critique of European Marxism's continuing ignorance of anarchism and its suppression by the former, see Kellermann (2011). One outstanding and rich publication on anarchism/syndicalism globally is van der Walt and Schmidt (2013).

the uprisings of 2010/2011: "[D]igital media allow new articulations of memory to emerge" and bear the "possibilities for facilitating 'alternative' social memories" (Keightley & Schlesinger, 2014). Print proofs of anarchists' sheer existence, such as the above-mentioned interview collection published in German and dating from before the uprisings, or small and hard-to-find booklets (e.g., the interview with two anarchists from Aleppo: Échos révolutionnaires de Syrie, n.d.), are limited or hard to access in the Arab region (Kalicha & Kuhn, 2010). Yassin-Kassab and Al-Shami's (founder of Tahrir-ICN) "Burning Country: Syrians in Revolution and War" (2016) is the only post-uprising account in an academic book format that highlights anarchists within the Syrian revolution. Thus, digital media can be treated as a space from which "counter-publics of memory" (Haugbolle & Hastrup, 2008) for an anarchist diaspora can emerge. However, the challenge is to find formats that are less ephemeral than a Facebook timeline, possibly in the form of blogs.

One outstanding case of an anarchist blogosphere concerns the Syrian uprising where bloggers made an effort to remember the "radical life" of Omar Aziz (Hassan, 2015): a Syrian anarchist in his 60s who returned to Syria from exile. Aziz engaged in establishing anarchist structures of self-governance in the form of local councils. He initiated the founding of four local councils (LCCs, i.e., Local Coordination Committees) and pushed to link them translocally with other councils across Syria (Yassin-Kassab & Al-Shami 2016, p. 68ff.). Through the local councils, Aziz intended to root the political revolution in the daily lives and to fill the vacuum of the absence of state without establishing new authoritarian modes of governance. The local councils were meant as a tool to overcome the binary of "the period of power, in which the regime still manages everyday activities, and the period of the revolution, in which activists work daily to overthrow the regime. The risk lies not in the overlap of the two periods, for that is the nature of revolutions, but rather in the absence of correlation between the spheres of daily life and the revolution itself" (Aziz via Mobayed, 2013). This is a clear example of the above mentioned logic of affinity, as the LCCs are intended (and indeed worked) as an organizational structure not to make one party's or one sect's position hegemonic, but instead to politicize everyday life and to help people self-organize society according to their needs and without recourse to state or authority. Aziz, alongside other activists, such as Razan Zeituneh, was concerned particularly with the suburbs of Damascus such as Deraya, of which Al-Shami spoke as the "Deraya Commune" in 2012 before it was crushed; the reference to the Paris Commune of 1871 has been made by Aziz himself in his last tweet (Al-Shami, n.d.). Aziz is credited for being the "main architect behind the idea of the local councils" that have spread largely in Syria from 2012 onwards (Al-Shami, 2017; Favier, 2016, p. 7; Yassin-Kassab, 2016; Yassin-Kassab & Al-Shami, 2016, p. 68ff.). His paper about local councils and social and political transformation against the state "constitutes the cornerstone for independent self-governance in most areas that achieved liberation from regime control" in Syria by 2013 (Hassan, 2013; Aziz via Mobayed, 2013). Omar Aziz lost his life in prison in Damascus in 2013, and if it were not for blogs such as Budour Hassan's (*Random Shelling*), Yasmeen Mobayed's (*Qawem*), Nadir Attasi's (*Darth Nader*), or Al-Shami's and others' blog (*Tahrir-ICN*), this part of the uprising's history could well have been forgotten. It is through these acts of remembrance that anarchists would be able to reconstruct their history beyond local boundaries.

Apart from blogs, Youtube offers a valuable space where stories can be archived in the form of videos. Posting a documentary about the Syrian insurrection against the Assad government on Youtube, a Spanish film collective archives the presence of anarchist ideas and activists that may otherwise have been confined to a very local memory at best (Camara Negra, 2015). Another documentary, "Le peuple veut la chûte du système" (Tarlacrea, 2013), is the most detailed piece of evidence that the anarchist collective Mouvement Désobéissance/harakat asyan in Tunisia existed: the film crew interviews them at length and accompanies them on demonstrations. However, and this points to the limitation of digital media as a tool for connective diasporic media practices, this outstanding documentary is not findable on specifically anarchist platforms, but – as of now – only on Youtube and without any reference to anarchism (uploaded by the activist, but not anarchist network Sidi Bouzid News), thus hardly visible to the anarchist diaspora unless you know what you are searching for. Thus, potentially accessible content does not necessarily and easily find its way into the common discursive space of the diasporic group. What Owens and Palmer stated about anarchist counter-publics in 2003 is still – if not even more – valid 14 years later: "access to the technology is not sufficient […] Few will discover most of this information without a specific interest in finding it" (2003, p. 340). Constraints, as opposed to affordances, are an issue that I want to elaborate in the conclusion.

7 Conclusion

I do not mean to romanticize media technologies as incubators or initiators for the *emergence* of an anarchist diaspora. Of course, it would be media-centric to claim that the collective self is constituted solely through media practices. But in light of far distances, high repression and quantitative marginality, digital media appear as one important space where diaspora is cultivated through the technologies of disclosure, examination and remembrance. However, further research will have to consider the very ephemeral nature and volatility of a great deal of anarchists' self-mediation practices: why is it that so many blogs and Facebook groups dealing with anarchism have been launched and then abandoned? A further issue to consider is the gap between potential and actual visibility: why are Arabic translations of classical anarchist texts or even books being accomplished with great effort, if the links to the download page are broken, if the sites are not maintained, or if the site limits access to downloads (especially in the case of the Egyptian Libertarian Socialist Movement)? Was Daniel Guérin's book translated into Arabic language for the second time (see Footnote 9) because the existence of the first translation was not known to the author? Why have anarchists in the region not resorted to a more broadly known tool, such as Indymedia, or other platforms in order to connect and become visible in a more sustainable way?[14]

Cammaerts (2015) points out that affordances always come with their counterpart: constraints. Censorship is the most obvious one, and examples of deleted posts on Facebook abound both in liberal democracies such as Great Britain, as well as in authoritarian countries such as Egypt (Cammaerts, 2015; Youmans & York, 2012). Clearly, corporate interests and politically motivated censorship is a serious issue especially for marginal(ized) communities. Youtube videos in which actors of the Egyptian Black Bloc read communiqués, explained and announced their actions in detail, were deleted.[15] However, in the course of my research I was surprised by the anarchists' very open handling of their contact information, not rarely displaying their gmail(!)-addresses in the info section of their Facebook(!)-pages. Real names are used by Egyptian anarchists despite experiences of state repression (Libertarian Socialist Movement, 2013). The affordance of visibility and the wish to network translocally/transnationally through digital media seems oftentimes to outweigh the fear of repression. "First and foremost: You are not alone" is a quote from CrimethInc.'s letter (2013), and I suggest that the notion of being linked to peers from the diasporic community is a central issue to self-mediation practices. The function of liking groups on Facebook gives an example of the importance of seeing and being seen, an important aspect of connectivity: "If seeing is an articulated activity, being seen is no less so" (Brighenti, 2007, p. 331). It is certainly easy to 'like' each other on Facebook, it needs only one click, and is minimally binding. However, looking at 'liking' through the diaspora lens, it appears as a not-so-trivial practice of seeing and being seen, and ultimately means that one is not alone. Not being alone is a recurring

14 In fact, in Egypt, anarchists attempted to establish an Egyptian branch of Indymedia, which failed due to Indymedia's internal conflicts having to do with the Egyptians' stance on Israel (Giraud, 2014).

15 Galián (2015, p. 366) also refers to this video, but it is unfortunately not retrievable anymore: https://www.youtube.com/watch?v=3AvvlzV5Cqs.

motive that I encounter not only explicitly in media texts, but also in discussions with anarchists when they talk about the meaning of their media practices. Posting and reading are substantially motivated by this question of belonging, by solidarity and 'affinity' that are central to anarchist politics (Day, 2004), and not only, or maybe even hardly, by rational, ends-oriented calculations of influencing people or convincing them, as a typical social movement lens would suggest.

Lastly, researching anarchism, anarchists, and their self-mediation practices means making a case for including the margins and the radical imaginaries into the academic history-writing of the transformation processes of the Arab uprisings and their aftermath.

References

afaq (2008, October 11). Appendix – The symbols of anarchy [section 3: Where does the circled A come from?]. An Anarchist FAQ. Retrieved from http://anarchism.pageabode.com/afaq/append2.html#circledA

Alkayial, S. (2013, February 17). عزيز الأوراق التأسيسية لفكرة المجالس المحلية بقلم الشهيد عمر. Retrieved from https://www.facebook.com/note.php?note_id=143690742461532

Al-Shami, L. (2013, August 23). The life and work of anarchist Omar Aziz, and his impact on self-organization in the Syrian revolution. Retrieved from http://www.fifthestate.org/archive/397-winter-2017/the-legacy-of-omar-aziz/

Anarchism in Arabic (2011-2013). Retrieved from http://anarchisminarabic.blogspot.de/

Anarchist symbolism (n.d.). In *Wikipedia*. Retrieved from https://en.wikipedia.org/wiki/Wikipedia:Citing_Wikipedia.

Arab Anarchists (2012, November 24). كتابات باكونين ترجمة : مازن كم الماز وحسن دبوق. Retrieved from https://www.facebook.com/Arab.Anarchists/posts/392317557512375

Arshinov, P. (1974) [1923]. *History of the Makhnovist Movement (1918-1921)*. Detroit: Black and Red.

ASyndicalist (2013, February 26). Egypt: The "Black Bloc" myth. Retrieved from https://libcom.org/forums/africa/egypt-black-bloc-myth-26022013

Atassi, N. (2013, September 6). Syrian Anarchist challenges the rebel/regime binary view of resistance [interview]. Retrieved from http://www.truth-out.org/news/item/18617-syrian-anarchist-challenges-the-rebel-regime-binary-view-of-resistance

Avrich, P. (1991) [1970]. *Kronstadt, 1921*. Princeton: University Press.

Ballenthien, J. et al. (2015). Editorial. *Forschungsjournal soziale Bewegungen: Zwischen Sichtbarkeit und Anonymität, 28*(3), 3-7.

Bamyeh, M. (2013). Anarchist Method, Liberal Intention, Authoritarian Lesson: The Arab Spring between Three Enlightenments. *Constellations, 20*(2), 188-202.

Brighenti, A. (2007). Visibility: A Category for the Social Sciences. *Current Sociology, 55*(3), 323-342.

Burkitt, I. (2002). Technologies of the self: Habitus and capacities. *Journal for the Theory of Social Behaviour, 32*(2), 219-237.

Bustani, H. (2014). Dissonances of the Arab Left. *Radical Philosophy, 184* (March/April), 35-41.

Camara N. (2015). Ecos del desgarro [documentary]. Retrieved from https://www.youtube.com/watch?v=Bx4PIlwITnU

Cammaerts, B. (2012). Protest logics and the mediation opportunity structure. *European Journal of Communication, 27(2),* 117-134.

Cammaerts, B. (2015). Technologies of Self-Mediation: Affordances and Constraints of Social Media for Protest Movements. In J. Uldam & A. Vestergaard (Eds.), *Civic Engagement and Social Media – Political Participation Beyond the Protest (p.* 97-110). Basingstoke: Palgrave Macmillian.

Clifford, J. (1994). Diasporas. *Cultural Anthropology, 9*(3), 302-308.

Cohen, R. (2008). *Global Diasporas: An Introduction.* London et al.: Routledge.

Couldry, N. (2004). Theorising media as practice. *Social Semiotics, 14*(2), 115-132.

CrimethInc. (2000). Alive in the Land of the Dead. Retrieved from https://crimethinc.com/2000/09/11/alive-in-the-land-of-the-dead

CrimethInc. (2013, February 9). Letter to the Egyptian Black Bloc. Retrieved from http://www.crimethinc.com/blog/2013/02/09/letter-to-the-egyptian-black-bloc/

Day, R. J. F. (2004). From Hegemony to Affinity: The Political Logic of the Newest Social Movements. *Cultural Studies, 18*(5), 716-748.

Day, R. J. F. (2005). *Gramsci is dead: anarchist currents in the newest social movements.* London et al.: Pluto Press.

de Jong, A. (2016, March 18). The New-Old PKK. *Jacbin.* Retrieved from https://www.jacobinmag.com/2016/03/pkk-ocalan-kurdistan-isis-murray-bookchin/

Échos révolutionnaires de Syrie: Conversations avec deux anarchistes d'Alep (n.d.). Hourriya – Cahiers anarchistes internationalistes (Ed.). Retrievable also online https://hourriya.noblogs.org/

El Guindy, Z. (2013, June 13). Meet the Black Bloc: Egypt's most talked about radical opposition group. *Ahram Online.* Retrieved from http://english.ahram.org.eg/NewsContent/1/151/73889/Egypt/Features/Meet-the-Black-Bloc-Egypts-most-talked-about-radic.aspx

Esenwein, G. R. (2005). *The Spanish Civil War: a modern tragedy.* New York: Routledge.

Favier, A. (2016). Local Governance under the Democratic Autonomous Administration of Rojava. In L. Narbone, A. Favier & V. Collombier (Eds.), *Inside Wars: Local Dynamics of Conflict in Syria and Libya* (p. 6-15). San Domenico di Fiesole: European University Institute. Retrieved from http://cadmus.eui.eu/bitstream/handle/1814/41644/Inside%20wars_2016.pdf

Fortier, A.-M. (2002). Queer diaspora. In D. Richardson & S. Seidman (Eds.), *Handbook of Lesbian and Gay Studies* (p. 183-197). London et al.: Sage.

Forschungsjournal Soziale Bewegungen (2015). Zwischen Sichtbarkeit und Anonymität. Protest, Bewegung und digitale Kultur, 28(3).

Foucault, M. (1997). *Ethics: Subjectivity and Truth* (p. 223-251). Edited by Paul Rabinow. New York: The New Press.

Galián, L. (2015). New Modes of Collective Actions: The Reemergence if Anarchism in Egypt. In F. Gerges (Ed.), *Contentious Politics in the Middle East: Popular Resistance and Marginalized Activism Beyond the Arab Uprisings* (p. 351-371). New York: Palgrave Macmillan.

Gibril, S. (2015). Contentious Politics and Bottom-Up Mobilization in Revolutionary Egypt: The Case of Egyptian Football Supporters in Cairo. In Fawaz Gerges (ed.), *Contentious*

Politics in the Middle East: Popular Resistance and Marginalized Activism Beyond the Arab Uprisings (p. 305-330). New York: Palgrave Macmillan.

Giraud, E. (2014). Has radical participatory online media really failed? Indymedia and its legacies. *Convergence: The International Journal of Research into New Media Technologies, 20*(4), 419-437.

Gordon, U. (2007a). *Anarchism and Political Theory: Contemporary Problems.* Retrieved from http://www.academia.edu/964092/Anarchism_and_Political_Theory_Contemporary_Problems

Gordon, U. (2007b). Anarchism Reloaded. *Journal of Political Ideologies, 12*(1), 29-28.

Gorman, A. (2011). "Diverse In Race, Religion And Nationality ... But United In Aspirations Of Civil Progress": The Anarchist Movement In Egypt 1860–1940. In S. Hirsch & L. V. D. Walt (Hrsg.), *Anarchism and Syndicalism in the Colonial and Postcolonial World, 1870-1940* (p. 1–32). Leiden: Brill.

Graeber, D. (2009). *Direct Action: An Ethnography.* Edinburgh et al.: AK Press.

Guérin, D. (n.d. [approximately 1996]). *Al-taharrouriyya: min al-'aqida ila al-mumarasa.* Translation by Georges Saad. No place. [Original: 1965. L'anarchisme. De la doctrine à l'action. Paris: Gallimard].

Guérin, D. (2012). *Al-Anarkiyya: min al-nazariyya ila al-mumarasa.* Translation by Hassan Dabbouq. Al-Archiv al-Arabiy. [Original: 1965. L'anarchisme. De la doctrine à l'action. Paris: Gallimard].

Haugbolle, S. & Hastrup, A. (2008). Introduction: Outlines of a new politics of memory in the Middle East. *Mediterranean Politics, 13*(2), 133-149.

Hall, S. (1986). The Problem of Ideology – Marxism without Guarantees. *Journal of Communication Inquiry, 10*(2), 28-44.

Hassan, A. (2013, April 12). تاريخ الحركة الأناركية فى مصر (tarikh al-haraka al-anarkiyya fi misr). Retrieved from https //www.youtube.com/watch?v=XUF-rRiBLig

Hassan, B. (2013, February 20). Omar Aziz: Rest in Power. Retrieved from https://budourhassan.wordpress.com/2013/02/20/omar-aziz/

Hassan, B. (2015, February 23). Radical lives: Omar Aziz. Retrieved from http://novaramedia.com/2015/02/23/radical-lives-omar-aziz/

Heck, R. (2015). Zwischen Eigentor und Aufstand: Ultras in den gegenwärtigen Revolten. *Kosmoprolet* (4), 158-203.

Hilal, J. & Hermann, K. (2014). *Mapping of the Arab Left: Contemporary Leftist Politics in the Arab East.* Ramallah: Rosa Luxemburg Foundation.

Holloway, J. (2002). *Change the World without Taking Power. The Meaning of Revolution Today.* London: Pluto Press.

Jarrar, E. (ed.) (2013). *The left and the Arab Revolutions.* Conference papers Cairo 24 to 25 April 2013. Cairo: Rosa Luxemburg Foundation.

Jerzak, C. T. (2013). Ultras in Egypt: state, revolution, and the power of public space. *Interface: A Journal on Social Movements, 5*(2), 240-262.

Kalicha, S., & Kuhn, G. (2010). *Von Jakarta bis Johannesburg: Anarchismus weltweit* (1st ed.). Münster: Unrast.

Katsiaficas, G. (1998). *The Subversion of Politics: European Autonomous Social Movements and the Decolonialization of Everyday Life.* New Jersey: Humanities Press.

Keightley, E. & Schlesinger, P. (2014). Digital media – social memory: remembering in digitally networked times. *Media, Culture & Society, 36*(6), 745-747.

Kellermann, P. (2011). *Marxistische Geschichtslosigkeit: Von Verdrängung, Unwissenheit und Denunziation: Die (Nicht-)Rezeption des Anarchismus im zeitgenössischen Marxismus.* Lich: Edition AV.

Khuri-Makdisi, I. (2010). *The Eastern Mediterranean and the making of global radicalism, 1860-1914.* Berkeley: University of California Press.

Kurz, R. (2007). Grau ist des Lebens goldener Baum und grün die Theorie. *EXIT!* (4), 15 – 106. [English translation available at https://libcom.org/library/grey-golden-tree-life-green-theory-robert-kurz].

LeVine, M. (2013, February 2). The revolution, back in black. *Al-Jazeera*. Retrieved from http://www.aljazeera.com/indepth/opinion/2013/02/201322103219816676.html

Libertarian Socialist Movement Egypt (n.d.). Photo. Retrieved from https://scontent-fra3-1.xx.fbcdn.net/v/t1.0-9/255269_499290463418515_1396584920_n.jpg?oh=815a7317115e9525ad1e0ffc79a59ee9&oe=58EED662

Libertarian Socialist Movement (2013, January 25). In response to the indictments in Alexandria. Rerieved from http://www.anarkismo.net/article/24774

Lim, M. (2009). Muslim Voices in the Blogosphere: Mosaics of Local-Global Discourses. In G. Goggin & M. McLelland (Eds.), *Internationalizing Internet Studies. Beyond Anglophone Paradigms* (p. 178–195). New York: Routledge.

Magazinredaktion (2013, March 18). Brief an den Schwarzen Block von Ägypten. Message posted to https://linksunten.indymedia.org/de/node/81387

Marshall, P. (2008). *Demanding the Impossible: A History of Anarchism.* London et al.: Harper Perennial.

Martin, F. (2009). That Global Feeling: Sexual Subjectivities and Imagined Geographies in Chinese-Language Lesbian Cyberspaces. In G. Goggin & M. McLelland (Eds.), *Internationalizing Internet Studies. Beyond Anglophone Paradigms* (p. 285–301). New York: Routledge.

Milstein, C. (2010). *Anarchism and its aspirations* (Vol. 1). Oakland: AK Press.

Mobayed, Y. (2013, September 14). Translated: "A discussion paper on local councils in Syria". Retrieved from https://muqawameh.wordpress.com/2013/09/14/translated-quota-discussion-paper-on-local-councils-in-syriaquot-by-the-martyr-and-comrade-omar-aziz/

Moynihan, C. (2013, January 25). A 'Black Bloc' Emerges in Egypt [New York Times Blogs]. Retrieved from http://thelede.blogs.nytimes.com/2013/01/25/a-black-bloc-emerges-in-egypt/?_r=0

NOT BORED!a (n.d.). Mustapha Khayati. Retrieved from http://www.notbored.org/khayati.html

NOT BORED!b (n.d.). Manifesto of the Algerian Group of the Lettrist International. Retrieved December 2016 from http://www.notbored.org/algerian-lettrists.html

Öcalan, A. (2013). *Democratic Confederalism.* London and Cologne: Transmedia Publishing.

Owens, L. & Palmer, L. K. (2003). Making the News: Anarchist Counter-Public Relations on the World Wide Web. *Critical Studies in Media Communication, 20*(4), 335-361.

Plant, S. (2000). *The most radical gesture: The Situationist Internationale in a postmodern age.* London: Routledge.

Radical Beirut (2013, May 17). A Letter to North American Anarchists. Retrieved from https://www.facebook.com/notes/radical-beirut/a-letter-to-north-american-anarchists/413180332114614

Ramonet, T. (2013). Ni Dieu ni maître. Une histoire de l'anarchisme, part 1 and 2 [documentary]. German title Kein Gott, kein Herr! Eine kleine Geschichte der Anarchie. Available on youtube https://www.youtube.com/watch?v=YyleVzZpIGU (French) and https://www.youtube.com/watch?v=vSnpsyUTb80 (German)

Rehmann, J. (2013). *Theories of ideology: the powers of alienation and subjection.* Leiden and Boston: Brill.

Rheingold, H. (1993). *The Virtual Community. Homesteading on the Electronic Frontier.* Reading: Addison-Wesley

Spiegel Online (2015, March 18). Krawalle bei Blockupy-Protesten rund um die EZB. Retrieved from http://www.spiegel.de/wirtschaft/soziales/blockupy-proteste-ausschreitungen-in-frankfurt-am-main-a-1024105.html

Stockman, F. (2017, February 2). Anarchists respond to Trumps inauguration, by any means necessary. Retrieved from https://www.nytimes.com/2017/02/02/us/anarchists-respond-to-trumps-inauguration-by-any-means-necessary.html?_r=0

Tahrir-ICN (n.y., December 4). ALGERIA: The Kabyle mentality [original document: Mohamed, Sail (1951). La mentalité Kabyle. *Le Libertaire N. 257].* Retrieved from https://tahriricn.wordpress.com/2013/12/04/algeria-the-kabyle-mentality-by-sail-mohamed/

Tahrir-ICN (2015, January 18). Call for a first Mediterranean anarchist meeting by FA, IFA and Le Communlibertaire [blog post]. Retrieved from https://tahriricn.wordpress.com/2015/01/18/call-for-a-first-mediterranean-anarchist-meeting/

Tahrir-ICN, manifesto (n.d.). "About". Retrieved from https://tahriricn.wordpress.com/about/

Tarlacrea, M. (2013). Le people veut la chûte du système. An V de la revolution tunisienne [documentary]. Retrieved from https://www.youtube.com/watch?v=8ndsbKNh5ng

The Invisible Committee (2009). The coming insurrection. Semiotexte Intervention Series.

The Invisible Committee (2014). To our friends. Semiotexte Intervention Series.

Tölölyan, K. (1996). Rethinking diaspora(s): Stateless power in the transnational moment. *Diaspora: a journal of transnational studies, 5*(1), 3-36.

Van der Walt, L. & Schmidt, M. (2013). *Schwarze Flamme: Revolutionäre Klassenpolitik im Anarchismus und Syndikalismus.* Hamburg: Nautilus. [English edition (2009). *Black Flame: The Revolutionary Class Politics of Anarchism and Syndicalism.* Wiley-Blackwell.]

Veneuse, J.-M. (2009). *Anarca-Islam* [Thesis submitted at Queen's University Kingston]. Retrievable online: https://theanarchistlibrary.org/library/mohamed-jean-veneuse-anarca-islam

Voline (1990) [1947]. *The Unknown Revolution, 1917-1921.* Montreal and New York: Black Rose Books.

Wakeford, N. (2002). New technologies and 'cyber-queer' research. In Richardson, D. & Seidman, S. (Eds.), *Handbook of Lesbian and Gay Studies* (p. 115-144). London et al.: Sage.

Yassin-Kassab, R. (2016, July 25). Against all odds, village republics take hold in Syria. *The National.* Retrieved from http://www.thenational.ae/opinion/comment/against-all-odds-village-republics-take-hold-in-syria

Yassin-Kassab, R. & Al-Shami, L. (2016). *Burning Country. Syrians in Revolution and War.* London: Pluto Press.

Youmans, W. L., & York, J. C. (2012). Social Media and the Activist Toolkit: User Agreements, Corporate Interests, and the Information Infrastructure of Modern Social Movements. *Journal of Communication, 62*(2), 315–329.

Zak, M. (2017, March 7). "Erinnert euch an mich" – Nestor Machno und seine ukrainische anarchistische Volksarmee [podcast]. Retrieved from http://www.deutschlandfunk.de/erinnert-euch-an-mich-nestor-machno-und-seine-ukrainische.1247.de.html?dram:article_id=380652

Power Dynamics in Online Communities: The Palestinian Case

Abir Kopty

1 Introduction

While there is a large amount of literature discussing the impact of new Information and Communication Technologies (ICT) and social network sites (SNS) on activism and social movements, less attention has been given to the implications of these technologies on the dynamics within these activism circles and social activist groups.

This article explores the impact of social media on Palestinian activism through a close look at Palestinian activist communities on Twitter. It draws on many scholars' suggestion that the Internet helps create communities (Norris, 2004; Sassenberg & Postmes, 2002), in particular virtual communities, and to democratize and decentralize movements (Van de Donk et al., 2004) as well as allowing freedom of speech (Groshek, 2009). The study aims to examine these assumptions and to contribute further to this discussion through exploring the dynamics between and within these online communities, and to shed light on power relations, trust, competition, conflicts, censorship and modes of domination.

Theoretically, the article relies on Pierre Bourdieu's theory of practice to examine power relations and the reproduction of hierarchies within the *field* of Palestinian online activism, particularly on Twitter, by exploring group hierarchies within this field and the individual-agent interrelations. The methodology of this article includes social network analysis of Palestinian activists' Twitter activity and interviews with eight Palestinian activists.

The analysis of the Palestinian Twitter map and interviews with Twitter activists in this article show the emergence of online communities, however, without necessarily entailing a 'sense of community'. Members of these communities would still define themselves as 'individual activists'. Additionally, these online communities are not necessarily 'flat', i. e., without hierarchies. Interviews and network analysis show that hierarchies do exist in online communities and that offline power rela-

C. Richter et al. (Hrsg.), *Digital Media and the Politics of Transformation in the Arab World and Asia*, Studies in International, Transnational and Global Communications, https://doi.org/10.1007/978-3-658-20700-7_4

tions are reproduced online. Sources of power in these communities could be the actors' *capital*, illustrated by their access to knowledge, information, networks and other resources, while competition to improve positions within the community is usually over gaining more followers and thus becoming more influential. In many cases, these power dynamics lead to conflicts among individuals or 'clusters' of actors, and have implications on freedom of speech on these platforms. Activists practice self-censorship not only due to surveillance by the authorities, but also due to 'online naming and shaming' practices by other online actors or followers.

2 Expanding Bourdieu's Theory of Practice to Digital Media Fields

Bourdieu's theory of practice is a significant framework through which to discuss the issue of reproduction of power relations and hierarchies within a social field. His theory aims to explain the relationship between the agent and the structure. Concepts such as *habitus*, *capital*, *field*, *doxa* and *symbolic power* form the principles of the theory of practice.[1]

The *habitus*, according to Bourdieu, is the system of dispositions or embodied feelings, thoughts, perceptions that are a result of the social agents' history, such as education, upbringing, etc., and that arise from certain social positions, such as class, gender, ethnicity, and so on. Further, Bourdieu argues that the habitus is a "structured and structuring structure" (Bourdieu, 1984, p. 170). It is structured by our past and present conditions, and it is structuring because it contributes in shaping our present and future practices. Habitus is not static, but can change and develop, and it is produced "without any conscious concentration" (ibid., p. 173). It is therefore a combination of our objective social conditions and our subjective experience (Bourdieu & Wacquant, 1992, p. 121) or, in Bourdieu's words, the "dialectic of the internalization of externality and the externalization of internality" (Bourdieu, 1977, p. 72).

Agents' practices according to Bourdieu are an outcome of the relationship between the field, the habitus and the capital (Bourdieu, 1984, p. 101). Each agent enters a social field with his or her specific habitus and capital. *Capital* is defined by Bourdieu as the "set of actually usable resources and powers – economic capital, cultural capital and also social capital" (ibid., p. 114). When entering a social field,

1 For a Bourdieusian approach to the Chinese context, see Lin, Hamm & Reinhardt in this volume.

these forms of capital (especially the economic and cultural) can become *symbolic capital* (Bourdieu, 1991, p. 238), a sort of symbolic status of honor and prestige.

The *field* can be any social structure or network, such as school, university or specific university department, work, club, sports, hospital, etc. According to Bourdieu, a field is where social agents are positioned.

It is "a field of forces within which agents occupy positions that statistically determine the positions they take with respect to the field, these position-takings being aimed either at conserving or transforming the structure of relations of forces that is constitutive of the field" (Bourdieu, 2005, p. 30). Fields are sites of "internal struggles" over domination (Bourdieu, 2005, p. 36), in which agents reproduce power relations and compete over their positioning in the hierarchy of the field.

This struggle between the agents defines the dominant and dominated positions and determines what practices agents are allowed or not allowed (Bourdieu, 1997 in Walther, 2014). The competition over positioning in the field is bound to the rules of the field, the *doxa*. Strategies of agents depend on the position they occupy in the field or the recognition they are granted by other agents, which influence their perception of the possibilities offered by the field and their choices. However, the issues the agents struggle with depend on the possibilities created by the previous struggles (Bourdieu, 1996, p. 206).

Doxa was defined by Bourdieu as the "universe of tacit presuppositions that we accept as the natives of a certain society" or "a system of presuppositions inherent in the membership in a field" (Bourdieu, 2005, p. 37). These rules are treated with "ordinary acceptance of the usual order which goes without saying" (Bourdieu, 1984, p. 424). On the other hand, they are not static. Members of the field shape its doxa. Those who have more power (i. e., capital) have dominance over shaping these rules, and those who have less power either accept these rules unconsciously or struggle to change them (Bourdieu, 2005, p. 30). Therefore, fields are structured by the power relations (struggle) between the agents within the fields, who are established by their habitus; and fields, in return, also structure the habitus.

If we take the political field as an example, where people discuss political opinions, Bourdieu stresses that the capacity to discuss politics is related to the feeling of self-competence, i. e., that you do not only have the technical capacity to express political views but are also entitled to do so. Such entitlement is, of course, defined by the doxa of the field. As a result, in such fields there might be an objective and subjective exclusion (Bourdieu, 1984, p. 399). Therefore, it is valid to assume that agents in a given field might practice self-exclusion as a consequence of their feeling of 'impotence'.

In other words, the competence – the positioning in the political field – is of course related to the capital and the habitus of each agent and the doxa of the field.

We can assume that the doxa in such a context defines, for instance, what counts as a legitimate political opinion, and influences who is entitled to express public opinion.

In this struggle over domination, Bourdieu suggests the mode of *symbolic power/violence* that is "gentle" and covert violence (as opposed to overt-direct violence), as "symbolic forms of domination" are exercised "upon a social agent with his or her complicity" (Bourdieu & Wacquant, 1992, p. 167; Bourdieu, 1990, p. 133). Symbolic power does not only need the dominator to practice it, but the dominated to accept and internalize it as objective and natural, and therefore not resist it. The basis for this violence is the power relations, which manage to impose meanings as legitimate (Bourdieu & Passeron, 1977, p. 4).

Bourdieu's theory of practice can be a valuable concept to study social movements and their re-configuration through digital media because we can view the digital media as a field, into which actors with digital capital enter, online communities can form, and hence hierarchies may be established. The theory helps understand how hierarchies and power are constructed in the online sphere and how these power structures influence the agents' interrelations and behavior, and how they may lead to self-censorship, conflicts and competition.

3 Digital Media, Social Movements and Communities: What Previous Research Tells Us and What Not

The existing body of scholarship has suggested a wide spectrum of attitudes to the impact of the Internet, digital and social media on activism and social movements – and these attitudes often seem to be contradictory.

3.1 Digital Media as a Field: The Utopian vs. Dystopian Perspectives

Digital media may have impacts on organizational dynamics and on relations between activists. It has prompted the development of "horizontal networks of interactive communication" that connect the local and global (Castells, 2007), it has enabled individuals to find multiple points of entry into varieties of political action (Bennett, 2003), and has helped in mobilization for collective action (Carty, 2011).

boyd and Ellison (2007) have stressed the role of social network sites in providing a new organizational framework for online communities. Many scholars have emphasized the ways in which the Internet and digital media have provided a particular opportunity to youth to exercise active citizenship (Rheingold, 2008). Norris (2001) argues that the Internet created an arena that provided people with flexibility, skills and innovative capacity they can use to mobilize, create actions and events.

The Internet has helped activist groups in different ways, including spreading information faster to wider audiences and across borders (Castells, 2001) and helping form transnational movements (Bennett, 2003), while reducing the costs of communication and organizing (Bimber, 2000; Earl et al, 2010; Leizerov, 2000). Castells (2001) describes the Internet as a flexible tool that can be used in many forms according to social practice, leading to a variety of social outcomes (p. 50).

While many have argued that the Internet can undermine the state's power to silence opposition (Masoud, 2011) and protect activists from state repression as was the case with Indymedia and the anti-globalization movement in Seattle (Kidd, 2003), or the case of the Zapatistas in which international exposure deterred the Mexican government from repression (Castells, 1997), others have pointed out that the governments are those who benefit from the Internet because they can track politically active citizens and control or undermine their actions through censorship, surveillance and propaganda (Morozov, 2011; Howard & Hussain, 2011). Garrett (2006) has also noted the risk in the dependency on new ICTs, especially in cases where governments and elites have the upper hand over the infrastructures on which ICTs rely.

Bimber (2000) claims that the Internet creates fragmented and pluralistic structures that exist for the duration of a single political effort instead of long-standing movement structures. Other scholars have argued that the Internet promotes "slacktivism" or "clicktivism", which refer to the "five-minute activists" who make quick pointless actions to feel good about themselves (Shulman, 2009; Morozov, 2009; Vitak et al., 2011). Participating in activism becomes easy when it is online, everyone can take part in different ways, or can join and leave groups and campaigns at any time, raising doubts as to the commitment and dedication of the participants, the value of their participation and the ability to sustain coherent movements (Morozov, 2009; Bennett, 2003; Van de Donk et al., 2004).

Additionally, scholars have argued that the Internet pulls people away from civic engagement in their communities (Slouka, 1995; Putnam, 2000), while others have argued that the use of social network sites breaks the state's monopoly over information (Lynch, 2011) and results in more informed, and therefore more engaged, citizens (Valenzuela et al., 2012; Elin, 2003). Also, the Internet helps people expand their networks and increase their political engagement (Gibson et al., 2000), and can encourage uninvolved people to transform from "baby activists" into "real activists" (Harlow & Guo, 2014).

This study attempts to expand the research and establish a deeper understanding of the field of digital media activism in the Palestinian case through examining the formation of communities/groups within the *field* and the power dynamics among and within these communities.

3.2 Agents Newly Ordered: A Space for Community Formation

Research has shown that the Internet promotes collective identity and helps in creating a sense of community (Norris, 2004). It can also reduce the attention paid to individual differences and thereby unify groups (Sassenberg & Postmes, 2002). Howard Rheingold (1993) coined the concept of "Virtual community" in his classic study of an online community. Rheingold (2002) argues that informational technology is providing the arena for communities to form around different social topics or political causes. These online communities may include communities that bring together geographically dispersed people around a certain agenda or people who live within the same geographic location (DiMaggio et al., 2001).

Wellman (2000, 2001) has argued that online social networks are fundamentally changing the nature of communities and relationships within these communities. He describes these emerging communities as "networked individualism" that allows individuals to join different political communities. However, other scholars have questioned the ability of digital communication to maintain the community binding and trust needed to sustain a social movement (Diani, 2000; Calhoun, 1998; Polat, 2005). In the present study, we look on how agents spread over the field of digital media activism in the Palestinian case and what kind of online communities can be observed.

3.3 Struggles Ahead: Hierarchies vs. Decentralization

Internet and information technologies seem to help create decentralized, non-hierarchical movements (Van de Donk et al., 2004, p. 7; Geser, 2001, p. 36-41), replacing hierarchical bureaucracy with flat, networked structures (Tapscott, 1999 in DiMaggio et al., 2001). The ability to access information and to achieve large-scale coordination at a low cost allows "loosely structured groups [to] operat[e] without managerial direction" (Shirky, 2008, p. 47), and has the potential to enhance equality (Bimber, 2000).

On the other hand, scholars have addressed the issue of digital divide and unequal access (Norris, 2001; Bonfadelli, 2002) and how digital divide may increase inequalities within society (Tilly, 2004). The digital divide includes the gaps in

Internet literacy, resources of infrastructure (Bonfadelli, 2002) and also economic, political and cultural gaps (Fuchs, 2009 in Harlow & Guo, 2014). Wilhelm (2000) argues that underprivileged ethnic or social groups may use the Internet less as compared to more privileged groups.

DiMaggio et al. (2001) suggested that issues of inequality on the Internet should not only be examined through the lens of accessibility, but also through that of access to attention. It is true that the Internet can be a space for a plurality of voices, but one should examine also the practices and structures that threaten such premises of equality. It will thus be interesting to investigate how the inequalities materialize in the Palestinian field of digital media activism.

3.4 The Online Doxa: Democracy and the Freedom of Speech

Digital media, including blogs, websites, SNS, are seen as alternative media and a source of information and as a tool for activism. As alternative media, they enable activists to counter the mainstream media or bypass its gatekeepers to broadcast their own messages to the public (Downing, 2001; Myers, 2000; boyd in Stein, 2009; Postmes & Brunsting, 2002). Further, many scholars view digital media as a digital "public sphere" (Van de Donk et al., 2004), that has the potential to promote democracy and pluralism (Groshek, 2009). It allows space for more critical voices (Lei, 2011), where people feel more comfortable to be their "true selves" online (Bargh et al., 2002). In addition, the Internet can be an empowering force for the less powerful to be able to express their opinions without being punished or sanctioned by the more powerful (Brunsting & Postmes, 2002).

Others have doubted the democratizing force of the Internet, calling attention to government surveillance and censorship (Morozov, 2011) and the role of powerful elites in shaping political material and discourse (Hindman, 2008). Activists and social movements are not the only ones using online communication networks. They too, have to struggle with domination of other powers, such as corporate media or political powers that are active in such realms. "The structures of power are rooted in the structure of society and these power structures are reproduced and challenged in the communication realm" (Castells, 2007, p. 257).

One of the urging questions this research explores is related to the freedom of speech in the digital fields. Who decides what or what not should be said online? Are there rules? And if so, who sets them? As reviewed above, commentators have argued that online communication and social media helps to promote democracy, create decentralized communities and break the traditional hierarchies in movements and groups, and enhance group unity within virtual communities. By using Bourdieu's theory of practice, this research aims to explore these perspectives further. In particular, the study aims to look at whether and how social media as a field of activism reproduces social hierarchies and power relations.

4 Palestinians and the Internet

There are very few studies discussing how the Internet in general and social media in particular impact Palestinian activism.

There are two important aspects that one should take into consideration when addressing the question of Palestinian online activism. The first one is the Palestinian transnational context. Due to the Israeli occupation of Palestinian land, and the displacement of Palestinians since 1948, about half of the Palestinians live in the diaspora while the other half lives inside the Mandate territory of Palestine (Israel, the West Bank, and the Gaza Strip). These different parts are either separated (like most of the West Bank, surrounded mostly by a separation wall and hundreds of checkpoints between villages, cities and lands) or isolated (like Gaza which has been under blockade from 2007-2017 after the Hamas movement won the Palestinian legislative council election). In the context of the article, this aspect is important because it examines hierarchies and power dynamics in the digital field between online communities as well as within communities, and explores whether the geographic location of the agent plays a role in its positioning in the field. The second important consideration is that with regards to Internet freedom, Palestinians, especially in the West Bank and Gaza, face two types of surveillance: one by the Israeli occupation and the other by the local Palestinian authorities. This is an important aspect especially when we look at the powers that dominate the field of digital media activism.

In *Palestine Online*, Myriam Aouragh discusses the development of the new ICTs in the Palestinian territory and the role of the Internet from 1996 to 2006 in analyzing its social and political implications. Given the diasporic character of the Palestinian society, the Internet has become an important tool in achieving the political aims of self-determination across territorial borders (Aouragh, 2011). One of the main implications of the Internet for the Palestinians is the reformation of collective identity: "Two related processes are important here: first, the communicative act itself – connecting Palestinians to each other for the first time on this scale since 1948, second, the content – through online discussions and exchange images – led to new ways of imagining and identifying with a nation" (Aouragh, 2011, p. 230).

Interestingly, during the Second Intifada (2000-2005), the Internet and mobile phones did not serve the objectives of political mobilization and activism (Bishara, 2009). Digital communication channels had instead two roles: first, in the Palestinian society, they provided a flow of information through news websites and email exchange, thereby serving as a tool for connection between people, asking for help and care for each other. Second, for the Palestinian diaspora, the Internet offered direct information about the homeland (Aouragh, 2011; Bishara, 2009).

Over the last decade, the Internet penetration among Palestinians has increased rapidly and consequently so did their online presence and their usage of social network sites. According to the Palestinian Central Bureau of Statistics, about 50 percent of Palestinian houses in the West Bank and Gaza were connected to the Internet in 2014. 75.1 percent of those connected to the Internet use social network sites. As for the Palestinian citizens of Israel, the available statistics from 2015 indicate that 90.4 percent of all computer users (above the age of 10) use the Internet and 76.9 percent of Internet users use social media (Qawasmi & Othman, 2016). According to the Social Studio report (2016), there were 1.6 million Facebook users, 493,000 Twitter users, and 480,000 Instagram users among a total of 4.87 million Palestinians that resided in the West Bank and Gaza in 2016.

Iazzolino (2010) has argued that the new ICTs have empowered many Palestinians to use the Internet for citizen journalism projects, alternative media projects, blogs and others, and has represented a significant platform for freedom of speech. However, reports of civil society organizations show that Palestinians cannot fully enjoy the emancipation premise of the Internet. During the latest uprising, between October 2015 and January 2016, the number of Palestinians arrested by Israel on the basis of "Incitement through social media" reached 150. In addition, multiple online activists were arrested by the Palestinian Authority in the West Bank or the Hamas government in Gaza (Qawasmi & Othman, 2016).

Hanafi (2005) has looked at a Palestinian virtual network of scientists and technologists abroad, and suggests that the Internet helps in the "reshaping of geography" by connecting diasporic communities to each other, without them going through the center, that is, through communities within Palestine, but also shows how these networks can be exclusive to include only educated, English speaking and middle class people.

In her work on the Palestinian blogosphere, Siapera (2010) explored the issue of power dynamics in this network. She found that the most popular blogs belong mostly to middle class Palestinians living abroad who hold university degrees. She argued that this urges us to look at the positioning of these blogs and bloggers "along a class, cultural and social hierarchy, which inevitably shapes their outlook". Siapera concluded that offline hierarchies operate in online environments. This is a very relevant observation that aligns with Bourdieu's theory that in any given *field* the struggle over power exists and shapes the hierarchies within the *field* between the agents whose background (*capital*) plays an important role in their positioning (Bourdieu, 1984; 2005).

5 Methodology

This study uses two main methods: social network analysis to map Palestinian communities on Twitter and semi-structured interviews with Palestinian Twitter activists. Social network analysis looks at social actors' (nodes) behaviors. It is a method to map relationships (ties) and flows between social actors and the patterns and implications of these relationships (Wasserman & Faust, 1994; Jamali & Abolhassani, 2006). Through network analysis, researchers can look into actors' positions within networks to explain power inequalities. The centrally located actors have more power because they have the shortest access to the largest number of actors and are empowered by their position while the peripheral actors have less power and are more constrained (Stevenson & Greenberg, 2000).

Interviews are a key qualitative research technique in ethnography (Hammersley, 1990) that aims to learn how the study participants understand and interpret their behavior (Rubin & Rubin, 1995). This study adopts the semi-structured interview method, which combines a list of predetermined questions around a set of central topics, and at the same time allows the interviewer to add open-ended exploration when new issues or topics emerge throughout the interview (Wilson, 2013, ch. 2). The interviews were conducted in Arabic and translated by the researcher into English.

In a first step, relevant Palestinian activists were asked to name two Palestinian Twitter accounts that they consider as a reference for political activism. The survey received about 20 responses, hence, started with the analysis of about 40 Twitter accounts. These accounts were analyzed using Twitonomy software in order to identify their connections (i. e., those who are mostly re-tweeted, replied to or mentioned by each of these accounts). Through this analysis, one could further explore Palestinian Twitter accounts. In order to limit the scope of the analysis, the study excluded Palestinian Twitter accounts that had fewer than 1000 followers.

In sum, about 400 Palestinian Twitter accounts were analyzed, for the period of October-November 2015, which witnessed a wave of uprisings and protests in Palestine, especially in Jerusalem and the West Bank. The accounts' profiles and tweets for the same period were downloaded and saved. Examining these profiles and tweets was important in identifying the activity and backgrounds of the concerned Twitter activists. The study used network analysis software to map the Palestinian activists' communities and their networks on Twitter. After filtering accounts that had fewer than two connections, the network ended up with about 900 nodes, that is the 400 Palestinian Twitter accounts initially identified (except those who have fewer than two connection) and the nodes they were connected to.

The network analysis was followed by conducting interviews with eight Palestinian Twitter activists over Skype. The questions included three main dimensions: 1) Do the agents in the digital *field* of Twitter see themselves as part of a community? 2) How do hierarchies and the struggle over positioning in the digital *field* materialize? 3) To what extent does the digital *field* contain a set of rules on what can/cannot be said, who sets these rules and how does that impact their sense of freedom of speech? The author of this study confirmed that all interviewees' identities would be kept confidential in order to guarantee their openness. Thus, this study anonymizes names completely and any information that might indicate their identity.

6 Network Analysis

Figure 1 (see next page) illustrates the visualized network of Palestinian activity on Twitter and the online communities that are formed in this space.

Three communities were identified that are both connected and disconnected. They are slightly connected through some Palestinian actors who lie in-between the communities and engage with more than one community, but at the same time, the three communities are functioning in distinctly separate realms and around different topics or needs.

- ***Community one (diasporic) on the right side of the map***: This community is dominated mainly by diaspora Palestinians and foreign pro-Palestinian activists, based mostly in the US and Europe.
- ***Community two (local) at the center of the map***: This one is dominated mainly by Palestinians who are living in the West Bank or are Israeli citizens. It also includes many Palestinians living in the Arab world and Gaza, but very few beyond those countries.
- ***Community three (Gaza) on the left side of the map***: Members of this community are almost exclusively Gazans with few connections to other Palestinians in other parts of Palestine.

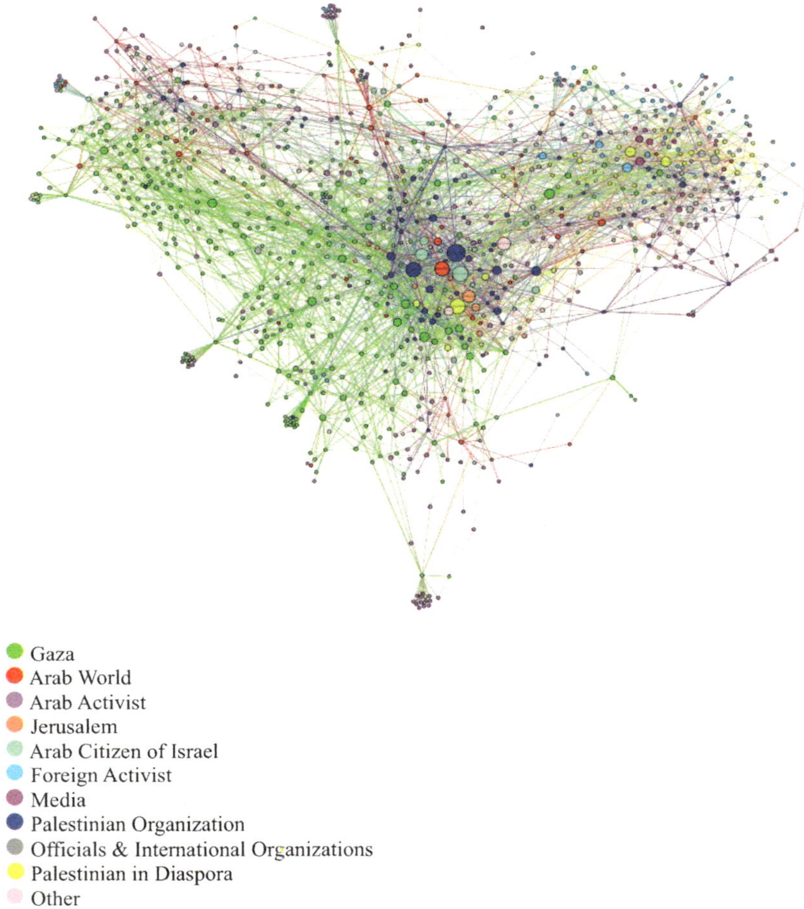

Fig. 1 Network of Palestinian activity on Twitter and the online communities. (Source: author)

Diasporic Palestinians (community one) consists of members who are mostly well educated, work in NGOs or media and have good networks with Western activists and journalists. They tweet mainly in English and engage largely with media outlets, human rights or advocacy organizations and politicians. Their access to such institutions, enabled by their jobs, positions and their language, grants them more power to influence and engage, and it is obvious that even without an organizational framework, they function within a strategy of influencing and countering Israeli propaganda, targeted at the Western media.

The 'local' Palestinians (community two) is the most central community within the three, that lies in-between the other two communities, has most connections to the other two, and has among its members the most central actors. This community faces offline movement restriction due to separation, isolation and entry denial policies by Israel, and therefore most of its members cannot meet in one physical place at the same time. Therefore, it is noticeable that they resort to the Internet to engage in conversations with each other or their peers in the Arab world, establish a sense of community, and to spread information and news, rather than focusing on influencing Western public opinion. This is also apparent as they mostly tweet in Arabic. The group's centrality can be explained by its closeness to the reality on the ground, and its access to events, actions and information, especially given that the period of the Twitter accounts' analysis is October to November 2015, where a lot of the protests and events were happening in the West Bank and Jerusalem.

The Palestinian Gaza group (community three) consists of mostly young or undergraduate Palestinians, who are communicating mainly with each other in Arabic. They communicate less with other Palestinians elsewhere, and the topics they discuss are mostly non-political, but rather social, religious or about sports. In reality, Gaza is the most isolated place in Palestine. It has been under blockade (air, land and sea) by Israel since 2007. Entries and exits outside of Gaza are almost impossible. It is obvious that this reality is reflected online as well, for an observer of online dynamics, Gaza's online Twitter community seems disconnected from the other Palestinian communities.

Drawing on Bourdieu, one can already identify power hierarchies between these communities. Because the local community has direct access to events and information and is geographically located in the context of happenings (a form of social capital and habitus), their position is at a central location in the network. The diasporic community has another source of power, and that is its network (social capital), i. e., access to international media and organizations and its members' positions, capacities and experience (habitus). At the same time, the Gaza community, which has less access, fewer capacities, and different interests in the topics chosen by the more dominant actors in the field, is marginalized and remains peripheral.

The following section examines the individual actors' positions within these communities. In order to examine the centrality of actors within the network and across the communities, the top twenty Twitter accounts with the highest "degree of centrality", "closeness centrality" and "betweenness centrality" were listed according to Wassermann and Faust's classification (1994). These are all measures to define actors' location in a social network and will help to identify where the most prominent actors are located. Actors who are the most important or the most prominent are usually located in strategic locations within the network.

Degree of centrality examines the degree of the actors' centrality, i. e., the nodes who have the most ties with other actors in the network. This of course underlines that actors with more centrality degrees have more power (Wassermann & Faust, 1994, p. 169).

Closeness centrality measures the actors' proximity or distance from other actors in the network. The closer the actor is to other actors, we assume that it can quickly interact with them, and hence, he or she is more central, and has a better position to communicate with other actors (Wasserman & Faust, 1994, p. 183).

Betweenness centrality measures the in-between or intermediary positions of the actors in a network. In other words, which actors lie on the pathway between a pair of actors, when these actors are not directly connected. This position makes the 'betweenness actors' have some control over the communication between the two actors (Wasserman & Faust, 1994, p. 188).

After listing the top 20 accounts that have the highest degree of centrality, 20 accounts that have the highest closeness centrality and 20 that have the highest betweenness centrality, they were sorted by community. As a result eight of the Palestinian actors who score high on the three types of centrality are from community three (Gaza), nine are Palestinian actors from community one (diaspora), and 19 are Palestinian actors from community two (local). Since the vast majority of community three (Gaza) does not use Twitter for activism, this community was excluded from further investigation. Because the Gazan group is too marginalized in the *field* of digital media activism, the focus remains on the centrality of the members of communities one and two.

Looking at the diasporic community, even though this community appears more diffused than the second, local community, one can still see some centralized actors and hierarchy. Looking at the list of the most central actors (based on measuring degree centrality, closeness and betweenness centrality), all of the nine most central actors are either journalists' or news websites' accounts based in the US, or belong to Palestinian, Arab American, or official Palestinian organizations.

The diffusion of community one compared to community two can be explained based on the type of activity each community practices. Community one works in a more strategic way, and engages with the media, organizations, and officials, and hence is not focused on forming a closed community.

In the local community, however, the ties are more condensed and central: it is mostly formed by Palestinians who have the need to be connected with each other, and that entails a more condensed and hierarchal structure. This community is mostly formed by activists, and therefore, most of the 19 actors who were on the top lists of degree, betweenness and closeness centrality are mostly individuals rather than organizations, journalists, or officials – except for two Palestinian media outlets. The majority of these actors live either in the West Bank, Jerusalem, or are Israeli citizens. Due to their proximity to events on the ground, one can clearly understand why those who are on the ground are more dominant and powerful.

It is worth noting here that, had the research been conducted for another period of time, results could have been different. One can assume that, had the period under research been during a Gaza war, the Gazan community could have been more central/powerful in the network due to its access to information and events on the ground.

To summarize, it becomes clear that there is a sort of community formation in the online field. In the interview section, we will explore whether actors actually have a sense of community. As for hierarchies between and within the communities, we have seen that they do exist. Community two has the most central positioning due to its proximity to information and events on the ground, and therefore has a sort of digital capital. Community one has the capital of capacity to make strategies and follow them, and hence the power to access media and international institutions, while community three is totally marginalized and isolated. The same goes for the most central actors: their positioning in the online field is determined by their access to information, their network, and their capital.

7 Interviews Analysis

To explore further the power dynamics in the online community, the study focuses, as a case study, on community number two, the local community, the most central and the most diverse. Eight members of community two were interviewed. Activists with different centrality degrees (high, medium and low) were chosen. Since the questions focus on hierarchies, power relations and freedom of speech, these choices were aimed at gathering insights from actors who have different positions within the network structure. In addition, and since this community is the most diverse Palestinian community among the three, interviewees were chosen from different geographical locations, two from within Israel and three from the West Bank, one from Gaza, and two from the diaspora. Three of them are women and five are men.

7.1 The Field according to the Agents: Collective Initiatives and Communities

For many of the interviewees, the Internet allowed Palestinians in different geographical locations to surpass all physical barriers to "revive the Palestinian identity", connect, and create "collective initiatives" and "unified actions" that were not possible before social media. One of the activists described this as "electronic family reunification".

As for the sense of community, it was clear that activists saw social media as a space enabling the creation of communities, and could identify online group formation. These groups might be formed on partisan or non-partisan bases. One of the activists named a few groups that were organized online and that had specific names and structures mainly formed by actors based in Gaza. Other groups had come together based on shared ideology or political opinion but did not have an organizational structure or a name. Many of the interviewees identified the local community from our network analysis as a group that belonged to the latter category, i. e., forming around political opinion, as one of the activists described: "This might not yet have a name or a structural form, but you talk about convergent visions".

Interestingly enough, even though most interviewees talked about a community that in our analysis featured as community two (local) and that was also seen as a group by the interviewed activists, they did not necessarily identify as part of this group. Most of them identified as "individual" activists, including two of the most dominant actors within this group (who have high degrees of centrality). They and the others said they did work with the group, participate in online collective actions of that and other groups, but would still identify themselves as individual activists. In their words: "I work as an individual, not part of a group", "I'm not part of a group, I'm active alone", or "I don't see myself as part of a group".

7.2 How the Struggles Materialize: Hierarchies and Power Dynamics

Many of the interviewees indeed acknowledged a certain hierarchy on Twitter, with one of them saying, "there are people more important than others on Twitter". This has an effect on the actions being taken in the field: When asked about how decisions are made within the activists' groups, interviewees said that sometimes actions happen spontaneously, without any organizational form. For example, sometimes a hashtag emerges spontaneously without any discussion or decision, and people follow.

Other times, though, actions or campaigns are organized. Most communications happen in online private channels between a group of people, they make a decision about a campaign or a hashtag, and then communicate with the larger group, and people usually follow. Some of them said they were part of this process, and others said they were not, and they just "receive messages to tweet about something or use a certain hashtag".

With regards to leadership and impact on the success of an action, some said it did matter who initiates the action because "someone with more followers will have more impact on decision making". Another activist said: "There is an elite on Twitter and they are influential. They decide. They navigate".

When asked what makes someone influential/dominant on Twitter, they identified some characteristics that can be considered, based on Bourdieu, as digital *capital*:

- *Number of followers:* because they can reach more people and get more attention than others.
- *Having trustworthy networks:* One of the activists mentioned that the connections you have with other highly followed actors make you influential. Also, being endorsed by a trusted actor, or having the backing of a political party, one's family or other legitimized institutions who recommend and retweet you.
- *Topics they discuss:* This could be when, for example, activists specialize in certain topics or discuss controversial issues.
- *Knowledge and access to information:* In order to receive and spread information exclusively and quickly, access to events and the activists' ability to report from the ground and publish instantly makes them powerful and followed. Another related aspect is the geographic location, which sometimes enables access to exclusive information.
- *Capacities:* such as writing competence, style in self-expression, and often also English as a communication language.

Most activists believe there is a competition on Twitter between "clusters" that want to have more power. One of the activists called them "gangs": "there is a sort of forming of gangs on Twitter – groups that compete with each other", which according to him, creates tension between them.

Most activists could also give examples of such tensions. They are usually related to political opinions. People might attack each other over a tweet, and in many cases, the argument escalates into an online "fight". In many cases, others who belong to the same 'clusters' of the involved join the fight, or they are tagged by the sides in order to join.

7.3 The Online Doxa: Rules for Expressing Opinions in the Digital Field

All activists agreed that they felt surveilled by the Israeli occupation, by the local authorities, either the PA in the West Bank or the Hamas government in Gaza, the Jordanian regime (for one activist who lives in Jordan) or the Turkish regime (for another activist who lives in Turkey). Activists risk arrest and detention because of their social media posts. They agreed they are not fully free to express their opinions on social media, and there are "multilayers of censorship": "I don't feel I have absolute freedom of speech. I can't express my opinion on certain issues" and "In the political affairs, it's clear why, I can't say my opinion on everything".

The only activist who tweets under a pseudonym said that since she does not write her opinions and uses the account to tweet the news only, she does not face much censorship; however, she asserted that on Facebook (where she uses her real name), she feels surveilled, and "avoid[s] writing a lot of things". She also said that she deleted all her blogposts from her blog because of the feeling of being surveilled by everyone: the occupation, the PA and even society.

Indeed, the activists agreed about the society as yet another source of surveillance, which may include the family ("My family asked me to not publish something against Jordan, and I had to delete my comment") or employers ("I'm a public sector employee, I can't say certain things"). One interviewee said that while he was an employee of a certain ministry, he tweeted against the minister, and consequently they stopped his salary for one month as a punishment. This, he testifies, stopped him from criticizing the minister or at least made him soften his public critique.

The followers also impose pressures: "as long as your followers are increasing the more restrictions you feel on what you can write". The practices might become more offensive and the activists might get virtually "attacked", through naming and shaming practices for their posts on social media. "There are things I was attacked for, maybe once or twice I deleted things after I got attacked", said one activist. "If they (the followers) don't like what you wrote, you will get attacked", mentioned yet another interviewee.

Thus, all the interviewees said that there are things that they refrain from writing, either to avoid any risk of arrest, losing their jobs, to avoid getting into an argument with others or being criticized and attacked, or due to the fear that someone will misuse their posts: "If you want to tweet an opinion that you know that most of your followers oppose, you might avoid doing so", said one of the activists.

However, when asked about whether they thought there were rules on social media that they should follow, most activists could not identify any rules: "I can't think of rules, there are rules that I put to myself. I don't curse for example".

Another mentioned: "No, I don't see people putting rules. There are no rules." or "Everyone decides for themselves." There seems to be the misleading idea that the doxa is shaped by flat access, where everyone is equal and have the same power.

8 Discussion and Conclusion

Social media helps in creating communities; however, these communities are not seen as solid and stable as long as they lack an organizational form. In the network analysis, the communities that were identified among the Palestinians had no organizational forms. However, during the interviews, several Twitter groups were mentioned that included social groups with an organizational form, or political groups that were formed and operated by political parties. Worth noting here is that the research aim and scope is not about identifying all Palestinian online communities, but rather about looking at the power dynamics between and within online communities. However, this exploration might serve as a suggestion for the direction of further research in that respect.

Some activists described the Palestinian online groups on Twitter as "clusters" that compete or clash with each other, but did not see them as sustainable communities. Even though most interviewees identified the group in which they operate as matching what has appeared in the network analysis, they would still define themselves as "individual" activists. This is particularly interesting in the discussion of communities, because even though we can see communities forming online, these opinions raise many doubts as to whether online communities indeed create a "sense of community". In *Bowling Alone*, Putnam (2000) argues that the Internet individualizes society and reduces the social *capital* of actors, while Norris (2004) argues that it brings people together and Sassenberg and Postmes (2002) posit that the Internet can also reduce the attention to the individual differences and unify groups. This research suggests that there is an intermediate position between these two divergent perspectives that calls for further investigation. People utilize and maintain their online network by joining groups and collective actions and at the same time consider themselves individual activists. One explanation could be that, generally, people are tired of structured forms of activism and seek to be free of constraining structures or ideologies.

As shown in the network and the interview analyses, hierarchies on social media do exist, either amongst or within groups. This challenges much of the existing scholarship (Van de Donk et al., 2004; Geser, 2001). These hierarchies depend on many factors. The first one, as suggested by the interviewees, is the number of followers. Indeed, looking at the network analysis, many of the most central actors have thousands of followers. Those who have around thousand followers and are still central, have other forms of capital, as suggested in the interview analysis, that help them improve their positioning in the hierarchy. These forms include, first, their networks – we could see it in the analysis of the diasporic community, who had access to sources of influence (power), such as international media outlets and organizations; second, their access to information as in the case of the activists in the local community who are at the heart of an event and report from there, or specialize in certain issues and post credible information about them; and third, the self-expression competence and the type of topics they discuss, such as taboo issues.

Drawing on Bourdieu, followers are digital capital the interviewees gain in the field as they compete to improve their position. As the analysis showed, they gain this position with the help of their habitus and capital, their position offline, their access to information and their network of trust. People who trust them (because they know them offline), can recommend them to others online and therefore help them to increase their "access to attention" and followers. Conversely, when online actors gain attention, i.e their content (posts) become popular and widely shared or discussed, or when they have high followership, this grants them power and influence that help them to improve their position in the network, which is reflected in their power to impact decision making, lead actions, or influence others on Twitter.

Another important finding that emerged from the interview analysis is that offline trust is crucial for building online trust, which confirms Diani's (2000) argument that face-to-face interaction is needed to build trust. This again suggests that offline hierarchies are re-produced in the online space as Siapera (2010) concluded in her work on the Palestinian blogosphere. Those who have a powerful network offline, and enjoy the trust of powerful people, can get a better positioning online. Other power dynamics that were demonstrated by the analysis include competition, conflicts, and censorship activists practice over each other. These dynamics can be seen as a constant struggle of activists to improve their positioning in the hierarchy of the field, i.e, the online network (Bourdieu, 1984, 2005).

The practice of self-censorship, especially as a result of the 'soft' or 'offensive' censorship of fellow online activists or followers, is by itself an illustration of Bourdieu's notions:

1. An actor is subject to symbolic power practiced by the dominating over the dominated with their complicity;
2. The activist wants to maintain or improve his or her positioning in the network and therefore avoids driving any controversy;

3. In the field, there are rules over what opinions are allowed or not allowed, legitimate or non-legitimate, that the actors follow, and these rules are set by external powers, i. e., the occupation or local authorities and the internal power dynamics in the field between the actors and
4. this leads to Bourdieu's notion of the feeling of self-competence or incompetence to express one's political opinion, and the entitlement to do so which may lead to self-exclusion.

In terms of 'rules' (doxa), the activists' denial of existing rules, even though they mentioned that there are certain things they avoid saying, political opinions they avoid expressing and that they shun confrontation, indicates that all actors accept these rules subconsciously (Bourdieu, 2005).

And lastly, the notion of the Internet as a free space is strongly challenged by this research, contributing to the existing scholarship on state surveillance (Morozov, 2011). However, this research suggests an additional important dimension, which is the self-censorship activists practice due to the censorship as well as the naming and shaming practices of other online actors.

To conclude, this research suggests that the scholarship on social media should widen and deepen the examination of the re-production of group hierarchies in the online space. The power dynamics illustrated by this and other studies may have significant implications for the transformation of political and social communities and social movements.

References

Aouragh, M. (2011). *Palestine Online, Transnationalism, the internet and the construction of identity.* London: I.B. Tauris.

Bargh, J. A., McKenna, K. Y., & Fitzsimons, G. M. (2002). Can you see the real me? Activation and expression of the "true self" on the Internet. *Journal of social issues, 58*(1), 33-48.

Bennett, W. (2003). Communicating global activism. *Information, Communication & Society, 6*(2), 143-168.

Bimber, B. (2000). The study of information technology and civic engagement. *Political Communication, 17*(4), 329–333.

Bishara, A. (2009). New Media and Political Change: The Case of the Two Palestinian Intifadas. Mediterranean Programme Series. EUI RSCAS; 2009/21.

Bonfadelli, H. (2002). The Internet and knowledge gaps: A theoretical and empirical investigation. *European Journal of Communication, 17*(1), 65–84.

Bourdieu, P. (1977) *Outline of a Theory of Practice.* Cambridge: Cambridge University Press.

Bourdieu, P. (1984). *Distinction: A social critique of the judgement of taste*. Cambridge, MA: Harvard University Press.

Bourdieu, P. (1990). *The logic of practice*. Stanford: Stanford University Press.

Bourdieu, P. (1991). *Language and Symbolic Power*. Cambridge, MA: Harvard University Press.

Bourdieu, P. (1996). *The rules of art*. Cambridge: Polity Press.

Bourdieu, P. (2005). The political field, the social science field, and the journalistic field. In R. Benson & E. Neveu (Eds.), *Bourdieu and the journalistic field* (p. 29-47). Cambridge: Polity Press.

Bourdieu, P. & Passeron, J. C (1977). *Reproduction in Education, Society and Culture*. London: Sage.

Bourdieu, P., & Wacquant, L. (1992). *An invitation to reflexive sociology*. Chicago, IL: University of Chicago Press.

boyd, d. m., & Ellison, N. B. (2007). Social network sites: Definition, history, and scholarship. *Journal of Computer-Mediated Communication, 13*(1), 210-230.

Brunsting, S., & Postmes, T. (2002). Social movement participation in the digital age: Predicting offline and online collective action. *Small Group Research, 33*(5), 525-554.

Calhoun, C. (1998). Community without Propinquity Revisted: Communications Technology and the Transformation of the Urban Public Sphere. *Sociological Inquiry, 68*(3), 373–97.

Castells, M. (1997). *The Power of Identity*. Malden, MA et al.: Blackwell Publishing.

Castells, M. (2001). *The Internet galaxy: Reflections on the Internet, business and society*. Oxford: Oxford University Press.

Castells, M. (2007). Communication, power and counter-power in the network society. *International Journal of Communication, 1*, 238-266.

Diani, M. (2000). Social Movement Networks Virtual and Real. *Information, Communication and Society, 3*(3), 386-01.

DiMaggio, P., Hargittai, E., Neuman, W. R., & Robinson, J. P. (2001). Social implications of the Internet. *Annual Review of Sociology, 27*(1), 307-336.

Downing, J. (2001). *Radical media: Rebellious communication and social movements*. London: Sage.

Carty, V. (2011). *Wired and mobilizing: Social movements, new technology, and electoral politics*. New York and Oxon: Routledge.

Earl, J., Kimport, K., Prieto, G., Rush, C., & Reynoso, K. (2010). Changing the world one webpage at a time: Conceptualizing and explaining Internet activism. *Mobilization: An International Quarterly, 15*(4), 425-446.

Elin, L. (2003). The radicalization of Zeke Spier: How the Internet contributes to civic engagement and new forms of social capital. In M. McCarthy & M.D. Ayers (Eds.), *Cyberactivism: Online activism in theory and practice* (p. 97–114). New York: Routledge.

Garrett, R. K. (2006). Protest in an information society: A review of literature on social movements and new ICTs. *Information, Communication & Society, 9*(2), 202–224.

Geser, H. (2001). On the Functions and Consequences of the Internet for Social Movements and Voluntary Associations. *Sociology in Switzerland: Social Movements, Pressure Groups and Political Parties*. Online Publications. Zurich, March, 2.

Gibson, R. K., Howard, P. E., & Ward, S. (2000). *Social capital, Internet connectedness & political participation: A four-country study*. Prepared for the 2000 International Political Science Association, Québec, Canada. Retrieved from http://citeseerx.ist.psu.edu/viewdoc/download;jsessionid=A7F36DA8F859F09FA0B5C9749C8C72DE?doi=10.1.1.11.8677&rep=rep1&type=pdf

Groshek, J. (2009). The democratic effects of the Internet, 1994—2003: A cross-national inquiry of 152 countries. *International Communication Gazette, 71*(3), 115-136.

Hammersley, M. (1990). *Reading ethnographic eesearch: A critical guide.* London: Longman.

Hanafi, S. (2005). Reshaping geography: Palestinian community networks in Europe and the new media. *Journal of Ethnic and Migration Studies, 31*(3), 581-598.

Harlow, S., & Guo, L. (2014). Will the revolution be tweeted or facebooked? Using digital communication tools in immigrant activism. *Journal of Computer-Mediated Communication, 19*(3), 463-478.

Hindman, M. (2008). *The myth of digital democracy.* Oxford: Princeton University Press.

Howard, P. N., & Hussain, M. M. (2011). The role of digital media. *Journal of Democracy, 22*(3), 35-48.

Iazzolino, G. (2010). Digital Shahid – From Broadcast Media to Citizen Journalism in Palestine. *Arab Media Society* (12). Retrieved from http://www.arabmediasociety.com/articles/downloads/20101211120136_Iazzolino.pdf

Jamali, M., & Abolhassani, H. (2006, December). Different aspects of social network analysis. In *2006 IEEE/WIC/ACM International Conference on Web Intelligence* (p. 66-72). Retrieved from http://ieeexplore.ieee.org/xpl/mostRecentIssue.jsp?punumber=4061321

Kidd, D. (2003). Indymedia.org: a new communications commons. In M. McCarthy & M.D. Ayers (Eds.), *Cyberactivism: Online activism in theory and practice* (p. 47–69). New York: Routledge.

Lei, Y. W. (2011). The political consequences of the rise of the Internet: Political beliefs and practices of Chinese netizens. *Political Communication, 28*(3), 291-322.

Leizerov, S. (2000). Privacy advocacy groups versus intel. A case study of how social movements are tactically using the internet to fight corporations. *Social Science Computer Review, 18*(4), 461-483.

Lynch, M. (2011). After Egypt: The limits and promise of online challenges to the authoritarian Arab state. *Perspectives on Politics, 9*(2), 301–310.

Masoud, T. (2011). The Road to (and from) Liberation Square. *Journal of Democracy, 22*(3), 20–34.

Morozov, E. (2009). Iran: Downside to the "Twitter revolution". *Dissent, 56*(4), 10–14.

Morozov, E. (2011). *The net delusion: The dark side of Internet freedom.* New York, NY: PublicAffairs.

Myers, D. J. (2000). Media, communication technology, and protest waves. In *Trabalho apresentado na conferência. Social Movement Analysis: The Network Perspective,* Ross Priory, Scotland (p. 22-25).

Norris, P. (2001). *Digital Divide: Civic engagement, information poverty, and the Internet worldwide.* Cambridge: Cambridge University Press.

Norris, P. (2004). The bridging and bonding role of online communities. In P. N. Howard & S. Jones (Eds.), *Society online: The Internet in context* (p. 31–41). Thousand Oaks: Sage.

Polat, R. K. (2005). The Internet and Political Participation Exploring the Explanatory Links. *European Journal of Communication, 20*(4), 435-459.

Postmes, T., & Brunsting, S. (2002). Collective action in the age of the Internet mass communication and online mobilization. *Social Science Computer Review, 20*(3), 290-301.

Putnam, R. D. (2000). *Bowling alone: The collapse and revival of American community.* New York: Simon and Schuster.

Qawasmi H. & Othman D., (2016). *Hashtag Palestine: Palestinian Social Media Activity during 2015.* 7amleh – Arab Center for Social Media Advancement. Retrieved from http://www.7amleh.org/en/article/62

Rheingold. H. (1993). *The virtual community: homesteading on the electronic frontier.* Reading, MA: Addison Wesley.
Rheingold, H. (2002). *Smart Mobs: The Next Social Revolution.* New York: Perseus.
Rheingold, H. (2008). Using participatory media and public voice to encourage civic engagement. In W. L. Bennett (Eds.), *Civic life online: learning how digital media can engage youth* (p. 97–118). Cambridge, MA: The MIT Press.
Rubin, H. & Rubin, I. (1995). *Qualitative interviewing: The art of hearing data.* Thousand Oaks, CA: Sage.
Sassenberg, K., & Postmes, T. (2002). Cognitive and strategic processes in small groups: Effects of anonymity of the self and anonymity of the group on social influence. *British Journal of Social Psychology, 41*(3), 463-480.
Shirky, C. (2008). *Here Comes Everybody! The Power of Organizing Without Organizations.* New York: Penguin.
Shulman, S. W. (2009). The case against mass e-mails: Perverse incentives and low quality public participation in the U.S. federal rulemaking. *Policy and Internet, 1*(1). Retrieved from http://www.psocommons.org/policyandinternet/vol1/iss1/art2/
Siapera, E. (2010). Networked Palestine: Exploring Power in Online Palestinian Networks. *Orient – Deutsche Zeitschrift fur Politik und Wirtschaft des Orients, 51*(1), 25-37.
Slouka, M. (1995). *War of the Worlds: Cyberspace and the High-tech Assault on Reality.* New York: Basic Books.
Social Studio (2016). *Social Media Report in Palestine.* Retrieved from https://socialstudio.me/wp-content/uploads/2017/04/SMRP2016-Eng.pdf
Stein, L. (2009). Social movement web use in theory and practice: A content analysis of US movement websites. *New Media & Society, 11*(5), 749-771.
Stevenson, W. B., & Greenberg, D. (2000). Agency and social networks: Strategies of action in a social structure of position, opposition, and opportunity. *Administrative Science Quarterly, 45*(4), 651-678.
Tilly, C. (2004). *Social Movements 1768-2004.* Boulder, CO: Paradigm Publishers.
Van de Donk, W., Loader, B. D., Nixon, P. G., & Rucht, D. (2004). *Cyberprotest: New media, citizens and social movements.* London: Routledge.
Valenzuela, S., Arriagada, A., & Scherman, A. (2012). The social media basis of youth protest behavior: The case of Chile. *Journal of Communication, 62*(2), 299–314.
Vitak, J., Zube, P., Smock, A., Carr, C. T., Ellison, N., & Lampe, C. (2011). It's complicated: Facebook users' political participation in the 2008 election. *CyberPsychology, Behavior, and Social Networking, 14*(3), 107-114.
Walther, M. (2014) *Repatriation to France and Germany, A Comparative Study Based on Bourdieu's Theory of Practice.* Wiesbaden: Springer.
Wasserman, S., & Faust, K. (1994). *Social network analysis: Methods and applications* (Vol. 8). Cambridge: Cambridge University Press.
Wellman, B. (2001). Physical place and cyberplace: The rise of personalized networking. *International Journal of Urban and Regional Research, 25*(2), 227-252.
Wellman, B. (2000). Changing connectivity: A future history of Y2. 03K. *Sociological Research Online, 4*(4). Retrieved from http://www.socresonline.org.uk/4/4/ wellman.html
Wilhelm, A. (2000). *Democracy in the Digital Age.* New York: Routledge
Wilson, C. (2013). *Interview techniques for UX practitioners: A user-centered design method.* Newnes: Elsevier Science.

Political Communication Chinese Style: The Elite Network in State-Regulated *Sina Weibo*

Zihao Lin, Andrea Hamm and Susanne Reinhardt[1]

1 Context and Research Background

It is a commonplace among scholars that the Internet plays an increasingly important role in Chinese public life (Hassid, 2012). This includes a strong focus on the articulation of an alternative political discourse (Gleiss, 2015). According to a nationwide survey, typical Chinese netizens are "politically opinionated, supportive of democratic rules and critical about party-state" (Lei, 2011). They form the so-called "new opinion class" (Zhou, 2009). The Twitter-like social network *Sina Weibo/ Sina Microblog* (Chinese: Xinlang Weibo), launched in 2009, has received huge attention, as it attracted 129 million monthly active users in December 2013 (Registration Statement, 2014). Carnesecca (2015) pins down different tools for expressing collective discontent in Chinese cyberspace, and reveals the "persistent connectivity and information carrying capacity of social media" (p. 120).

While some scholars are cheering for social media's democratic potential, referring to a utopian perspective on digital media and politics, others remain rather suspicious and follow a dystopian trend in evaluating social media,[2] especially with corroborating evidence of the Chinese Communist Party's (CCP) strict online content censorship (Chen et al., 2013; Fu et al., 2013; King et al., 2013). Jiang (2014) terms the evolution of the Chinese cyberspace during the last two decades a "cat and mouse game" (p. 3), that is, a constant interplay of state regulation and bottom-up activism.

In this research, we understand a microblog platform as a social field, that is, in a Bourdieusian sense, a multidimensional space constructed by differentiation or

1 Authors contributed equally.

2 For a detailed literature review on utopian vs. dystopian perspectives see the contribution of Abir Kopty in this volume.

C. Richter et al. (Hrsg.), *Digital Media and the Politics of Transformation in the Arab World and Asia*, Studies in International, Transnational and Global Communications, https://doi.org/10.1007/978-3-658-20700-7_5

distribution of properties between or among the agents. We frame the launch of Sina Weibo as the emergence of a new social field that was immediately interconnected with existing social, political and economic fields within the Chinese regime. Agents and groups of agents that enter a social field are defined by their relative position within the social world (Bourdieu, 1985). On the one hand, the CCP paternalistically regulates the Chinese cyberspace, turning against the idea of Internet autonomy. On the other hand, the booming social networking technology in contemporary China creates room for bottom-up activism. The microblog elite, however, possesses digital power, which distinguishes it clearly from the bottom-up grassroots users. Following Bourdieu, we see microblog elites as agents of action. Exploring their networks and political stances, our overarching research questions are: Which agents belong to the elite on Sina Weibo and how do they differ from each other? What kind of digital capital do they have? What kind of political discourses do they engage in? To approach these questions, we conduct a social network analysis.

2 Conceptual Framework

2.1 The Microblog Platform as a Social Field

Agents' properties can be described as a field of forces, i. e., structural power relations imposed on all agents entering the field (Bourdieu, 1985). The state represents a fundamental force in both the hierarchy of Sina Weibo and all other fields of Chinese society. Indeed, in 2010, the State Council Information Office (SCIO) of China puts forward the concept of "Internet sovereignty" (SCIO, 2010). It claims that "[w]ithin Chinese territory the Internet is under the jurisdiction of Chinese sovereignty. [...] Citizens of the People's Republic of China and foreign citizens, legal persons and other organizations within Chinese territory must obey the laws and regulations of China and conscientiously protect Internet security" (as cited in Jiang, 2010, p. 72). According to the Sina Weibo Service Protocol and the Weibo Community Regulation, certain information is deemed illicit:

> "Users have the right to publish the information, but are prohibited from publishing information containing the following: (1) against the basic principles established by the Constitution; (2) harming national unity, sovereignty and territorial integrity; (3) disclosing state secrets and endangering national security or harming national honor and interests; (4) inciting ethnic hatred, ethnic discrimination, undermining national unity, or against ethnic customs and habits; (5) violating the state religion policies or propagating cult and superstition; (6) spreading rumors, disturbing social

order or undermining social stability; (7) advocating obscenity, gambling, violence, pornography, murder, terrorism or abetting a crime; (8) inciting illegal assembly, association, procession and demonstration to disturb social order; (9) other content against national laws and administrative regulations"
(Article 13, Weibo Community Regulation, 2015, own translation).

The concept of *Internet sovereignty* of the Chinese government signals the tendency of the SCIO to take the newly emergent cyberspace under strict regulation. The service provider Sina functions as the surrounding technology agent in the microblog field. It is crucial that the technology agent shapes the infrastructural conditions of such a virtual space out of its own interest of economic profit: as a private company, Sina is doing its best to attract registered users and to keep the information flow running efficiently. Simultaneously, however, the technology agent has to succumb to the regulation of the state according to Internet sovereignty and is lacking autonomy to a certain extent. The state and Sina are two agents embedded in a tensed social field, in which each agent desires to reach its either economic or regulatory goals. The state plays a multi-faceted role in the social field of Sina Weibo. On the one hand, the Chinese state impacts Sina Weibo indirectly, as the Weibo platform integrates state sovereignty into its community regulation. On the other hand, we find that several state channels appear as a group of agents within the Weibo platform, behaving as elite users, as will be detailed out in the later section.

In 2012, Sina Weibo introduces a real-name registration (RnR) and a verification system that urges new users to hand in personal information to the service provider. Later, the platform announces to enforce regulation when misconduct on behalf of the users is detected (Weibo Community Regulation, 2015). The real-name registration, the state-sponsored anti-rumor campaign[3], and the Community Regulation represent platform entry permissions, i. e., principles of differentiation that state and technology agents jointly set upon the users of Sina Weibo. "[S]tructuring principles of a world view", as Bourdieu (1985) noted, "are rooted in the objective structures of the social world" (p. 729). As customers of a social networking service, the bloggers are constantly reminded to obey certain non-negotiable user policies defined by the service provider, e. g., to observe national laws as the red line.

3 A campaign targeted at Weibo opinion leaders charged of spreading "online rumors": http://www.globaltimes.cn/content/806540.shtml

2.2 Digital Capital and Elite-Grassroots Division in the Social Field

According to Bourdieu (1985), capital exists either in material form or as power over the field. Agents utilize their properties to win a favorable position in the social space. In other words, the social field is a set of positions defined by a system of coordinates as well as agents that are distributed within the dimensions according to their volume of capital. In digital social media, we assume that the key coordinate takes the form of *digital capital.* Broadly defined, digital capital in Sina Weibo incorporates connectivity and visibility. Connectivity means the position of a particular agent in a network made up of several nodes. Visibility describes the volume of effective contribution an agent has to the information flow. Digital capital is an effective indicator of influence in the microblog field: An agent's position on Weibo can be understood as the outcome of competition of its ability to be heard (Lee, 2011).

Despite longstanding arguments that social media's network structure is intrinsically flat, egalitarian and grassroots-centered (Castells, 2007), we conceptualize Weibo as a hierarchical social field based on an uneven distribution of digital capital. The competition for digital capital on the microblog platform as a newly emergent social field is contingent on the hierarchies within other existing political, social, and economic fields. This hierarchy is implemented by Sina's complex verification system. It consists of two main categories, i. e., identity/individual verification (based on real, recognizable, individual identity) and official/organizational verification (for government organs, enterprises, media, schools, NGOs). Being verified comes with advantages, including special services of fan management or the priority to be shown in other users' search results (Weibo, 2016). Sina's introduction of its verification system constructs an artificial distinction between the verified celebrity and the unverified grassroots, based on the symbolic capital of a given agent. Symbolic capital refers to different forms of capital (economic, cultural, political) that are perceived as legitimate in terms of prestige or reputation (Bourdieu, 1985). The mechanism starts with individuals and organizations that already enjoy huge *offline prestige*, e. g., a top-500 corporate CEO, a blockbuster film star, or a mass-circulation press agency. Then, technology-savvy agents from different fields enter the microblog field through the verification system and compete for new capital, i. e., *digital capital,* to increase their cards at play (Figure 1).

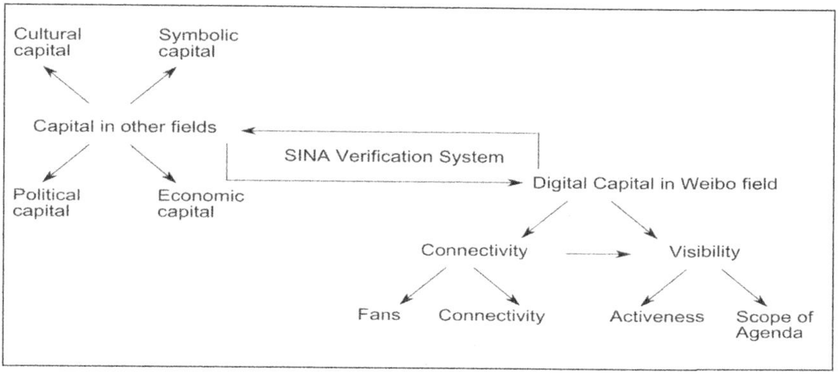

Fig. 1 Reproduction of capital through Sina verification.
This graph illustrates the genesis of digital capital and how it can be transferred back to the original field. (Source: authors)

Empirical results show a trend towards the centralization of discursive power in a small group of channels in the Chinese microblogosphere (Li, 2012). In previous studies, the so-called *big Vs* refer to giant channels that possess extraordinarily high fan numbers. Their behavior is thought to have elitist characteristics, and they – rather than bottom-up activists with substantial agendas but much fewer followers – play a decisive role in determining the visibility and flow of an issue in digital networks (Zeng & Huang, 2012). This suggests that the big V, unlike grassroots users with low fan numbers, obtain certain properties that place them in a favorable position in the power relations. Big Vs will utilize this position to maintain or strengthen capabilities of action (Bourdieu, 1985). Based on this insight, we conceptualize big Vs as the microblog elite, since they enjoy privileged property in the sense of digital connectivity and visibility. By contrast, grassroots users are agents with little digital capital in the form of fans, and thus are excluded from competition for influence. The "digital subalterns" do not have their own voice and become completely dependent on the elite (Kent, 2008). An elite channel's absolute fan number, together with its connections to other elite agents, allows it to exert influence on its followers, and thus on different groups within the network.

The two concepts of *elite agent* and *opinion leader* resemble each other but are still distinctive. Opinion leaders are perceived to "have superior competency and more experience with the subject than an average person" (Lee & Cotte, 2009, p. 2), defined with an emphasis on ability and knowledge. They contribute to the formation of public opinion through knowledge and to information diffusion in general. However, scholars can identify opinion leaders only on issue-specific occasions. By contrast, an elite agent is influential within the cyber field due to its digital capital, that is, a structurally favorable position within the network. A central network location "is the key element in identifying social capital" (Lin, 1999, p. 36). While elite channels do not necessarily seek to become opinion leaders, the structural advantage guarantees them such privilege. Grassroots users are not capable of becoming opinion leaders unless they reach a certain degree of visibility in the information flow, i. e., having enough fans. Generally, they have to seek help from elite channels.

2.3 Digital Elites and Political Discourse

Agents constantly perform in order to impose their view of the world, or the view of their own position in this world – their social identity (Bourdieu, 1985). On Weibo, "the new opinion class" (Zhou, 2009) is a popular group label employed by grassroots users who produce their bottom-up worldview in cyberspace. Li (2012) uses the term *nonsymmetrical mode* to describe the digital presence of the big V. Loaded with the grassroots as fans, big Vs only follow other public figures in their fields and engage in active interaction only with them.

We define political discourse as organized speech that reflects certain implicit or explicit assumptions about the power relations pertaining to the field. We assume that elites coming from different fields tend to strategically utilize their digital capital in order to present world views in their own favor. That is, elite agents, out of their particular interest, endeavor to make certain agendas more visible than others.

According to the approach from Kelly & Etling (2008), within the political agenda, we differentiate between a *cultural politics agenda* and a *power politics agenda*. Agents that develop a cultural politics agenda in their channel communicate values that shape society. In the context of China, the cultural politics involve topics such as minority rights, animal protection, language, religious freedom, doctor-patient-tensions, feminism, Americanization, ethnicity, etc. By contrast, users maintaining a power politics agenda in their channel deal with topics related to the government's decision-making (Kelly & Etling, 2008). For China, this includes one child policy, local and central government policy, party decisions, state-owned enterprises, environment and climate law, corruption, One-China policy, etc.[4] To express *apolitical* views, that is, to escape from cultural or power politics discussions, signals an implicit, passive, or silent acceptance of the existing power structure.

4 Topics can migrate between the cultural politics agenda and the power politics agenda, depending on whether the Chinese government is mentioned in the discourse.

To summarize, we put the ideas into a field model that characterizes Sina Weibo (Figure 2). To begin with, the state and law enclose the whole social space, indicating their power as an ultimate arbitrator of all agents within it. The inner circle represents the territory of technology agent (Sina), who is responsible for setting rules of entry permission and for maintaining the space. The microblog elite consists of an ensemble of big nodes. The elite agents come from different fields, take up central spots in the network location, and compete or cooperate with other elites for more digital capital (connectivity and visibility). The grassroots agents are scattered particles in the digital field. They possess the lowest quantity of capital, and thus have little power to bargain for visibility or influence.

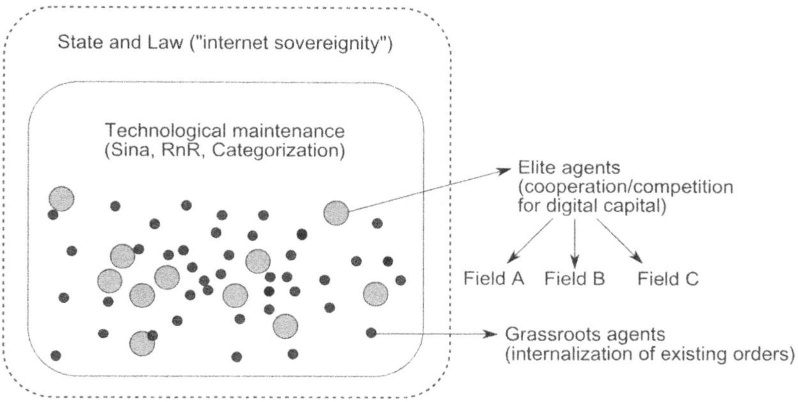

Fig. 2 Sina Weibo field model.

This graph shows the environment in which elite and grassroots agents are embedded, i. e., the. regulatory context as well as the entry and network conditions. (Source: authors)

3 Methodology

3.1 Operationalization

We argue that social network analysis (SNA) is a suitable method to visualize the relationships and explore the structure in which elite agents reproduce their world-views. Social network analysis takes social systems into consideration, and thereby focuses on the relationships among the units that make up the system (Borgatti et al., 2013). An agent's relative position in the network defines the limitations as well as the opportunities that he or she encounters.

The first aim is to examine who forms the digital elite on the Sina Weibo platform and how those elite agents are connected to each other; consequently, the most relevant task is to create a category system to organize the various elite agents. The categories are linked to different social fields, which means that the agents from one category are prominent in the corresponding social field. However, some categories such as state channels and public intellectuals belong to the same political field and are only distinguished by their professions.

An open coding process followed, which we started with eleven channel categories. These are inspired by category sets offered from former empirical studies on social networks (see Lotan et al., 2011; Zeng & Huang, 2012). During the coding process (that is explained in the following section), we observed that the data matrix with these initial categories was distributed unequally. On the one hand, five of the categories (i. e., activist, NGO, lawyer, religious leader and academia) only contained their starting points. On the other hand, the initial category 'other' was surprisingly large because many service channels from Sina appeared, constituting a new category that had not been mentioned in the literature before. Weibo service channels can easily be identified by the name prefix "Microblogging" (Chinese: Weibo), as well as by the profile information stating "official products of Sina". Hence, we organize the elite channels in the following category system for further analysis:

- *State*: Political parties, ministries, police, individuals/organizations that are primarily known for their relationship to the government
- *Media*: Media organizations/channels, journalists, media persons, media owners, etc.
- *Weibo services*: Services from the Weibo platform itself
- *Entertainment/arts*: Artists, authors, musicians, actors, amusing channels, etc.
- *Business*: CEOs, business people, company owners, etc.
- *International*: with international influence outside China, e. g., a foreign embassy
- *Public intellectuals*: Scientists/scholars, NGOs, religious leaders, lawyers, etc.
- *Other*: accounts that do not clearly fit into any other category

Additionally, to understand the potential of elite agents to engage people in massive discussion or to promote shared values, we evaluate the elite agents' digital capital. Digital capital is operationalized as connectivity and visibility.

On the one hand, one agent's connectivity can be measured by his or her *number of fans* and by his or her *influence network* that corresponds with the in-degree (= the number of incoming connections [fans] to one node in a directed network, see social network analysis). These two variables carry different meanings. A channel with a huge number of fans can reach a certain number of grassroots users that follow it. This influence is upgraded when this agent also has a connective influence within the elite network, which means a high in-degree. By contrast, if an agent is isolated from other elites, his or her ability to spread information will be less effective regardless of the individual fan base.

On the other hand, visibility can be measured by the *agent's activeness*. The potential of elite users to engage people depends on their activeness (i. e., number of posts a user addresses to his fan base). This means that a highly active user provides a high amount of information, and thus creates a dynamic connection with his or her fans that can lead to further engagement of the grassroots users for their community icons.

Finally, visibility can be categorized by an *agent's scope of agenda*. We want to know about the particular political discourses the identified agents engage in. Not all elite channels on Weibo will have the same agenda. Because of Weibo's commercial tendencies, we assume that there will be a certain number of channels without a political agenda in the elite network. These users do not participate in controversial public discussions. Nonetheless, there will be channels with political contents that can be classified as belonging to either cultural or power politics.

3.2 Method

In this study, an explorative social network analysis of the elite on China's largest microblog platform Sina Weibo is conducted. In the network, each elite agent represents a node, and an edge is defined as a following relation between two agents. In this manner, a complex graph of nodes and their various interconnections is generated.

To collect the network data, a node list of the Weibo elite is required. The number of fans is the most accessible variable for identifying the Weibo elite. We set the elite criterion at having at least one million fans. Different starting points from all channel categories are chosen from previous literature and media sources.[5] Considering online and offline symbolic capital, we choose one or two starting points per channel category, from which the network is generated in a two-level coding process. The data was collected manually in an one-time data crawling procedure in April 2016.

5 We chose the elite network starting points based on reviewing the following sources: Bloomberg, 2001; Foster, 2009; Jiang & Tang, 2015; Kong, 2013; Kuo, 2016; Lee, 2003; People's Daily Online, 2016; Sheng & Gao, 2013; Wang, 2015; Xu, 2016; Zeng & Huang, 2012.

First, each elite channel is matched with one of the eight channel categories outlined above based on its profile information. For example, the channel *@Official Weibo of Fans' Headlines* (Chinese: fensi toutiao guanfang weibo) is categorized as a Weibo service because its profile information indicates that this channel is operated by Sina. Second, skimming the first 15 posts on both the popular and the complete feeds of a channel, we classify the agenda of this particular channel profile as *apolitical agenda*, *cultural politics agenda*, or *power politics agenda*. The advantage of the popular feed is that it provides more stable information, since it consists of the most popular postings of all time that exhibit the most 'likes', 'shares' and comments. By contrast, the complete feed changes quickly, depending on the latest posts of a blogger. Finally, in a content analysis, the political agenda is marked with up to three keywords per channel. Moreover, we collect more detailed information (number of fans, posts and followings, level of certification, etc.) for descriptive statistics.

To create the network graph, the open-source software *Gephi* is used. This program has been utilized in similar studies (e.g., Kelly & Etling, 2008). We make use of the *Force Atlas* algorithm, which is also recommended for SNA by the developers (Gephi.org, 2011). The basic principles of Force Atlas are the following:

- Nodes reject each other if not interconnected
- Interconnected nodes attract each other
- All nodes are drawn to the center of the graph by so-called 'gravity'
- Nodes with high interconnectivity in the elite network are located in the center of the graph – nodes with a low degree of connectivity are located in the periphery

The node size is defined by in-degree. In the network graph, the node size visualizes the number of elite fans an elite agent possesses (the connective influence within the elite network), which equals the in-degree. The node color illustrates either the channel category or its agenda. The edges have the blended color of the two nodes which are connected by them.

4 Results

The result of our analysis is a network graph that consists of 291 channels. A clear majority of them is the 125 red entertainment/arts nodes, which represent more than 40 percent of the channels. Furthermore, there are 45 blue media channels and 39 yellow Weibo service channels. With smaller portions, there are 29 business channels, 22 public intellectuals, 13 state channels, 5 international channels and 13 channels categorized as 'other'.

We find 173 channels owned by individuals and 118 organizational channels. This relates closely to the distribution of channel certification levels. 168 channels are certified as 'blue V', which means 'private channels', while 116 channels are certified as 'yellow V', which covers 'professional channels'. We also find a small minority of seven channels that are not certified, five of them belong to the entertainment/arts sector, and two of them are categorized as 'other'.

The average number of posts per channel is roughly 11,200. State and media channels are the most active in posting, with each category having averagely more than 20,000 posts per channel. Thereafter, international channels' and public intellectuals' numbers of posts are higher than the general average. By contrast, Weibo services, entertainment/arts and business channels appear to be less active than average.

In the following section, we show first the connectivity among elite agents, and second the kind of political agenda that is set by them.

4.1 The Elite Network of Sina Weibo

Regardless of the nodes' category indicated by color, the network shows a high interconnectivity between almost all channels (CENC, Figure 3). Considering the categories, the CENC consists of three main areas: the red entertainment/arts, the blue media and the yellow Weibo services. The areas create three factions that are each characterized by a dominating color which allows its clear distinction. Nevertheless, single nodes from one faction appear to be scattered over the other two factions. For example, blue media nodes are dispersed within both the red entertainment/arts faction and the yellow Weibo service faction. The same can be observed for single nodes from the other two factions.

Among these, the Weibo service faction contains the biggest nodes of the network that can be found in the upper right corner of this faction. These Weibo services have the highest in-degree. Moreover, they occupy, together with some smaller entertainment/arts nodes, the most central positions in the CENC. Both characteristics lead to high connectivity. By contrast, the media faction is distributed in rather peripheral positions on the upper right side of the graph. Additionally, it appears to be the least densely connected faction, whereas the red entertainment/arts faction appears to be the most densely connected one. In general, the density between the three factions varies. As both the entertainment/arts faction and the media faction are each separately highly connected with the Weibo services, the density between the two of them is much lower (Figure 3).

Regarding the remaining categories in the CENC, the light green state channels are located within the blue media faction, hence those two categories are strongly interconnected. Similarly, most of the light red public intellectuals can be found within the media faction; however, they occupy a comparatively peripheral position. Additionally, singular public intellectuals are located within the red and the yellow factions. Generally, it can be observed that most of both the state channels and the public intellectuals are located at the upper right periphery of the CENC. This corresponds with a low number of incoming connections from elite agents from other factions of the network. The five international channels do not take up a specific area. Three of them are located within the media faction. The other two can be found within the Weibo service faction. The business nodes can be found in the right part of the network, mainly within the media and Weibo service factions. Only a handful of business channels can be found at the boarders of the red entertainment/arts zone (Figure 3).

4.2 Agenda in the Elite Network

A second map shows the elite network colored by channel agenda (CENA). In the CENA graph (Figure 4), a great number of the channels have an apolitical agenda (pink area). A frequency analysis reveals that nearly two thirds of the elite channels possess apolitical agendas, i. e., 186 channels are coded not to contain any political content in their complete or popular feed during our period of data coding. Conversely, 105 channels are political; within those, 34 are coded to display culture politics, whereas 71 contain power politics.

The upper blue part of the CENA is the political area, containing the media, state and public intellectual channels as well as a minority of entertainment/arts channels. While the lower pink part appears to be the apolitical area, mainly consisting of entertainment/arts and Weibo services, the channels related to power politics are grouped in the upper half of the CENA.

The distribution of the channels according to their agendas can be described as a binary division that creates two poles: one power political pole and one apolitical pole. However, the border between the two areas is not sharp. This means that nodes with power politics agendas reach far into the apolitical area and vice versa. Hence, the interconnectivity between the two poles is not null. Moreover, it can be observed that the agents with a cultural politics agenda (green) are scattered over the whole network without a distinctive pattern, which corresponds with a connectivity to both power political agents and apolitical agents.

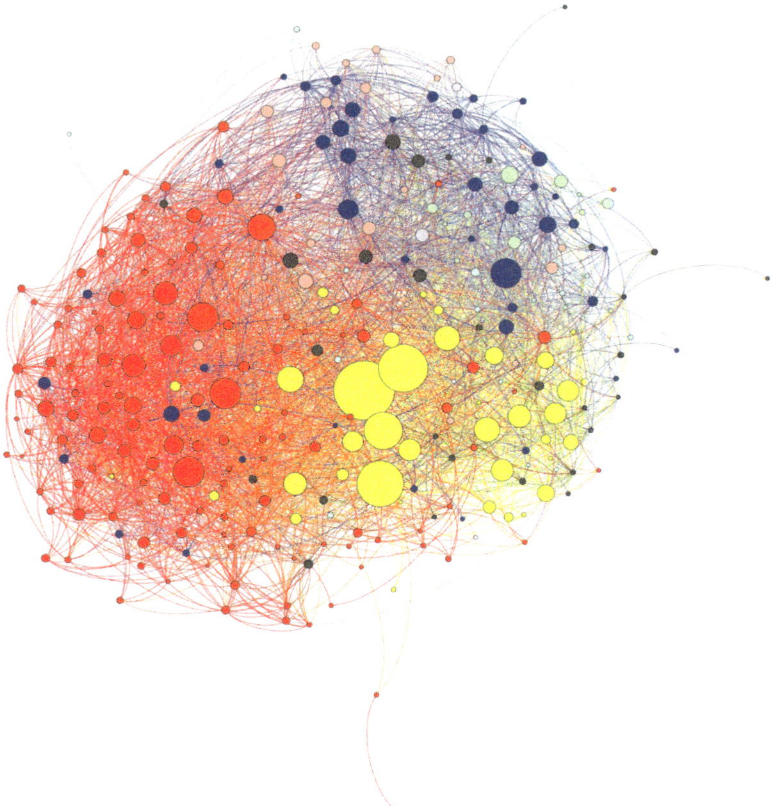

Fig. 3 The complete Weibo elite network colored by channel categories (CENC). The CENC graph (n = 291 channels) was created with the Force Atlas algorithm by Gephi. It is colored by the following channel categories: Entertainment/arts (red), media (blue), Weibo service (yellow), business (black), public intellectuals (light red), state (light green), international (light violet), others (light blue).[6] (Source: authors)

6 The colors assigned in the visualization are used to maximize the contrast between different sectors and contain no further symbolic meaning.

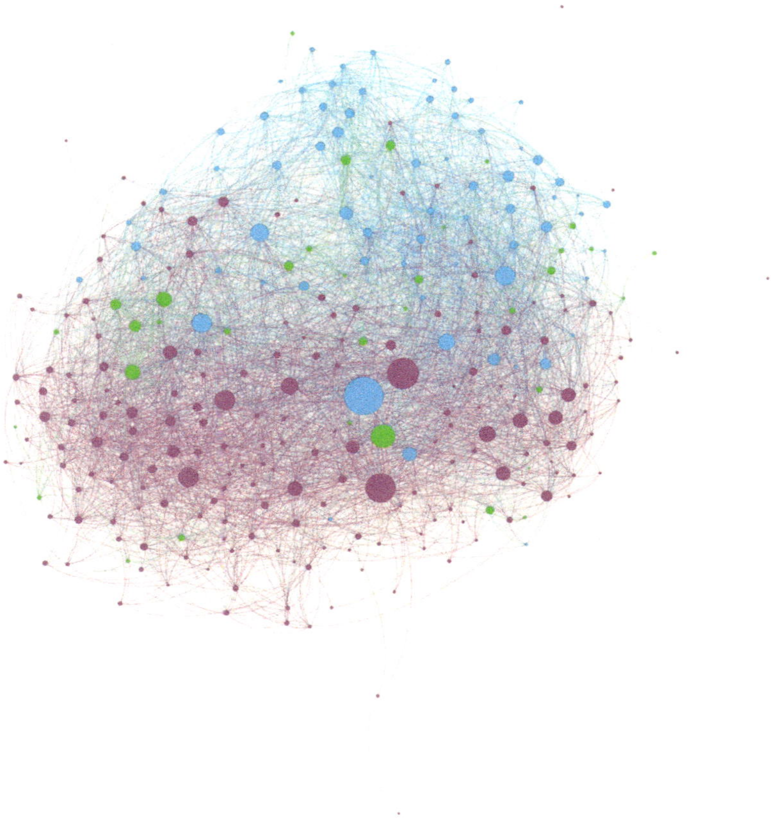

Fig. 4 The complete elite network colored by channel agenda (CENA): apolitical agenda (pink), cultural politics agenda (green) and power politics agenda (blue). (Source: authors)

Linking the distribution of the channel categories (Figure 3) to the two poles (Figure 4), it can be stated that the power political pole is widely dominated by public intellectuals, state, media and international channels, whereas in the apolitical pole, entertainment/arts channels and Weibo services prevail. The business agents, however, are spread across both poles. Some Weibo services are found to have a political agenda. The node with the highest in-degree in the elite network is a Weibo service with a power politics agenda.

Looking now at the edges of the political agenda elite network colored by channel category (PENC, Figure 5), it can be stated that the political agenda elite network is less densely connected than the complete network (compare Figure 3). However, at the upper center and the upper right, the political network is much denser than at the bottom left part of the graph. In the dense part, more channels with a power politics agenda are situated. At the bottom of the graph, some isolated channels can be found. Their weak connection to the other elite agents with a political agenda can be observed given the few edges that reach them as well as their peripheral position on the map. All of the peripheral nodes have a rather small size (= in-degree), which means that they have low connective influence within the elite network because of low numbers of elite fans, and that most of the isolated nodes have a cultural politics agenda.

Because of their large nodes, it is still the three factions that visually dominate the PENC: entertainment/arts (red), media (blue), and Weibo service (yellow) channels (Figure 5). However, it is the channel categories media, entertainment/arts and public intellectuals that are most frequent.

In the PENC, state channels (light green) are all grouped in the upper right area, while the public intellectuals (light red) are more scattered across the graph (Figure 5). These two categories are rather distanced from each other. Only four of the 19 public intellectuals reach into the area of state channels. Although few of the state and public intellectual channels reach into the center of the graph, in general these categories occupy more peripheral positions in the network.

Compared to state channels and public intellectuals, the media channels (blue) in the PENC generally have bigger nodes, which means they are more often subscribed to by elite users. The media nodes are distributed around the nodes of public intellectuals and state channels. On the one hand, media channels are situated near the state channels. These 'state-near' media channels are mostly organizational ones. On the other hand, media channels are also positioned around the nodes of public intellectuals. These 'intellectual-near' media channels are rather individual ones. The few international channels are positioned in the middle between the state channels and the public intellectuals. Likewise, the business channels with a political agenda are situated in this intermediate zone. However, there are some business channels that reach into the very right area of the PENC near the state channels (Figure 5).

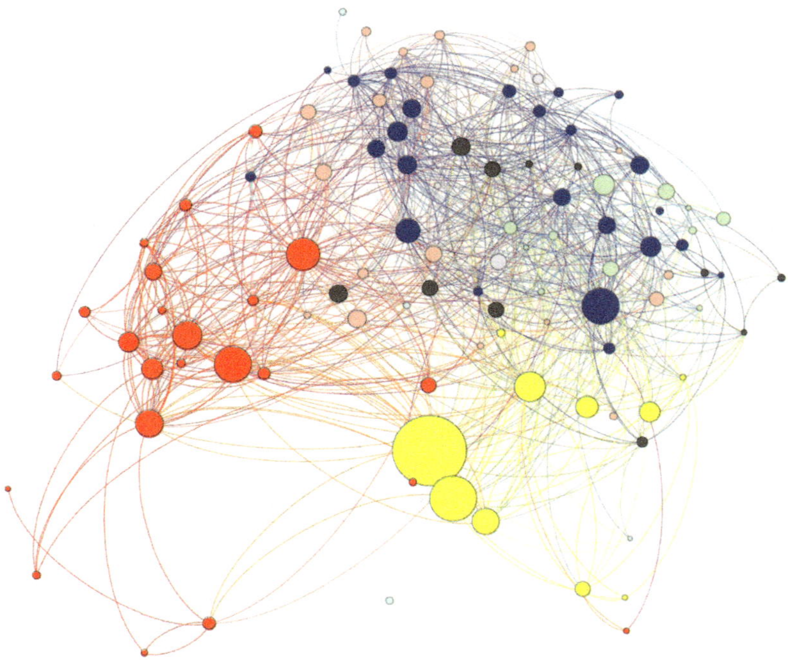

Fig. 5 The political agenda elite network colored by channel category (PENC). Apolitical channels are filtered out. The graph shows the following channel categories: state (light green), media (blue), Weibo service (yellow), entertainment/arts (red), business (black), international (light violet), public intellectual (light red), other (light blue). (Source: authors)

Separated from all other categories, the left area of the PENC graph is composed of the entertainment/arts channels (red). They generate a less dense zone compared to the others. The reason for that is the small number of entertainment/arts channels with a political agenda. Some smaller nodes of the entertainment/arts channels appear to be isolated at the bottom. In the CENC (Figure 3), these isolated nodes are in the middle of the entertainment/arts zone.

Compared to their position in the CENC (Figure 3), the Weibo services (yellow) in the PENC (Figure 5) are now positioned in the lower right area. Looking at the edges, they are still intensely connected with all the nodal categories. They are positioned in between the areas of entertainment/arts and state channels. This means technically that they are highly 'followed' by nodes from both categories, while the state and the entertainment/arts channels are not following each other.

4.3 Topics Visible in the Political Agendas

As described in the chapter above, each channel that has a political agenda is analyzed more deeply. For the explorative content analysis, up to three prevailing keywords from the content of a given channels' complete and popular feed are summarized. Altogether, they provide a picture of the discourse and topics in the Weibo elite network. However, they do not indicate if a user deals with a topic in a positive, negative or neutral way.

Using the online tool Tagul, an intuitively comprehensible graph is created (Figure 6). The keywords have the following frequencies (selection of terms that appear at least five times): international politics (16), police enforcement (15), public health (15), public security (14), peacekeeping force (10), education (9), environment (9), lost kid (9), economic policy (7), corruption (6), national identity (6), Beijing transportation (5), financial policy (5) and police violence (5).

Fig. 6 Word cloud generated by the frequency analysis of keywords.

The graph shows the topics that channels that hold a power politics or a culture politics agenda have communicated about. The font size illustrates the frequency (= the bigger, the more frequent). (Source: authors)

The keywords relate to both power politics and cultural politics. While international politics, police enforcement, public security and peacekeeping force are the most frequent topics categorized as the power politics agenda, the culture politics agenda is mostly comprised of topics such as public health, education, environment and lost children.

5 Discussion

In the on-going scholarly discussion about the role of social media under authoritarian context, the overarching assumption of the utopian school is that non-elite agents no longer need to succumb to the state monopoly of information. In this manner, they are free to participate in bottom-up connective actions. Nonetheless, by identifying and examining the microblog elite, our analysis of Sina Weibo critically contravenes the utopian model in several perspectives.

5.1 Fans as Capital: Gaps between the Microblog Elite and the Grassroots

Social capital is crucial when it comes to mobilizing and engaging people in a certain political action. The same applies to virtual campaigns in the online world. Contrasted to the "We are the 99 %" narrative in the Twitter blogosphere (Bennett & Segerberg, 2012) that depicts a bottom-up mechanism of grassroots organization, Chinese scholars (Li, 2012; Zeng & Huang, 2012) and the results of our research suggest the difficulty of applying this logic to Weibo. Rather, the observation is that in the beautiful new world of the Internet, the power hierarchy is, if not worse than in the non-digital world, still unevenly constructed.

We argue that on Weibo, a profound division or distinction between elite and grassroots agents is institutionalized by the real-name registration (RnR) as well as the Sina Weibo verification system. Although real-name registration is a prerequisite for every user in Sina Weibo, registered netizens can decide for themselves whether or not to display their real identity publicly in their profile. The verification system, by contrast, is a bonus service that offers extra credibility to those who want to emphasize who they are, and thus attracting more fans based on it. In our network, only seven out of 291 elite actors are non-verified and only three of the 105 political elite agents do not have a level of certification at all. It is clear that for the majority of influential figures, the real-identity verification is embraced as a basic step in gaining online credibility. This is in line with Bourdieu's idea (1985) that reputation, prestige, or symbolic capital stemming from one field can be used as capital in another field. Elite agents, especially those from the entertainment sector, gain a great deal of digital power based on their existing capital in the offline world.

Grassroots agents are put in a less favorable position in the competition for attention and visibility the moment they enter the cyberspace. The right to talk is not equal to the power to be heard (Zhang, 2011). On Weibo, whether information wins more visibility depends not only on each individual's fans and 'following' network, but also the platform's algorithms which recommend information to netizens not in these networks. These privileges are reserved for verified channels, and thus exclude those who want to remain anonymous in the social network. The differences between the grassroots' connective action and the viral movement led by opinion leaders have been analyzed by several scholars (Li, 2012; Zeng & Huang, 2012). A good example from a previous study is salient in the Yihuang Demolition issue (Zeng & Huang, 2012). *@ZhongRujiu's* experience of being bullied by the local police caught no huge attention because of the channel's low number of fans. Only when the elite channel *@Deng Fei* reposted the original Weibo-message, this incident grew viral.

Li (2012) predicted the centralization of discursive power, in which the verified microblogging elite predominantly follow and interact with other influential elite channels and rarely with grassroots users. Even with sufficient Internet access, the "digital subaltern" (Kent, 2008) cannot speak up or gain visibility without the help of these elite channels. In our study, we find corroborating indicators for this argument: on average, the analyzed elite channels follow 602 users, whereas they have nearly 10.8 million fans, which is almost 18,000 times the number of channels one agent follows. Thus, the input-output relation of an average elite microblog is extremely asymmetric. Moreover, the high connectivity of the elite network enhances the influence of individual elite channels even more. They represent the largest circulated 'press' that generates news and plays the role of gatekeeper for the public. At this point, it seems fitting to celebrate the information communication technology's potential to decentralize state power as Howard and Hussain (2013) did. Nonetheless, social media bring about new inequality that does not favor the oppressed, namely, the augmenting gap, in terms of digital capital, between the technology-savvy elite and the grassroots activists.[7] The most followed actor under examination is a Weibo service channel that has nearly 191.6 million fans, which

---

7 For a similar conclusion with regards to urban/rural divides and the integration of topics of the poor and marginalized classes, see Merlyna Lim's contribution; for a discussion of intersecting digital divides, see Anna Antonakis' article in this volume.

is more than one tenth of China's population. Moreover, this channel is massively connected with other elite channels. Hence, our results suggest that big Vs are not lone wolves in the formation of an elite network. They rather form alliances and cooperate with each other in order to increase digital capital and influence.

5.2 Division and Hierarchy among Elite Agents

Unsatisfied with the existing utopian model that tends to oversimplify new media as a dualistic battlefield between regime and citizens, we used an inductive categorization process to discover the spectrum of elite actors in our network. Several possible categories that we had expected to be salient in the network eventually turned out peripheral, such as NGOs, religious figures, and lawyers.

We explore Weibo services as a group of agents that has not yet been addressed in current literature, but their noticeable existence as well as their striking influence is intriguing. In terms of connectivity, the Weibo service channels represent the number one category.[8] They constitute the third biggest group and possess an average fan base of 26.1 million, over twice the size of the runner-up – the entertainment sector. In the elite network, the Weibo service channels take up a core spot in terms of bridging actors from different sectors. According to the weak tie thesis (Burt, 1992), they literally become the intermediaries of transport between different sub-communities that could otherwise be completely isolated from each other.

The entertainment/arts sector is salient for two reasons. First, it is the biggest category in terms of number of nodes in our elite network, making up nearly 43 percent of the channels in the network. Secondly, they formulate a closed subgroup far away from the state agents, public intellectuals, and certain media channels. Although various entertainment/arts practitioners occupy the elite network, the average number of fans of this category is only second – after the Weibo service channels.

The actors from the categories media, state, and public intellectuals are more commingled as a whole. Media organizations and practitioners represent the second biggest category in terms of the number of nodes in the elite network. Screening out some tabloid channels that connect more to the entertainment/arts sector, they form their own community together with the state actors and the public intellectuals.

8 Nonetheless, criticism has been put forward from users that some *Weibo Service* channels are automatically and mandatorily added to individuals' following-lists after Sina Weibo's system upgrade and cannot be removed. This partially explains their surprisingly high fan bases. See some complaints here: https://www.douban.com/group/topic/78850953/.

An interesting observation is that despite being relatively peripheral in the elite network, the public intellectuals and the state actors are the most 'caring' ones, following respectively 1270 and 1010 channels on average, nearly two times the number of followings of media channels. This implies the scholars' and officials' tendency towards a broad interest in information input from various agents. In terms of activeness (Liu & Liu, 2011), the elite media channels have the highest average number of posts, followed by the state and the public intellectuals. This means that they endeavor more to run their channels as a source of information output. In comparison, the elite users of the more influential categories (biggest fan bases), such as entertainment/arts and Weibo service, post far less actively on average.

5.3 Talking about Power: Three Elite Political Discourses

Bourdieu (1985) argues that in the "subjective" side, the social field is structured "because the schemes of perception and appreciation available for use at the moment in question, especially those that are deposited in language, are the product of previous symbolic struggles and express the state of the symbolic power relations" (p. 727). That is, shortly put, agents compete in a field to impose their own worldviews on others. Although our elite network turns out to be quite densely connected as a whole, leaving few outliers in marginal positions, we still identify the existence of several sub-communities that are worth discussion. According to content analysis, we find that elites have different strategies in choosing their agendas. To begin with, the entertainment/arts sector is huge but remains a pretty much isolated 'controversy-free' zone. Moreover, in terms of channels with political agendas, the state actors and the public intellectuals deviate from each other, whereas the many media channels 'pick their side' from either one of the groups. These communities show utterly divergent patterns in their information flow. The Internet does not only circulate anti-regime grievances, but also pro-regime narratives and hedonistic escapism.

Based on the observation above, we argue that more specified studies of factions or polarization as a result of fragmented elite networks are needed. Within the networks where information flows, Weibo constitutes a discursive field where different agents compete for the power to promulgate their understanding of the power relations within the social space. It is a discursive field where conflicting worldviews are expressed in an isolated manner. We conclude that there are three mutually exclusive driving forces: the escapist entertainment, the establishment, and the state-critical (Figure 7).

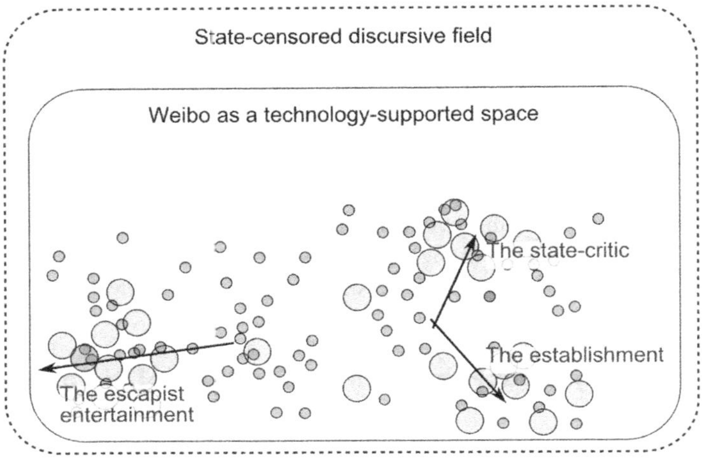

Fig. 7 Three divergent discourses in the elite network. (Source: authors)

Following Bourdieu, they constitute three distinct classes of similar agents "who occupy and who, [are] being placed in similar conditions and subjected to similar conditionings, have every likelihood of having similar dispositions and interests and therefore of producing similar practices and adopting similar stances" (1985, p. 725).

On the one hand, the digital elite stemming from the entertainment industry aims to increase cultural capital and economic capital. This incentive keeps them fan-oriented and away from sensitive political discussions. Being an escapist in the digital field means making use of existing rules while not challenging them. This becomes obvious in the large, isolated, and broadly apolitical entertainment/arts sector in our network. Over 80 percent of actors, singers, filmmakers, etc. disappear from the network when we filter out the apolitical channels. It is to be noted that the identification of the public agenda lies in our coding of the most popular and the latest 15 posts from each channel. When an actor is deemed apolitical, there are two possibilities: (1) he or she does not talk about public controversies at all, or (2) he or she once tried it in the past, but the content did not win enough acknowledgements and failed to become popular. The reason for the entertainment/arts sector's retreat from public discussion is apparent: Sina Weibo has always been a highly commercialized platform since its beginning (Zhou, 2011). Online digital capital can be used in various ways: not merely does it point to the mobilization potential, but it constitutes also an ideal tool for a marketing-oriented "fans economy", that is, the possibility for stars to make profit by advertising products to their fans (Jin et al., 2011; Wu, 2016). Due to the fans economy, digital capital mostly helps increase the elite agents' economic capital. In order to win favor with their fans, a common strategy for celebrities from the entertainment industry is to stay away from heated disputes and post more about light-hearted content.

On the other hand, the pro-regime supporters and the state-critics are diverging and constantly in competition with each other. 86 percent and 85 percent of elite channels in state and public intellectual categories, respectively, hold political agendas, and the majority involves power politics related to government decision-making. The state actors and public intellectuals form two densely connected sub-communities that do not much overlap. The pro-state elite are more assertive in promoting the legitimacy of the existing power relations because they benefit from such structure. The critical public intellectuals, challenging the state for the legitimacy of their own elite status, push alternative agendas. Other elite agents, such as media channels and business people, are more equivocal in their attitude toward the state; their strategies vary from alliance with the establishment or with the state-critics to complete escape from political discourse.

Through the word cloud (Figure 6), we have a glimpse of the elite political agendas with huge visibility on Weibo. Topics framed in state terms (such as international politics, public health, and police enforcement) are highly visible, whereas controversial ones (such as human rights and religious freedom) that potentially challenge current power relations remain rather marginalized. It needs to be pointed out that all the online discussions on Weibo, however fierce and critical they may seem, are under direct regulation of Sina and the ultimate jurisdiction of the Communist Party. What Morozov termed as "authoritarian deliberation" (Morozov, 2009) and Tang and Iyengar (2011) as mediatization "as a strategy of governance" (p. 4) is coming true in China's micro-blogosphere: the prestigious state actors as well as the party press possess a prodigious capability to mobilize fans on Weibo (*@Xinhua news agency*, *@People's Daily*, and *@Jiangning Public Security Online* being the most densely connected and influential media channels in our network). The subject of police enforcement that we categorized under the political agenda is a typical case as it generally covers everyday practices of the public security department, the traffic squad, and police officers. Out of 15 elite channels that address this topic, eight are state actors or related to the party press. *@Forensic Qin*, a legal medical expert as well as a best-selling detective storyteller, depicts and reposts numerous vivid police stories on his microblog. In sharp contrast, the less spread agenda of police violence is promulgated by *@Xu Xin*. This activist lawyer reposts several videos showing police hooliganism and physical conflicts in cities of Shanghai, Dali and others. It is to be noticed that the establishment elite users do not always post about all-positive, state-propaganda agendas: They can also be critical to a certain point. *@People's Daily*, for instance, posted an in-depth article that describes the problem of gender stereotypes in China's primary education system on Children's Day 2016.

Although the influential public intellectuals formed a community that can offer the netizens a broader scope of alternative news, this potential must be observed together with the increasing force of potent state-sponsored national discourse that is also gaining legitimacy. Obern (2013), for example, argues that Chinese netizens are critically involved in national and domestic issues on social media to challenge the official narrative. This view might need some adjustment as in our network the official narratives set by the regime-related elites actually resurge in a more empathetic, dynamic, and personalized manner.

6 Conclusion

In this article, we explored Sina Weibo as a newly emergent social field in contemporary China. Building on the genesis of digital capital, Weibo constitutes a hierarchical space where technology-savvy elites from different fields harvest millions of fans. The Sina Weibo verification system forms an influence network which is exclusive to grassroots users, and allows the elite users to make their worldviews dominant.

Through the analysis of 291 Weibo elite channels, we found out that agents from the entertainment/art field are the dominating elite group in terms of their connectivity with the influence network. However, the state actors and public intellectuals, competing for higher visibility of their worldviews, are the most active and assertive in online discussions. Based on our social network and agenda analysis, we conclude three visible discourses of escapists, the establishment, and state-critics.

It remains to be seen how the three divergent discourses will evolve in China's microblogosphere in the future. We believe that a thorough reevaluation of the utopian school of Internet is necessary. Faced with rather divergent elite communities, the political escapists, the pro-regime as well as the state-critical thinkers might each separately build connections with channels that better suit their beliefs, and become ignorant about or intolerant of the other groups.

References

Bennett, W. L., & Segerberg, A. (2012). The logic of connective action: Digital media and the personalization of contentious politics. *Information, Communication & Society, 15*(5), 739-768.

Bloomberg. (2001). Hu Shuli. Retrieved from https://www.bloomberg.com/news/articles/2001-07-01/hu-shuli

Borgatti, S., Everett, M., & Johnson, J. (2013). *Analyzing social networks*. London [u. a.]: Sage.

Bourdieu, P. (1985). The Social Space and the Genesis of Groups. *Theory & Society, 14*(6), 723-744.

Burt, Ronald S. (1992). *Structural holes: The social structure of competition*. Cambridge, MA: Harvard University Press.

Carnesecca, C. (2015). Voice of the Masses: The Internet and Responsive Authoritarianism in China. In L. Lisheng, H. Kriesi & D. Kübler (eds.), *Urban Mobilizations and New Media in Contemporary China* (p. 117-132). Farnham & Burlington: Ashgate.

Castells, M. (2007). Communication, power and counter-power in the network society. *International Journal of Communication, 1*(1), 238-266.

Chen, L., Zhang, C., & Wilson, C. (2013). Tweeting under pressure: analyzing trending topics and evolving word choice on sina weibo. *Proceedings of the first ACM conference on Online social networks* (p. 89-100). New York: ACM.

Foster, P. (2009). Leading dissident 'exiled' to Chinese northwest. *The Telegraph*. Retrieved from http://www.telegraph.co.uk/news/worldnews/asia/china/4974333/Leading-dissident-exiled-to-Chinese-northwest.html

Fu, K., Chan, C., & Chau, M. (2013). Assessing Censorship on Microblogs in China: Discriminatory Keyword Analysis and the Real-Name Registration Policy. *Internet Computing, IEEE, 17*(3), 42-50.

Gephi.org. (2011). Gephi Tutorial Layouts. Retrieved from https://gephi.org/users/tutorial-layouts/

Gleiss, M. S. (2015). Speaking up for the suffering (br) other: Weibo activism, discursive struggles, and minimal politics in China. *Media, Culture & Society*, 37(4), 513-529.

Hassid, J. (2012). Safety valve or pressure cooker? Blogs in Chinese political life. *Journal of Communication, 62*(2), 212-230.

Howard, P., & Hussain, M. (2013). *Democracy's fourth wave? Digital media and the Arab Spring*. Oxford [u. a.]: Oxford University Press.

Jiang, K., & Tang, Z. (2015). Wei boqingjingxiawangluoyuqing guan jianjiedianshibiejikuosanmoshi fen xi [Research on Identification of Network Public Opinion's Key Nodes and Analysis on Diffusion Modes in the Context of Micro-blog]. *Library and Information Service, 59*(20), 105-111.

Jiang, M. (2010). Authoritarian informationalism: China's approach to Internet sovereignty. *SAIS Review, 30*(2), 71-89.

Jiang, M. (2014). The Co-evolution of the Internet, (Un) Civil Society & Authoritarianism in China. Retrieved from https://papers.ssrn.com/sol3/papers.cfm?abstract_id=2379092

Jin, Y., Wang, R., & Chen, X. (2011). Qi ye weiboyingxiaoxiaoguo he fen sishuliang de duan qi hu dong moxing [A Short-term Interactive Model on the Relationship between Enterprise Microblogging Marketing Effect and Followers' Number]. *Journal of Management Science, 4*, 71-83.

Kelly, J., & Etling, B. (2008). Mapping Iran's online public: Politics and culture in the Persian blogosphere. *Berkman Center research publication: no. 2008-01*. Retrieved from https://cyber.law.harvard.edu/publications/2008/Mapping_Irans_Online_Public

Kent, M. (2008). Digital Divide 2.0 and the Digital Subaltern. *Nebula, 5*(4), 84-96.

King, G., Pan, J., & Roberts, M. E. (2013). How censorship in China allows government criticism but silences collective expression. *American Political Science Review, 107*(02), 326-343.

Kong, L. (2013). Lun mi su li xin wen jiang de zhongguoshijiao [The Chinese Perspective of the Missouri Awards for Distinguished Service in Journalism]. *Modern Communication, 9*, 49-52.

Kuo, A. M. (2016). The Politics of Religion in China. Insights from Fenggang Yang. *The Diplomat*. Retrieved from http://thediplomat.com/2016/08/the-politics-of-religion-in-china/

Lee, K. (2003). Jia Zhangke. Sense of cinema. Retrieved from http://sensesofcinema.com/2003/great-directors/jia/

Lee K. (2011). *Weibo gai bian yi qie [Weibo changed everything]*. Shanghai: Shanghai University of Finance & Economics Press.

Lee, S., & Cotte, J. (2009). Network Centrality and Opinion Leadership. Retrieved from http://ojs.acadiau.ca/index.php/ASAC/article/viewFile/514/423

Lei, Y. W. (2011). The political consequences of the rise of the Internet: Political beliefs and practices of Chinese netizens. *Political Communication, 28*(3), 291-322.

Li, B. (2012). Wei bo yi jian ling xiu qun ti "xiao xiang su miao" ["Portraits" of microblogging opinion leaders]. *Journalism Review*, (9), 19-25.

Lin, N. (1999). Building a Network Theory of Social Capital. *Connections, 22*(1), 28-51.

Liu, N. (2004). Yuan hen jieshi, dong yuan jiegou he li xingxuanze – you guan zhongguo du shi di qujitixing dong fa sheng kenengxing de fen xi [Interpretation of Resentment, Mobilization Structure and Rational Choice: An Analysis of the Possibility of Collective Behavior in China's Urban Areas]. *Open Times, (4)*, 57-70.

Liu, Z, & Liu, L. (2011). Wei bo wang luo yu qing zhong de yi jian ling xiu shi bie ji fen xi [Recognition and Analysis of Opinion Leaders in Microblog Public Opinions]. *Systems Engineering, 29*(6), 8-16.

Lotan, G., Graeff, E., Ananny, M., Gaffney, D., Pearce, I., & Boyd, D. (2011). The Revolutions Were Tweeted: Information Flows During the 2011 Tunisian and Egyptian Revolutions. *International Journal of Communication, 5*, 1375-1405.

Morozov, E. (2009). The Internet: A room of our own? *Dissent, 56*(3), 80-85.

Obern, C, (2013) The Expression of Alternative Nationalism in China's Weibo. *Honors Projects*. Paper 1.

People's Daily Online (2016). People's Daily microblogging influence government index report. Retrieved from http://vdisk.weibo.com/s/q0w1lmSsJ4k9T

Registration Statement (2014). Retrieved from https://www.sec.gov /Archives/edgar/data/1595761/000119312514100237/d652805df1.htm#toc

Sheng, Z., & Gao, S. (2013). Zhong guo wei bo yi jian ling xiu, te zheng, te xing yu fa zhan qu shi [Opinion Leaders of Chinese Microblogs: Features, Types and Development Trends]. *Journal of North Eastern University (Social Science), 15*(4), 381-385.

State Council Information Office of People's Public of China [SCIO] (2010), Zhongguo hu lian wang zhuang kuang [The Internet in China]. *People*. Retrieved from http://politics.people.com.cn/GB/101380/11813818.html

Tang, W., & Iyengar, S. (2011). The Emerging Media System in China: Implications for Regime Change. *Political Communication, 28*(3), 263-267.

Wang, J. (2015). NGO 2.0 and social media praxis: activist as researcher. *Chinese Journal of Communication, 8*(1), 18-41.

Weibo Community Regulation. (2015). Retrieved August 22, 2016, from http://service.account.weibo.com/roles/gongyue

Weibo.com (2016). Weibo Renzheng [Weibo Verification]. Retrieved from http://verified.weibo.com/verify

Wu, Q. (2016). Fen sijingjiyuweibo de duo weijiazhiyanjiu. [Research of Fans economy and multiple values of Weibo]. *Journal of Advertising Study*, (1), 64-69.

Xu, X. (2016). Zhan ling wang luo zhi di dian [Occupying the Bottom of the Internet]. Retrieved from https://commondatastorage.googleapis.com/letscorp _archive/archives/101386

Zeng, F. & Huang, G. (2012). Wang luo yi jian ling xiu she qu de gou cheng, lian dong ji qi zheng ce ying xiang: yi wei bo wei li [The constitution, interaction, and the policy implication of cyber opinion leader community: in the case of Weibo]. *Open Times*, (4), 115-131.

Zhang, Z. (2011). Weibo shidai de cao gen huayuquanbaozhang [The safeguard of the grassroots' discursive power in the micro-blogging era]. *News Research*, (6), 6-8.

Zhou, H. (2011). Wei boyingxiaoxianzhuangyu fa zhan tai shichu tan [the status quo and trends of microblogging marketing]. *News World*, (4), 100-101.

Zhou, R. (2009). "Xin yi jian jie ceng" zai wang shang jue qi [The rise of "the new opinion class" in the Internet]. *Yan huang chun qiu*, (3), 52-57.

Internet-mediated Communication in Activists' Internal Networks: The Case of Iranian Women's Rights Activism

Mina Naeli

1 Introduction

This study provides firsthand empirical evidence about impacts of Internet-mediated communication on Iranian activist groups. It concentrates on women's rights activism, which is one of the most prominent and dynamic activist circles in the country. Since the early 2000s, women's rights activist groups have intensely relied on digital communication for their public outreach as well as for building or strengthening internal relations (Tohidi, 2009; Akhavan, 2011; Shirazi, 2012). Women's rights activism in Iran comprises groups that operate independently on a regular basis but act jointly when a common cause is at hand. The literature on women's rights activism shows that for the activist groups, mass mobilization has rarely been an option. Instead, they have focused on the internal organization of their resources and on the formation of coalitions with other groups. This observed phenomenon explains the research objective to evaluate the impacts of Internet usage on the women's rights groups' intra- and interrelations.

2 Women's Rights Activism

The 1905–1911 Iranian constitutional revolution period and the establishment of a constitutional monarchy, which proposed a vision of Iran as a modern society, became a departure point for women's social and political participation (Yeganeh, 1993). In the first place, women participated in the revolution as part of nationalist forces, regardless of specific women's issues. But as time passed, they started to raise their specific gender demands, such as the right for girls' education (Jahanshahrad, 2012). Since then, active social and political participation of Iranian women in all

C. Richter et al. (Hrsg.), *Digital Media and the Politics of Transformation in the Arab World and Asia*, Studies in International, Transnational and Global Communications, https://doi.org/10.1007/978-3-658-20700-7_6

major transformations have made Iranian governments ever since consider them as a strong political constituency and as agents of change. Particularly from the 1979 revolution onwards, Iranian women's rights activism has succeeded in putting women's legal equality on the national agenda (Sameh, 2010). During this time, to battle for the rights of their compatriot women, the activists founded well-defined groups, such as NGOs, as well as loosely defined groups, created special purpose coalitions and campaigns, and used media to gain the awareness and support of the public.

The most influential independent women's rights groups after the 1979 Islamic revolution were *Jameye zanane enghelabe eslami* (The Women's Society of the Islamic Revolution) and *Moaseseye Zanane mosalman* (Islamic Women Institute), which launched the monthly *Payam-e Hajar* magazine (Hagar's Message) (Mir-Hosseini, 2002). Within the structure of the revolutionary state, the Islamic feminist groups gained more participatory opportunities and public attention than their secular counterparts, such as *Etehade Enghelabi Zanane Mobarez* (Revolutionary Unity of Militant Women), a women's organization of the Communist Party of Workers and Peasants, which published their *Sepedih Sorkh* (The Red Dawn) journal. During the first decade after the revolution, Muslim women's rights activists and their publications opposed the discriminating laws regarding marriage, divorce, and child custody, which from their perspective were the result of misguided male interpretations of Islam's holy texts (Barlow & Akbarzadeh, 2008).

With the end of the Iran-Iraqi war in 1988, the death of Ayatollah Khomeini and the presidency of Hashemi Rafsanjani, a new era called the "Period of Construction" began (Bahramitash, 2007). The new economic, social and demographic post-war realities, and the need to mollify the restive, youthful population, pushed the government to enhance the freedom of the press and NGOs (Vakil, 2013). By the mid-1990s, numerous non-governmental or quasi-governmental organizations dealing with women's issues were created (Fazaeli, 2007). Among several hundred new journals and magazines that began publishing was the independent *Zanan* (Women) magazine, which later became the main platform for women's rights discourses (Kian, 1997). *Zanan,* operated by a number of high-profile women's rights activists, critically discussed socio-political, legal and economic issues from the perspective of women's interests and presented new approaches for addressing women's problems (Jahanshahrad, 2012).

Iran entered a political and social transformation era with the victory of the reformist candidate, Mohammad Khatami, in the 1997 presidential election followed by the domination of the reformists who won the majority of the seats in the 2000 parliamentary election (Iran country profile, 2015). The empowerment of the civil society and democratic entities, such as NGOs and the press, during eight years of Khatami reformist administration, gave social – mainly women's, laborers', and students' rights activists an unprecedented collective aspiration for building a more democratic society (Behravesh, 2014). In 1997, there were 67 women's NGOs, which rose to 337 in 2005. By 1999, in addition to numerous women's journals published locally, 13 women's journals and newspapers were being published at the national level (Mahdi, 2004). The reform movement also resulted in women's unprecedented political participation in the top government posts, the parliament, and the local councils (Bahramitash, 2007). Women's rights activists' media and NGOs explicitly supported the candidacy of reformist women, who in return would become their clear voice in politics and could lobby for their cases in decision-making bodies (Mohammadi, 2007). The collaborative efforts of women's legal establishments, parliamentarians, media and NGOs during this period pushed policy makers to lift some of the restrictions on women's legal rights (Vakil, 2011, p. 108). For instance, the legal age of marriage for girls and boys was raised, and the reform on child custody law entitled women to have the custody of their boys and girls up to age seven[1] (Esfandiari, 2010).

In 2005, Mahmoud Ahmadinejad won the election against his reformist rivals with the support of the lower classes that might have found the reform rhetoric too abstract to be relevant to the realities of their lives. The growing presence of women in the public sphere had become a serious source of concern for Ahmadinejad's administration (Amir-Ebrahimi, 2008). To decelerate this process, his administration reinforced its intimidation of women's rights activists, mainly by targeting women's press and NGOs. The activists, however, continued their efforts in spite of the clampdowns. One of the biggest women's rights coalitions, known as women's coalition for election, formed in April 2009, a few months before the disputed presidential election. Instead of endorsing one specific candidate, they presented their issues to all four nominees and demanded a response from each. The coalition received the support of 40 organizations and 700 women's rights activists or followers, which turned it into the largest pre-election coalition of women in Iranian history (Shojaei, 2012).

After Ahmadinejad had led various efforts during his two term presidency to steadily reverse progress made with regard to press freedom and the opening up of the civil society sphere under Khatami, the 2013 election of a moderate political figure, Hasan Rouhani, offered Iranians new hope for change. The composition of Rouhani's government and statements made by him and his ministers signaled a deliberate endeavor to deviate from Ahmadinejad's policies and to ease restrictions

---

1 Previously, the law entitled the mother to have the custody of boys aged up to two years only. With the new legislation, the court decides if the mother or father should receive the custody once children reach the age of seven (Koolaee, 2012).

on the society (Menashri, 2013). Women's rights activists' evaluation of the election of Rouhani was cautiously optimistic. With promises of eliminating discriminative and gender-segregating policies, his presidency provided much needed hope and energy for the activists (Vakil, 2013). In the context of this new political environment, and in contrast to the previous eight years of Ahmadinejad's rule, women's rights activists began to meet more openly. Their conventions, which had been canceled during the previous eight years due to state repression and a general sense of hopelessness, resumed (Thmasebi, 2013).

It is currently more than one decade that the Internet has been added to the women's rights activists' contention tools. Since 2002 women's rights activists have started to use the Internet as a new means of public communication (Akhavan, 2011; Shirazi, 2012). Also, it has been reported that women's rights activist groups have employed the Internet as an internal communication channel since the first term of Ahmadinejad's presidency. For instance, within the 2009 pre-election coalition, the Internet, and specifically e-mails, were largely utilized for networking and for mobilizing (Tohidi, 2009). The empirical results of this study confirm the noticeable existence of digital communication within and across the women's rights activist groups. It will be shown that the Internet's impacts on the activists' internal relations have emerged from the utilization of the Internet for both internal communication and for raising public awareness.

3 Online Communication Within and Across Activist Groups

This research is situated within studies that investigated the Internet usage within networks of activist groups and individuals. Apart from 'grand theorizing', the majority of the existing empirical studies is about activism experiences with the Internet in the context of Western democracies. The increasing amount of literature on activism in the Arab countries mainly focused on activists' use of the Internet for public mobilization and largely neglected to shed light on its role in internal communication.

The Internet has been praised widely as a cost-efficient communication channel (e.g. Bennett, 2003; Bimber et al., 2005; Juris, 2005; Nielsen, 2009) which can overcome limitations of space and time (e.g. Ayres, 1999; Deibert, 2000; Bennett, 2003; Juris, 2005). This opportunity is expected to decrease the transaction costs of coordination (Clark & Themudo, 2006) and to facilitate the participation of marginalized actors and groups in decision-making (Eagleton-Pierce, 2001). However, scholars discussed that the same qualities which make online communication cheaper and easier can generate new costs for activist networks. For instance, Nielsen (2009) identified three interrelated problems associated with reduced up-front costs of communications, more communicators, and more forms of communication: redundant communication (over-communication), discrepant information (mis-communication), and more communication than individual activists and their groups can deal with (communication overload).

Regarding the effects of the Internet on interpersonal and group relations, it has been argued that online technologies facilitate the adoption of decentralized, non-hierarchical activist approaches (Bennett, 2003; Surman & Reilly, 2003). There is, however, the potential of new tensions within activist organizations because the existing hierarchical balance is challenged by formally excluded actors who gain new importance online (Surman & Reilly, 2003; Clark & Themudo, 2006).

In terms of communication across activist groups, as Surman and Reilly (2003) stressed, online technologies have both driven and benefited from the increased enthusiasm of civil society organizations about collaboration. Numerous studies provided evidence about the contribution of e-mail lists and websites to collaborative networks of activist groups (e.g., Eagleton-Pierce, 2001; Van Aelst & Walgrave, 2002; Simi & Futrell, 2006).

The relation between the Internet use and the participation of individual activists in collective action is addressed in studies about online collective identity and the increasing debates around the so-called slacktivism. Melucci (1995) defines collective identity as the interactive and shared process by which social actors construct collective action. This process "involves cognitive definitions concerning the ends, means, and field of action". Thus, it refers to "a network of active relationships between the actors, who interact, communicate, influence each other, negotiate, and make decisions". It also requires "a certain degree of emotional investment, which enables individuals to feel like part of a common unity" (p. 44-45). It has been suggested that the Internet promotes collectivity[2] by encouraging perception among individuals that they are members of a larger community sharing the same goals (Bennett, 2003; Garrett, 2006).

However, in recent years in light of the growing role of social media within activism, the concern about reverse impacts of the Internet on activists' participation and collective identity is increasingly voiced in debates about slacktivism.

2 For a discussion of social media as a tool for the creation of the collective self through the theoretical lens of the diaspora see Almut Woller's contribution in this volume. For a critical stance on the social media's ability to foster a sense of community among activists see Abir Kopty's contribution in this volume.

Slacktivism has become somewhat of a buzzword. In an extremely negative sense it has been described as "feel-good online activism that has zero political or social impact" (Morozov, 2009, p. 3) and "five-minute activism" (Earl & Kimport, 2010, p. 74) by people who are unwilling to get their hands dirty and engage in actual efforts to achieve real social and political goals (Christensen, 2012). As a not entirely ineffective phenomenon, slacktivism was also referred to as "low-risk, low-cost activity via social media, whose purpose is to raise awareness, produce change, or grant satisfaction to the person engaged in the activity" (Rotman et al., 2011, p. 821). Critics of slacktivism have related the slacktivists' concern with social or political issues to the fulfillment of "selfish and narcissistic" purposes rather than to contributing to the achievement of societal benefits (Morozov, 2009; Breuer & Farooq, 2012). Moreover, slacktivism can satisfy previously active people's motivation to take real civic action and distract them from making more meaningful contributions (Morozov, 2009; Lee & Hsieh, 2013; Skoric & Poor, 2013).

This study advances the argument that the changes occasioned by new media can be specific to different social and political contexts (e. g. Michaelsen, 2011; Harp et al. 2012; Harlow & Harp, 2012). In the last decade, the usage of the Internet by Iranian activists has exploded. Still, the Internet's impact on the internal networking of activists has remained an unexplored topic. Particularly regarding the case of women's rights activism, there are plenty of articles focusing on the growing use of the Internet; however, most of them are written by the activists themselves and lack empirical data and evidence. Very few scholarly articles that represent empirical analysis of the case (Khiabany & Sreberny, 2010; Akhavan, 2011; Shirazi, 2012) focus on the implications of the Internet for the activists' public relation efforts. This is the first study which seeks to empirically shed light on uncovered aspects of the Internet usage within the internal network of Iranian activists.

4 Method of the Study

Individual, face-to-face, and semi-structured interviews were conducted with eleven women's rights activists, three males and eight females. The interviews were conducted in Tehran between October 2014 and January 2015. I considered activists who at the time of the interviews were active participants of one or more activist organization which aimed "to influence public policy, organizational action, or social norms and values" (Smith, 1997, as cited in Smith & Ferguson, 2001, p. 292) in the field of women and family. I selected women's rights activists with different lengths of involvement in activism in order to reflect diverse viewpoints of generations. Having gotten involved with women's rights affairs before the 1979 revolution, three activists had over 30 years of experience in women's rights activism, four had between ten and 20 years, and four young activists had less than ten years of experience. In addition, to uncover the experiences of those contributing in different spheres of activism, the interviewees were selected from heterogeneous occupational categories. Among the interviewed activists were a lawyer, a women's workshop instructor, a website manager, a website developer, a social worker, two NGO managers, two journalists, two gender study researchers, and two podcast producers. And finally, to avoid being restricted to the viewpoints of activists in the capital, two interviewees were selected from women's rights groups operating in smaller cities.[3] Although, this is not to say that the interviewed activists who were based in Tehran had no operations in other cities.

The analytical technique applied to the processing of the interview transcriptions was thematic analysis. Drawing on Braun and Clarke's (2006; Braun et al., 2015) pragmatic view of the method, the transcripts were initially coded to identify the key common viewpoints and experiences in the data. In this research, the codes were derived while reading through the transcripts, as the thematic analysis was principally based on an inductive approach. The lists of codes were reviewed to identify the codes that form a potential pattern of interpretation related to the research question. These codes were grouped to form the main overarching themes. The interviews were conducted and transcribed in Farsi. I then translated the statements that are quoted in the article into English. The four themes generated from the analysis differentiate between applications and impacts of three most utilized online platforms by women's rights activists: e-mail groups, websites, and social networking sites (SNSs). It was initially not planned to investigate the different types of online technologies utilized by the women's rights activists. However, this distinction emerged during the analysis of the interviewees' testimonies.

5 The Internet's Impacts on Women's Rights Activists' Internal Relations

My findings about Internet usage by women's rights activist groups uncovered that e-mail groups are the main Internet technology employed for internal communication. For the great majority of the interviewees, e-mail and in particular e-mail

3 For a discussion about the urban/rural contrasts in activist formation see also the contribution of Anna Antonakis about the Tunisian case in this volume.

groups, were the first and foremost tool for expressing and exchanging their views on various aspects of activism. The interviewees' experiences suggest that over recent years, a large number of the decisions related to activism had been made within these virtual groups. Besides the usage of e-mail groups for dialogue and decision-making, the interview analysis found that these online groups are also used for organization and broadcasting of activities within and across activist groups. What is important to note here is that in spite of networking potentials of SNSs, there was no interview evidence to suggest that activist groups have employed any of these sites for internal communication and organization.

There was a common assumption among all the interviewees that the major means of the activists' public communication are websites and SNSs, deployed to raise public awareness about women's issues, activist groups' objectives and the details of their activities. According to some of the respondents, the websites of the women's rights groups are also utilized by the activists themselves for the collection of women's rights-related practical and theoretical information.

The four overarching interview themes in this article demonstrate that the utilization of e-mail groups, as internal communication channel, and websites and SNSs, as public communication media, have brought about different impacts on the activists' internal relations. The first theme illustrates how e-mail groups have facilitated women's rights activist groups' collective decision-makings. The second theme shows that both activist websites and e-mail groups have encouraged collaboration across various activist groups. In the third theme it is discussed that the activist websites have empowered activist groups by improving knowledge of their members. The fourth theme demonstrates that utilization of SNSs by individual activists to communicate with public has damaged the activists' collectivity.

5.1 Theme One: E-mail Groups Facilitate Collective Decision-Making

According to all eleven interviewees, the e-mail groups enable more Iranian women's rights activists to exert influence on their groups' decision outcomes by circumventing two restrictions that had previously undermined the groups' collective decision-making processes: namely, geographical barriers and costs of offline meetings.

Iranian women's rights activism is dispersed across several provinces of the country, which have their particular female publics with a variety of demands. E-mail groups gave the activists the ability to participate in the activism debates without being confined to their geographical locations. "E-mail groups make decision-making more democratic because the activists who live in other cities and cannot attend meetings in Tehran found the opportunity to take part in the debates", said interviewee 2. The importance of this participation for women's rights activism was illustrated by interviewee 10:

> *"For NGOs and campaigns it is always critical to have the contribution of women [rights'] activists in smaller cities. This is because the demands of Iranian women include a wide spectrum of issues. The only way to identify and address the issues of different cities and minorities is through local activists."*

This interviewee explained that prior to the usage of e-mail groups, face-to-face meetings were a major venue for activists' internal deliberation. For this reason, the women's rights activists in the capital had been to a large extent prevented from contacting local activists from other parts of the country, which caused the latter group's dissatisfaction: "They believed that activists in Tehran are not aware of their particular difficulties and concerns". She emphasized that e-mail groups significantly addressed this communication gap and paved the way for participation of the dispersed activists in the debates.

The respondents went further to suggest that the opportunity that e-mail groups provided for the participation of scattered activists had prepared the ground for the creation of a collective identity and trust among the women's rights activists who had no physical contact. From the perspective of interviewee 11, physical proximity was a determinant factor in building trust and collective identity among the activists. She maintained that over recent years, e-mails have to a great extent eliminated the problem of physical distance between activists: "Now our collective identity is to a lesser extent dependent on our physical interaction and local environment." Interviewee 3 noted that "these [e-mail] groups have prevented the geographical gap from widening the mental gap". He firmly believed that the e-mail groups have informed the dispersed activists about each other's demands and expectations and have assisted the groups in agenda-setting that encompasses the priorities of "wider groups from wider geographical locations".

The financial cost of offline meetings was named as the other significant barrier due to which the groups could not facilitate the participation of certain members in their deliberations. Interviewee 7 pointed at the possibility that e-mail communication would give the groups to save the expenses of offline gatherings. When I asked him to explain the activist groups' budget sources and why cost reduction is of great importance to them, he replied by separating registered NGOs from informal groups and specific case-based campaigns:

> *"Budgeting has always been a very challenging issue. Normally, the NGOs are in a better situation. They have their own offices and defined sources of funding. Particularly those which work on social trauma cases can receive stipends from the government. They [the NGOs] definitely deal with financial issues, but the problem is much more serious for the [informal] groups and the campaigns. They mostly run on their members' contribution. One may devote her office or her home while others account for other costs."*

Interviewee 10's testimony suggests that before the formation of e-mail groups, there was little room for contribution of younger activists in the key debates due to the groups' financial constraints: "As the groups could not afford the cost of large gatherings, they had to limit the invitations to those who were more influential due to their experience and reputation." The analysis suggests that the participation of young activists and geographically dispersed activists, who were largely absent from offline meetings, in the groups' debates have increased the quality of decision outcomes. Interviewee 5 explained: "With the growth of e-mail interactions, the diversity of opinions increased, so we witnessed more creativity in the decisions." Interviewee 9 remarked that e-mail groups "help us to scrutinize a subject and be aware of its hidden aspects because it is discussed from different perspectives". More specifically, she acknowledged the constructive role of young activists in decision-making:

> *"Their contributions have been greatly influential...They have unframed minds so they look at the issues from different angles... Because they spend more time on the Internet and, unlike us [the older activists], they know how to search for the best sources of information, they are more aware of the events and discourses that are taking place globally."*

The interview analysis shows that the enhancement in decision-making outcomes is also related to the fact that in the activist groups and campaigns, the members, even the most experienced ones, do not resist challenging ideas. I asked the interviewees who provided the most details about brainstorming in e-mail groups to explain if the viewpoints of the participating activists are treated similarly regardless of their age, experience, and position within the leadership committees. The following quote from interviewee 2 represents the most common answer:

> *"It cannot be said that such factors as age or the length of activism were determining factors in decision-making. In these groups, there are high-profile activists like X and Y. But no one feels like she/he should not reject their idea*

because of their position…In most cases, the members used to agree on stronger logics and not ideas that were stated more regularly or were presented by the famous members."

5.2 Theme Two: The Activist Websites and E-Mail Groups Stimulate Interactivity and Collaboration across the Activist Groups

The review of women's rights activists' activities and the statements by the interviewed activists shows that a culture of cooperation exists within the entire network of women's rights activism. NGOs and informal groups advocate collaboration and networking rather than separation and competition. It is this culture and the tendency to build coalitions and partnerships that make e-mail groups and websites effective tools in facilitating interactivity across the activism network.

As mentioned, besides using e-mails to process the debates, Iranian women's rights groups also use their e-mail lists to coordinate their actions and to distribute information about their collective actions. Most of the interviewees who were subscribers to different activist e-mail groups referred to these online groups as the most common means of receiving and distributing notices of events and initiatives. Although they reported that this online technology is also used for intra-group planning and announcements, the greatest part of their testimonies was related to the opportunity that it has provided for collaborations across activist groups. The activists' e-mail groups have formed a network over which the activists from different groups can come together and organize their programs jointly. As an example, interviewee 2 maintained: "A few months ago I was added to an e-mail group. It was formed by activists from three [women's] groups in which programs for the commemoration of the International Women's Day had been talked about." Interviewee 8 explained that in multiple cases she signed statements that the activist groups had distributed through e-mail groups.

The interactivity of groups within the activism network is also facilitated by the websites that these groups maintain to communicate with people. It was mentioned that in addition to dissemination of information about women's issues, the activist websites spread details about their affiliated groups. The interview evidence suggests that this utilization of the websites enables the groups to become aware of each other's aims and activities. Interviewee 10 noted: "Websites gave the groups their own independent voice. We become aware of each other without having to hold physical meetings and visits." She emphasized that many of the activist groups are operating informally without any office. "We recognize these groups primarily through their websites. These websites do not only transmit information. They construct bridges between different ideologies and groups inside the activism." Interviewee 11 focused on the relations that the websites have created among various women's groups across the country:

> *"We can find information about the activities of hundreds of big and small organizations which operate in the country to assist women in resolving their difficulties. Having this information we [members of the group she cooperated with] can identify the groups that share goals with us, the ones that can help us in the pursuit of our objective."*

5.3 Theme Three: The Activist Websites Foster Personal Empowerment

The evidence generated from the interviews shows that the groups' websites have advanced the activists' personal empowerment by training them, both theoretically and practically, on issues related to women's rights. Talking about the impact of her fellow activists' articles on her abilities to follow her legal cases, interviewee 9 said: "In many cases, the articles that were shared by my friends' websites notified me about the aspects of the laws which I had ignored." Interviewee 11 explained that the activists' websites provide specific articles and e-books that "enhance the activism's theoretical foundation". She also mentioned that these websites actively publish articles that are self-critical of activism: "The faults in dealing with the obstacles, the weaknesses that exist in the organizations' intra-relations, criticism of women's campaigns and how they could have been more effective and so on." From her perspective, such articles help activists to learn from their faults. Interviewee 8 explained that the "academically compiled materials" of the websites assist her in creating her workshops' agenda and discussions: "For example, the e-books that very systematically present statistics about domestic violence."

The activists interviewed in this research paid great attention to the knowledge-building potential of the translated articles available on the activist websites. Interviewee 4 elaborated on a very common trend among the women's rights activists to translate academic and opinion articles about women's activism:

> *"It has been many years that we have an eye on the activities and breakthroughs of women's [rights] activists in other countries, particularly the regional and Muslim countries. Unfortunately, except for the reform era [eight years of Khatami's presidency], there has been a very limited relationship between*

> *Iranian and regional activists. To fill this gap, since the beginning the activist websites have been publishing translations of articles about activists and transformation related to women's issues in the region. This is because we always feel an overwhelming desire to learn from their strategies."*

Acknowledging the efforts by the women's rights activists, particularly the researchers and journalists, to identify and translate articles written in other languages, interviewee 9 noted: "Compared to the 1980s and the 1990s, the activists are much more informed about regional and international transformation and uprisings. Now we feel that we are moving in a brighter way."

Besides their visitors, the websites also empower the activists who participate in their maintenance. This was the notion held by four interviewees who had the experience of cooperating with the activist websites. Interviewee 6 explained that each website, like other forms of publication, produces a new group of authors or provides more publications from existing authors. He remarked that the new authors learn how to write and manifest their ideas. The experienced ones grow by subjecting their opinions to public judgment and "in this way, they revisit their viewpoints". Interviewee 11 said she always encourages activists in smaller cities "to launch their own websites and not be content with just cooperating with website teams in Tehran." This is because her experience of cooperating with a number of the women's websites has shown her that maintaining these websites increases the activists' sense of responsibility. Additionally, the content management activities "boost their ability to recognize and organize opinions, to analyze the situation, and to improve their writing capabilities". Interviewee 4 explained why the management of a prominent women's campaign "was a precious experience and a sort of personal empowerment" for her:

> *"I took the responsibility of the job in which I had no experience. I had to learn news report writing skills, and other responsibilities as a website manager. Well, I had the experience of writing articles but not news articles. I used to check other websites to see how they portray their events so that they would gain maximum attention. I got help from the activists who had journalism experience to teach me these skills."*

5.4 Theme Four: The Individual Women's Rights Activists' Use of SNSs Creates Internal Tensions

The experiences of interviewed activists demonstrate that there are differences between the individual and collective utilization of SNSs. The women's rights groups' social networking profiles are their supplementary communication platforms and are employed in a very similar way to their websites. Simultaneously, SNSs serve as the personal communication channels of the individual women's rights activists, that is, principally for informal expression of their personal views. At numerous points during the interviews, particularly the younger respondents explained that social media platforms have offered them a way to garner their own audiences. Their experiences reveal that while the leading activists have dominance over the analytical discourses on the activist websites, SNSs are the desired platform for the inexperienced young activists to express their personal viewpoints. Therefore, the advent of SNSs in Iran has decentralized the activists' public communication, giving more opportunities to the low-profile activists to participate in building a public opinion about women's rights activism. Despite these opportunities for enhancing the activist groups' public relations, exclusive public communication platforms that SNSs provide for the individual women's rights activists have given rise to internal tensions.

There was an assumption among six out of the eleven interviewed activists that utilization of SNSs has increased individualism in two main ways: 1) individualism in the distribution of information, and 2) over-presentation of the activists' individual identities and viewpoints. With regards to the first factor, the interview evidence demonstrates that tensions have been created by the activists' attempts to share opinions that can be perceived by the public as a collective standpoint of (or as information from) the groups they belong to. Interviewee 5 explained that "one of the serious problems is that in these spaces [SNSs], the personal opinions of activists are demonstrated to a great extent". She clarified that she meant specifically the activists who introduce themselves as group members, but publish viewpoints that are not in line with the collective position that has been taken by the group. She emphasized that this trend has caused challenges and disagreements within activist groups, and cited the following example:

> *"When Mrs. Mollaverdi*[4] *was selected as the vice president [for women's affairs], we had not yet gained any official position about her appointment. But some*

4 In 2013, Shahindokht Mollaverdi, a legal scholar and a well-known women's rights activist, was appointed by president Rouhani as the vice president for Women and Family

> *fellows published posts to support her. That created the impression that our group had approved her. After this we had serious arguments that if we want to write as members of the group it has to be on the group's page."*

While the first aspect of individualism concentrates on the activist groups' internal disputes, the second is concerned with the spread of rivalry and division among the activists who maintain social media profiles. Interviewee 3 took the firm position that contrary to the websites, because of the existence of personal profiles, SNSs have highlighted the difference in opinions: "Instead of concentrating on commonalities, we concentrate on the differences. Instead of focusing on common objectives, we lay emphasis on showing ourselves." Interviewee 11 remarked that while the websites focus on presenting awareness-building materials, on social networking sites the emphasis is on presenting personal opinions and analyses. Interviewee 6 compared the impact of activists' social networking profiles with that of e-mail groups. He noted that in the e-mail groups, conversations accelerated alignment and convergence. This is while "we can see many personal disputes among the activists from different groups on social media. They publicize their criticism of each other, which is not interesting for the public audience." Similarly, interviewee 8 emphasized the negative consequences of SNSs on activism, saying that "these networks [SNSs] have caused some internal divisions". I asked her whether the divisions were created on these online networks or were the reflection of differences on-the-ground, to which she replied:

> *"Yes. These differences definitely emerge from disputes in the real world. But when they enter social media they get expanded. In the e-mail groups we try to find a common solution, but on Facebook because the activists are talking in front of public eye their concern is primarily to defend their positions".*

Some of the respondents explained that since the growth of SNSs in the country[5], some activists "were imprisoned by these spaces and preferred to use them as their main activism platform even when they were offered opportunities for real world activities". Interviewee 4 voiced this drawback and related it to the sense of popularity that activists gain through SNSs: "They ask themselves, 'when I have thousands of followers on board, why should I leave these spaces [SNSs] and go back to where few might know me?'" The emergence of online activities that focus mainly on gaining

Affairs.

5 At the time of the interviews, Facebook, Twitter, and Google plus were the most popular and utilized social media among the interviewed activists and the Iranian public.

popularity and approval of the public is what interviewee 3 named "the branding of activism". Along seven other interviewees, he noted the growth of such forms of activities by women's rights activists on SNSs.

The tension arises when, in search for more endorsement, some activists over-represent their activities and/or the issues at hand through direct and uncontrolled communication channels that SNSs offer them. Some of the interviewees discussed that propagation of own activities and ideas on SNSs gives some activists and their issues "fake importance" in public eye and pushes the activists who have less online social networking activity to the margins. Interviewee 8 noted:

> *"Some [women's rights] activists, whom I know in person, don't have considerable activities on-the-ground. But just because they are always on the Internet they create this perception that they are among the most active of us. People have many times come to me asking, 'What is X doing?' I've replied: 'Nothing special. She is not participating in the actions.' 'Are you sure? She is always on Google Plus and seems so active'... she is not making as much effort as the activists who deal with a variety of difficulties of real activities, but she is seen more by the public – in contrast to many activists who are involved in big projects, but are not used to promoting themselves on social networks [SNSs]."*

Interviewee 5 stressed that some of these activists not only build on their own activities, but try to collect credit from the activities that had been conducted collectively. Besides gaining public recognition, she declared that over recent years, this online behavior has provided some activists with international opportunities, such as academic scholarships and research grants from international foundations: "Tensions were created between these activities and the groups they belonged to. Other activists asked why we should make the effort while others are using the opportunities personally."

The interview analysis also suggests that the attention for public endorsement on SNSs has distracted some activists from their collective responsibilities and has propagated individualism in practice. The two NGO managers interviewed for this study remarked on this pitfall. Interviewee 7 noted that social media's commentary features have made particularly younger activists reactionary in the way that "they spend numerous hours on these sites to present their personal defense". Similarly, interviewee 1 asserted that the younger members of her NGO "dedicate a great amount of time, which should be devoted to the NGO activities, to social networks". Related to this discussion is also the concern raised by interviewee 3. He declared that the "phony popularity" the activists receive on SNSs makes them ignorant of the necessity of collective action: "They have forgotten that the real changes have always been achieved by offline collective organization. I am very much looking forward to seeing the time that they get disillusioned with these networks and get back to their real groups."

Finally, the interview evidence suggests that in recent years there is a dispute between the activists who overwhelmingly dealing with online audiences in social media and those who in contrary spend a larger portion of their time on interacting with the offline society, over prioritizing the activism's demands. Five interviewees discussed that the dispute has emerged from the fact that activists who are mainly dealing with online publics defines women's rights activists demands differently from the other activists because on social media they have not access to the voices of people from all social groups of society. In addition to problems of the digital divide and media literacy, they were concerned about discrimination against some social segments of society on SNSs. They proclaimed that the Iranian social media space does not offer all societal groups equal opportunities to contribute to social and political discussions. Interviewee 3 said that what he could see on these sites was "a kind of centralization of discourses around the issues of the urban middle class and elimination of the voice of marginalized groups." From his perspective, Iranian social media has not only alleviated, but also reproduced the existing exclusion of particular social groups such as ethnic minorities, rural and lower classes:

> *"If a user from a small city or village writes about his issues, will he receive the same public attention? No! So, it is not all about the digital divide. This means that even when these groups enter these spaces, their voices are shut down... Users in these networks [SNSs] have built their own mainstream and they don't give a place to other voices. This exclusion exists in the society and magnifies on the Internet."*

Interviewee 5 referred to this exclusion by calling it "the classification of social demands". She noted: "If I was a working class woman who lived in Pakdasht [small town near Tehran], could I find the confidence to write about my troubles on these networks [SNSs], where I could hardly find issues of my social class? No!"

The emerged dispute became more evident by statements of interviewees 11, 4 and 10. Interviewee 11 noted that "the users' discussions on social media are the problems of the middle class. When we check them against the realities of the society, we find out that there are many issues that are of greater priority for other social classes." One of the main criticisms she has always expressed to her fellow activists who cite discussions on SNSs is that "you are reproducing the hardships that the lower class has always faced with in voicing its requirements. This is while a social activist is supposed to eradicate this deprivation." Interviewee 4 noted that the activists who "immigrated" to SNSs are becoming ignorant of the sufferings of the people who have no voice on SNSs, for instance working class women who "do not care about women's participation in the political structure, but worry about their economic situation". Interviewee 10 asserted: "Instead of talking with people who could not find a place in this [online] space, we [women's rights activists] flee to this [online] space where users just echo what they have in common."

6 Concluding Remarks

This article explored how more than a decade-long utilization of cyberspace has affected the characteristics of the women's rights activists' internal relations. The examination of the Iranian case provides the ground for comprehending the evolution of the impacts that has been brought about by the application of e-mail groups, websites, and SNSs. The more conventional types of Internet technologies, such as e-mail groups and websites, have improved collaboration and collective identity within and across women's rights activist groups, whereas the growth of the activists' personal social networking profiles has threatened the collectivity of the activism.

This article revealed that websites and SNSs serve the activists' external outreach, while email groups add a further communication opportunity to the women's rights activists' internal relations. E-mail groups have been the main Internet technology employed for the groups' intra- and intercommunication. The interviews provided no evidence to suggest that when women's rights groups use e-mail groups for internal communication, they struggle with any of the three challenges that, according to Nielsen's (2009) empirical research, may be entailed by the low cost of online communication: overcommunication, miscommunication, and communicative overload. The absence of these negative consequences is most probably related to the tendency of the women's rights groups to apply e-mail technology in a collective form. Also, contrary to the activist groups examined by Nielsen, the women's rights groups I observed do not employ other forms of online communication such as websites and SNSs for distribution of internal messages. Utilizing e-mail groups as a mere online platform for internal communication prevents the publication of identical messages – and thus also the problem of overcommunication; eliminates the dissonance between different online media – preventing the danger of miscommunication; and reduces the number of contacts generated from numerous means of internal communication – thus avoiding communicative overload.

By giving voice to geographically dispersed and young activists, e-mail groups provide the activism with more diversity of viewpoints. For the women's rights groups, elucidation of this diversity has not resulted in the difficulty in reaching consensus or the tendency to split (see Clark & Themudo, 2006). On the contrary, the comparison of different views on these virtual meeting spaces bridges the differences within physically disconnected activists and boosts the outcome of decision-making. The e-mail groups owe this success to the consent of the groups' leaders or high-profile activists to let the younger and the local ones challenge their perspectives. It is related to the fact that contemporary women's rights NGOs and informal groups are loosely organized. Thus, this research adds to the scholars' previous discussion about the ability of the Internet to promote non-hierarchical activist groups (Bennett, 2003; Surman & Reilly, 2003), by suggesting that there is also a vice versa relation: a non-hierarchal organizational form facilitates the Internet adoption for more collective and democratic decision-makings.

The second theme showed that the activist websites reinforce the pre-existing collaborative network of the women's rights groups. The third theme, however, suggested that the application of websites to this collaborative network has not been only about organization and coordination. The array of activist websites adds a layer to this network over which the activism knowledge is mobilized and shared across the women's rights groups. While scholars overwhelmingly studied the knowledge-building potential of activists' online spaces for public audiences and participants, the consequences of these spaces for the activists' personal empowerment are severely understudied. The case of this research suggests that, besides affecting public awareness, the content of activist websites also enhances the knowledge of the member and non-member activists. Moreover, behind these websites are teams of activists who improve their personal capabilities by practicing new technical and media skills, which are required for Web management.

This article provided empirical evidence for the line of theoretical inquiry that asks to what extent the Internet promotes collective identity among social actors, that results in the formation of collective actions. The findings make it clear that three characteristics of collective identity in Melucci's (1995) definition (shared definition, interaction or negotiation, and a sense of unity) are reinforced by more conventional forms of online communication: e-mail groups and websites. The e-mail groups create a virtual space for more regular discussions over "the ends, means, and field" (Melucci, 1995, p. 44) of the real-world actions of the women's rights activists. They provide the ground for "mutual recognition" (p. 45) between the activists who conventionally had little contact opportunity. The websites inform the activist groups about each other's causes, and e-mail groups facilitate their negotiation over the aspects of their collectivity. The success of these two forms of online platform in promoting collectivity can be also explained based on the notion of Diani (2000) that virtual networks operate at their best in the promotion of collectivity when they are backed by real social linkages. The virtual networks, built through the activist e-mail groups and websites, are affiliated with real-world groups that govern the decision-making and organizing process. The women's rights groups use digital media more as a means of managing participation and coordinating goals rather than inviting self-organization of action (Bennett & Segerberg, 2012).

The fourth interview theme demonstrated that the utilization of SNSs based on an individualistic logic weakens women's rights activists' collective identity. Skoric and Poor (2013) proclaimed that the comprehension of slacktivism lacks a defensible basis, since most of the literature about slacktivism is merely commentary and not founded on data. The findings presented about activists' individual social media profiles provide empirical evidence for two lines of argumentation among existing theories about slacktivism and its impacts on collectivity of activism. First, it was referred to by Morozov (2009) and Breuer and Farooq (2012) that in slacktivism, the primary focus is shifting from contributing to the achievement of a public good to the persuasion of "selfish and narcissistic" objectives. This notion particularly ties in with the case of this research. While e-mail groups facilitate debates for finding mutual solutions, SNSs serve as a stage on which women's rights activists act to promote the legitimacy of their own perspective. While the websites are used by the activist groups to identify others with similar interests, the personal profiles on SNSs make it possible for some activists to promote their personal activities in order to – as Breuer and Farooq (2012) stated – gain social prestige. Second, the claim that slacktivism satisfies the activists' motivation to take real civic action and distracts them from their previous commitments (Morozov, 2009; Lee & Hsieh, 2013; Skoric & Poor, 2013) finds evidence in the usage of SNSs by women's rights activists. The interviewees' testimonies suggest that since the growth of SNSs, the activist groups have lost the active participation of some of their members who decided to remain active on social media and not get back to on-the-ground activities. It was also noted that by devoting a substantial portion of their time to getting involved with their online audiences, some of them, in particular young activists, have been distracted from their collective commitments.

SNSs give the individual Iranian women's rights activists the ability to communicate directly with the public. This article suggests that the activists should take advantage of this opportunity with caution to avert backlashes on their groups. In recent years, there have been conflicts within activist groups over the power that individual women's rights activists have gained through these sites in disseminating information. Thus, this study reaffirms the notion suggested by Surman and Reilly (2003) that by de-centralizing the power over content, the Internet has created new tensions within civil organizations, particularly with regards to the use of SNSs.

This article's findings raise concerns about the fact that by encouraging individualism and interest in gaining personal popularity, personal social networking profiles can threaten activists' collective identity. The collective identity and network, which has been underpinned by an array of women's rights groups' websites and e-mail lists, can be entangled in tensions that arise from the growth of individual online social networking activities. As Treré (2012) noted, this finding "reminds us that future scholars must take particular care not to fall prey to fascination with the newest online applications...and avoid the trap of the attractiveness of the latest, cutting-edge applications for activism" (p. 2372).

References

Akhavan, N. (2011). Exclusionary Cartographies: Gender Liberation and the Iranian Blogosphere. In R. Bahramitash, & E. Hooglund (Eds.), *Gender in Contemporary Iran: Pushing the Boundaries* (p. 62-82). London: Routledge.

Amir-Ebrahimi, M. (2008). Transgression in narration: The lives of Iranian women in cyberspace. *Journal of Middle East Women's Studies, 4*(3), 89-115.

Ayres, J. M. (1999). From the streets to the Internet: The cyber-diffusion of contention. *The Annals of the American Academy of Political and Social Science, 566*(1), 132-143.

Bahramitash, R. (2007). Iranian Women during the Reform Era (1994-2004): A Focus on Employment. *Journal of Middle East Women's Studies, 3*(2), 86-109.

Barlow, R., & Akbarzadeh, S. (2008). Prospects for feminism in the Islamic republic of Iran. *Human Rights Quarterly, 30*(1), 21-40.

Behravesh, M. (2014). Iran's Reform Movement: The Enduring Relevance of an Alternative Discourse. *Digest of Middle East Studies, 23*(2), 262-278.

Bennett, W. L. (2003). Communicating global activism. *Information, Communication & Society, 6*(2), 143-168.

Bennett, W. L. & Segerberg, A. (2012). The logic of connective action: Digital media and the personalization of contentious politics. *Information, Communication & Society, 15*(5), 739-768.

Bimber, B., Flanagin, A. J., & Stohl, C. (2005). Reconceptualizing collective action in the contemporary media environment. *Communication Theory, 15*(4), 365-388.

Braun, V. & Clarke, V. (2006). Using thematic analysis in psychology. *Qualitative Research in Psychology, 3*(2), 77-101.

Braun, V., Clarke, V., & Terry, G. (2015). Thematic analysis. In Rohleder, P. & Lyons, A. C. (Eds). *Qualitative Research in Clinical and Health Psychology* (p. 95-113). Basingstoke: Palgrave Macmillian.

Breuer, A. & Farooq, B. (2012). Online Political Participation: Slacktivism or Efficiency Increased Activism? Evidence from the Brazilian Ficha Limpa Campaign. Retrieved from https://ssrn.com/abstract=2179035

Christensen, H. S. (2012). Simply slacktivism? Internet participation in Finland. *JeDEM-eJournal of eDemocracy and Open Government, 4*(1), 1-23.

Clark, J. D. & Themudo, N. S. (2006). Linking the web and the street: Internet-based "dot-causes" and the "anti-globalization" movement. *World Development, 34*(1), 50-74.

Deibert, R. J. (2000). International plug'n play? Citizen activism, the Internet, and global public policy. *International Studies Perspectives, 1*(3), 255-272.

Diani, M. (2000). Social movement networks virtual and real. *Information, Communication & Society, 3*(3), 386-401.

Eagleton-Pierce, M. (2001). The internet and the Seattle WTO protests. *Peace Review, 13*(3), 331-337.

Earl, J., Kimport, K., Prieto, G., Rush, C. & Reynoso, K. (2010). Changing the world one webpage at a time: Conceptualizing and explaining Internet activism. *Mobilization: An International Quarterly, 15*(4), 425-446.

Esfandiari, H. (2010). The women's movement. In R. Wright (Ed.), *The Iran primer: Power, politics, and U.S. policy* (p. 45-48). Washington, DC: United States Institute of Peace Press.

Fazaeli, R. (2007). Contemporary Iranian feminism: Identity, rights and interpretations. *Muslim World Journal of Human Rights, 4*(1), 1-24.

Garrett, R. K. (2006). Protest in an information society: A review of literature on social movements and new ICTs. *Information, Communication & Society, 9*(2), 202-224.

Harlow, S., & Harp, D. (2012). Collective action on the Web: A cross-cultural study of social networking sites and online and offline activism in the United States and Latin America. *Information, Communication & Society, 15*(2), 196-216.

Harp, D., Bachmann, I. & Guo, L. (2012). The whole online world is watching: Profiling social networking sites and activists in China, Latin America and the United States. *International Journal of Communication, 6*, 298-321.

Iran country profile (2015). Retrieved from http://www.bbc.com/news/world-middle-east-14541327

Jahanshahrad, H. (2012). A genuine civil society and its implications for the Iranian women's movement. *Women's History Review, 21*(2), 233-252.

Juris, J. S. (2005). The new digital media and activist networking within anti–corporate globalization movements. *The Annals of the American Academy of Political and Social Science, 597*(1), 189-208.

Khiabany, G. & Sreberny, A. (2010). *Blogistan: The internet and politics in Iran*. London: I.B. Tauris.

Kian, A. (1997). Women and politics in post-islamist Iran: the gender conscious drive to change. *British Journal of Middle Eastern Studies, 24*(1), 75-96.

Koolaee, E. (2012). Women in the Parliament. In Povey, T. & Rostami-Povey, E. (Eds.), *Women, Power and Politics in 21st Century Iran* (p. 137-152). London: Ashgate.

Lee, Y. H. & Hsieh, G. (2013). Does slacktivism hurt activism? The effects of moral balancing and consistency in online activism. *Proceedings of the SIGCHI Conference on Human Factors in Computing Systems* (p. 811-820).

Mahdi, A. A. (2004). The Iranian women's movement: A century long struggle. *The Muslim World, 94*(4), 427-448.

Melucci, A. (1995). The Process of collective identity. In H. Johnston & B. Klandemans (Eds.), *Social Movements and Culture* (p. 41-63). Minneapolis, MN: University of Minnesota Press.

Menashri, D. (2013). Hassan Rouhani: Iran's New Hope for Change. *Strategic Assessment, 16*(2), 7-21.

Michaelsen, M. (2011). Linking up for Change: The Internet and Social Movements in Iran. In Schneider, N. C. &, Gräf, B. (Eds.), *Social Dynamics 2.0: Researching Change in Times of Media Convergence* (p. 105-125). Berlin: Frank & Timme.

Mir-Hosseini, Z. (2002). Debating Women: Gender and the Public Sphere in Post-Revolutionary Iran. *Civil Society in the Muslim World: Contemporary Perspectives*, 95-100.

Mohammadi, M. (2007). Iranian Women and the Civil Rights Movement in Iran: Feminism Interacted. *Journal of International Women's Studies, 9*(1), 1-21.

Morozov, E. (2009). Foreign policy: brave new world of slacktivism. *National Public Radio.* Retrieved from http://www.npr.org/templates/story/story.php?storyId=104302141

Nielsen, R. K. (2009). The labors of Internet-assisted activism: Overcommunication, miscommunication, and communicative overload. *Journal of Information Technology & Politics, 6*(3-4), 267-280.

Rotman, D., Vieweg, S., Yardi, S., Chi, E., Preece, J., Shneiderman, B., Pirolli, P. & Glaisyer, T. (2011). From slacktivism to activism: participatory culture in the age of social media. *CHI'11 Extended Abstracts on Human Factors in Computing Systems* (p. 819-822).

Sameh, C. (2010). Discourses of Equality, Rights and Islam in the One Million Signatures Campaign in Iran. *International Feminist Journal of Politics, 12*(3-4), 444-463.

Shirazi, F. (2012). Information and communication technology and women empowerment in Iran. *Telematics and Informatics, 29*(1), 45-55.

Shojaei, M. (2012). *Central Role of The Women's Movement in the Civil Society.* Retrieved from http://melimazhabi.com/?maghalat=زنان-در-جامعه-مدنی ارزش-هسته‌ای-جنبش-

Simi, P., & Futrell, R. (2006). Cyberculture and the endurance of white power activism. *Journal of Political and Military Sociology, 34*(1), 115-141.

Skoric, M. & Poor, N. (2013). Barriers to Entry and Online Political Activism. *Proceedings of the Conference for E-Democracy and Open Government* (p. 343-349).

Smith, M. F. & Ferguson, D. P. (2010). Activism 2.0. In R. L. Heath (ed.), *Handbook of public relations* (p. 395-408). Thousand Oaks et al.: Sage Publications.

Surman, M., & Reilly, K. (2003). Appropriating the Internet for Social Change: towards the strategic use of networked technologies by transnational civil society organizations. Social Science Research Council. Retrieved from http://library.uniteddiversity.coop/Effective_Organising/Appropriating_the_Internet_for_Social_Change.pdf

Tohidi, N. (2009). Women and the Presidential Elections: Iran's New Political Culture. Retrieved from http://www.juancole.com/2009/09/tohidi-women-and-presidential-elections.html

Treré, E. (2012). Social movements as information ecologies: Exploring the coevolution of multiple Internet technologies for activism. *International Journal of Communication*, 6, 2359-2377.

Vakil, S. (2011). *Women and politics in the Islamic republic of Iran: action and reaction.* London: Continuum.

Vakil, S. (2013). The Iranian women's movement: agency and activism through History. *Orient-IV.*2013. Retrieved from www.sanamvakil.com/wp-content/uploads/2014/07/Orient_IV_2013.pdf

Van Aelst, P. & Walgrave, S. (2002). New media, new movements? The role of the internet in shaping the 'anti-globalization'movement. *Information, Communication & Society, 5*(4), 465-493.

Yeganeh, N. (1993). Women, nationalism and Islam in contemporary political discourse in Iran. *Feminist Review, 44*, 3-18.

Feminist Networks in Times of Multi-layered Transformations: Perspectives from Tunisia

Anna Antonakis

1 Introduction

In Western scholarship and policy analysis, Tunisia has been singled out since its independence in 1956 as a "model for modernity" in the region of the Middle East and North African (MENA) with the first president after independence, Habib Bourguiba introducing progressive women's rights. With the uprisings in 2010/2011, Tunisia again stood out, and this time as the country where the so-called Arab Spring started and information and communication technologies (ICTs) were used to overthrow dictatorship. Here, the narrative of the "Facebook revolution" took its starting point where ICTs were framed as tools of emancipation and empowerment. At the same time, the following politics of transformation accompanied by social media has been far less investigated.

Tunisia offers indeed a fascinating case because of the strong censorship of the Internet that was lifted on 13 January 2011, the night before Zine El-Abidine Ben Ali fled the country to Saudi Arabia. The formally restricted public sphere has diversified rapidly after the uprisings: a vibrant landscape of initiatives, unions, associations and various types of other organizations could emerge. New private media outlets and initiatives were created and communicated different opinions and values (Antonakis, 2015). In this context of increasing pluralism, also the hegemony of sexist power structures could be challenged nationally in more diverse ways, including the usage of digital media. A feminist analysis requires the inclusion of the economy of international communication structures to exhibit patriarchal backlashes further. Feminist digital security scholars lay out in their article "sexing the Internet" how "different kinds of political and economic tensions within a nation-state can be mediated by contesting morality issues and related gender and sexual issues in the digital realm" (Jensen et al., 2012, p. 66). They argue that a gendered analysis of ICTs reproducing sexist hierarchies implies

C. Richter et al. (Hrsg.), *Digital Media and the Politics of Transformation in the Arab World and Asia*, Studies in International, Transnational and Global Communications, https://doi.org/10.1007/978-3-658-20700-7_7

a "defamiliariz[ation]" from an exclusive focus on nation states in the research on digital censorship and surveillance (Jensen et al., 2012, p. 68). In response to the growing critique and concerns raised by scholars in the field of digital security, the communication infrastructure of the social media used by the activists is taken into consideration in this study. Against this background, I aim to investigate how women in Tunisia can negotiate gender through digital media in times of national and international transitions.

One might rightfully ask whether a country-based approach to analyze politics and media in transformation can be fruitful in light of post-colonial dependencies and interwoven communication infrastructures. This article argues that the analysis of transformation should incorporate both the national context and its local specific scriptures of power and resistance without losing sight of international developments in the ecology of media systems.

Six years after the 2010/2011 uprisings, it appears that women obtained the rights and the empowerment tools to negotiate their position in the Tunisian society and participate in the political process. However, I argue that this analysis relies on normative assumptions that is common especially in knowledge production from Western countries. If we truly want to keep track of the politics of transformation in Tunisia, it has to be analyzed within a local-global nexus and regard gender with an intersectional approach. Gender constitutes only one category of oppression that needs to be analyzed in its intersection with other categories such as locality, class, race and so on (see Smith, 1978, p. 156; Crenshaw, 1989, p. 140; Walker, 1992). In order to explore meaningful answers to the research question, I believe that employing these lenses can also help to uncover a 'modernist bias' that research especially from Western countries tends to reproduce.

'Modernity' is in my analysis associated with three major interlocking trajectories. I argue that they need to be investigated to exhibit the portrayal of the Tunisian nation as a model for modernity before and after the uprisings. In this regard, I refer to this process as 'modelization'. First, this modelization is concerned with gender politics in Tunisia. It was analyzed often with regards to its national progressive family legislation, the personal status law (CSP) and the constitution that accorded the country an "exceptional" position since the 1950s not only with regards to its neighbouring countries, but also European countries such as Switzerland and France[1] (Borsali, 2012, p. 30; Brand, 1998; Charrad, 2008; Marzouki, 1993, p. 94). Second, a policy of market liberalization initially had a slow start in the 1970s, but had been increasing in its effectiveness since 1986 with the introduction of the structural adjustment programs (SAP) aiming to install the internal and external

1 This includes political and body rights.

equality by means of state interventions (Bellin, 2002; Khiari, 2004). Tunisia has repeatedly been pointed out as an "economic model" by the International Monetary Fund (Bond, 2012) and in 2007, Tunisia was ranked the "most competitive country of Africa" as well as the 30th most competitive country in the world in the global competitiveness report (Schwab, 2007, p. XVII). Third, modernity is associated with the developments in technology and ICT optimism.

This article's aim is to shed light on the paradox that lies behind this modelization. The U.S. Gender studies scholar Doris Gray sees the progressive women's rights codification and the oppression of Islamic movements as the two main pillars for Western support of the authoritarian regime in Tunisia: "[t]he reasons for which the West continued its support for the dictator, were Tunisia's exemplary status of women's rights combined with the fact that Islamists, successfully portrayed within and outside Tunisia as akin to terrorists, were either in jail or in exile" (Gray, 2012, p. 286).

The three trajectories of a Western-framed idea of modernity outlined above legitimized European and US support for the authoritarian regimes. Thus, changes and stagnation in the country need to be under close scrutiny to prevent a re-modelization of the country that would prevent critical investigations while the country's population struggles with structural oppression, unemployment and political frustrations. I will focus on the first and third trajectory, bringing into dialogue research on intersectional theory with development in technologies. In doing so, I aim to provide a novel conceptual understanding of the study of gender and feminist movements and ICTs with regards to national and international transformations in Tunisia.

In the following article, women's and human rights actors are regarded as central actors trying to renegotiate gender in the transitional process in Tunisia in various ways within national and international communication infrastructures coded within hierarchical settings. Possibilities and options to participate unfold and developed within the nation state but are positively and negatively impacted by international developments as well.

2 Shifting the Focus to Behind the Screens: ANT and Feminist Inquiries

One useful approach to investigating the complex relationship of technologies, politics and feminism in development and after historical junctures is the Actor-Network Theory (ANT). In ANT studies, technological objects are given "equal status to humans". Under this broad approach, "narratives of politics, power, technology and transformation" can be re-constructed, favoring and facilitating empirical research, to "make sense of complex situation" (Bueger & Stockbruegger, 2017, p. 44).

Within this approach, German feminist scholars Carstensen and Winker discuss the Internet as "an idea to increase the possibilities for empowerment of feminist networks" (Carstensen & Winker, 2007, p. 109). They warn of technological determinism and simplification when constructing research designs. If the impact of the Internet on feminist politics were the only relation under investigation, they argue, then this would introduce the Internet as a "stable, fixed technology with definite effects". In order not to fall into this trap, they employ the approach of a sociology of technology. For the German context they ask "how feminist actors construct and use the Internet on the one hand, how the Internet actively intervenes and restricts or extends the scope of possibilities on the other hand and thus how they interact as co-players and opponents within societal power relations" (Carstensen & Winker, 2007, p. 11). Following up on their considerations, I attempt to address three challenges that derive for feminist activists from both the international Internet infrastructure itself and those that are embedded within the national societal power struggles.

Against this background, I think that the three "algorithmic harms" identified by Zeynep Tufekci (2015, p. 207f.) should be additionally taken into consideration by any scholar working with the data generated by Facebook or investigating the relation of social media and society in more general terms. Tufekci critically comments on the rapid developments in big data collected by companies and governments. Drawing from the ANT, Tufekci problematizes the algorithms employed on the Facebook platform as "actants (…) in that they are computational agents that are not alive, but that act with agency in the world" (ibid.). In order to grasp the novelty of this new category of actors, she introduces the term "computational agency" (CA) of algorithms and identifies three "algorithmic harms" which I will try to investigate in the present case in more detail: 1) the lack of visibility, 2) information asymmetry and 3) the hidden influence of algorithmic gatekeeping, which can be understood as traditional "editing".

I call for deploying qualitative methods within an intersectional paradigm to *shift the focus to behind the screens* and to the actors using social media and their specific constituencies. This is in line with the perspective provided by Richter and Badr (2016) calling for more "people centered analysis of social media" (p. 11). At the same time, the study of algorithms and those who program them bears interesting insights.[2] These two perspectives from behind the screens constitute important dimensions that bring back in subjective positionalities of users and coders within their specific context and hereby the asymmetrical reproduction of access to knowledge and power. However, applying both perspectives would go beyond the scope of this chapter.

For this study, I rely on over 40 explorative and guided interviews with feminist activists, journalists and scholars in Tunisia. The interviews were conducted between 2012 and 2016 in different cities of Tunisia to also give a broader picture and circumvent to a certain degree the capital bias that especially Western research in the regional studies maintains. The interviews included three major parts. These revolved around four themes and were usually discussed in this particular order during the interview: Firstly, respective understandings of the developments since December 17, 2010 (the day of Muhammed Bouazizi's immolation)[3] with reference to specific 'events' important for gender politics and their positioning of the activists within these (judgments of elections, constitutional process, national women's day 2012); secondly, explanations about their own activism; and thirdly, more specifically feminist activism in the particular post-2011 political setting (discussions of feminist and women's politics terminologies, strategies, perceived influences) and finally, media and social media (media use for information, communication and mobilization). In this article, I employed qualitative content analysis to evaluate the last part of the transcribed text in particular.[4]

An argument for my qualitative, de-centralized and actor-centered approach is of epistemic nature: In the fields of political science and area studies, an elitist paradigm is about to quietly be reproduced, with regards to the selection of actors in the fields of study – newer studies, often drawing from marketing research, use quantitative methods to identify 'influential users' on social media. In my perspective, selection mechanisms need to be addressed because if categories such as followers, retweets and mentions in globalized networks determine the 'influence' of actors online and consequently become objects of study, they do already have visibility (or

2 See also the contribution from Abir Kopty in this volume who combines a quantitative network analysis with interviews with the actors behind the network nodes.

3 There are different ideas about the starting point of the Tunisian 'Revolution', raising the issue of change and continuities: The local population in the governorate of Gafsa would see in the uprisings of 2008 the start of the revolutionary demands for work, liberty and national dignity that have not been fulfilled until today.

4 I conducted these interviews as part of my doctoral research in which I focused on the first two topics discussed with the respondents.

'digital capital').[5] I hold that taking into consideration non-institutionalized voices and also those who are not framed as 'VIPs' on social media can give greater insights into its employability for social change.[6] Most of the users that are relevant for local change do not necessarily appear in the analysis of quantitative data as Top Ten or top 100 participants in terms of hashtags or as bloggers reaching wide audiences.

3 Theoretical Approaches

3.1 Political Economy of Global (Digital) Media

Two intertwined trends – digitalization and globalization – have deeply transformed the ways we communicate. Adding to that, a third trend – monopolization of the Internet (DiGiacomo, 2016) – can be observed when analyzing the digital media ecologies defining our Internet infrastructure. According to a study from Oxfam in 2017, four of the eight wealthiest people in the world are CEOs of companies fostering innovation in ICTs: Microsoft, Amazon, Oracle and Facebook (Oxfam, 2017). With the growing monopoly of Internet businesses such as Google or Facebook, used by millions of people, the communication flows are being managed by capitalist US companies with multifaceted consequences that need yet more empirical investigations. Jodi Dean's theory on "communicative capitalism" appears appealing in this regard. It "designates the way values heralded as central to democracy take material form in networked communication technologies" where "rhetorics of access, participation, and democracy work ideologically to secure the technological infrastructure of neoliberalism" (Dean, 2007, p. 226). The concept speaks to the modernization trajectory related to technology optimism that also the Tunisian government relies on.

Many authors do not fit in either of those camps, but rather analyze the technology as a tool that led to an information revolution but is now shifting away from an open design to more monopolized structures. This "counterrevolution" would "push mainstream users away from a *generative* Internet that fosters innovation and disruption, to an *appliancized* network that incorporates some of the most powerful

5 However, in such an elite-centered study Lin, Hamm and Reinhardt in this volume exhibit how grassroots actors are marginalized within the digital social field, therewith identifying the power relations in this field in the Chinese context.

6 At the same time, this study can draw from interviews with representatives of this digital, visible elite in Tunisia, such as Lina Ben Mheni.

features of today's Internet while greatly limiting its innovative capacity – and, for better or worse, heightening its regulatability" (Zitrain, 2008, p. 8). Following up on the ANT, Zeynep Tufekci and other scholars and practitioners in the field of digital security raise concerns about "the ethics of algorithmic and experimental manipulation in online platforms, especially those like Facebook which play an oversized role in directing content, including news and civic information" (Tufekci, 2015, p. 205).

In light of these theoretical ideas, the narrative of the Tunisian 'Facebook revolution' cannot only be read as an expression of modernist technology determinism, but it also has to be understood as great PR for the corporation and as an instrument to attract new users[7] by giving the social media platform a sort of revolutionary legitimacy: The company would be associated with social uprising and the overthrow of a dictator.[8] In this field, the focus on the 'Facebook revolution' did de-politicize the discussion of the Tunisian uprisings: highlighting the tools rather than the origins of the uprisings, the attention was shifted away from global socio-economic injustices to new communicative realms that surely played their role during the crucial days of the uprisings in 2010/2011 (Antonakis, 2012). These were, however, often analyzed independently of the communication infrastructure provided by what was to become a 'new global political player' in the years to come.

Departing from this approach, the argument presented here incorporates the idea that national political changes as well as social media infrastructure provided by international companies permeate and define the communication context that must be investigated when studying change.

3.2 ICTs and Emancipation: For Whom? An Intersectional Lens in the Study of Digital Divides

In the following section, I argue that studies on ICTs and their potential for emancipation can profit from an intersectional lens, taking into account intersecting structures of oppression, influence on access, and resources to manipulate technologies.

---

7 As of 2016, in Tunisia the Internet penetration rate equals the Facebook penetration rate according to Internet World Stats (2016) with 51 percent of the population. The terms Internet and Facebook are used by many interchangeably on the daily basis.

8 Indeed, during a critical time of the uprisings, when the ATI (Association Tunisienne Internet, the Tunisian government's agency responsible for communications) was fishing the accounts of the opposition at the beginning of January 2011 (Antonakis, 2012; Ragan, 2011), the company interfered to protect the users from state censorship, according to an investigative report from January 2011 (Madrigal, 2011).

The theoretical debate on the Internet and how it impacts our modes of economic, political and cultural production can broadly be separated into two camps: The Internet 'optimists', who argue that with the development of the Internet, information and knowledge, which can be framed as power, have been made more easily accessible to everybody. The Internet is thus seen as a participatory tool for emancipation and liberation that leads to a "Global Village" (McLuhan, 1962).[9] This strand of thought has been labeled the "enlargement model" (Agre, 2002). On the other hand, 'pessimists' point to the reinforcement of existing hegemonic ideologies, such as sexisms, racisms and classism: the new communication infrastructure connecting billions of people worldwide reproduces these structures and mostly supports already existing power structures. Here, the Internet is also regarded as a breeding ground for anti-democratic, racist and sexist movements.

In this context, feminist scholars have started early on to investigate the impacts of ICTs on patriarchal power structures affecting gender relations in society and to analyze the potential of the new technologies with regards to emancipation, opening a spectrum of scholarship celebrating the Internet as a feminine space or viewing it as a space where patriarchal power structures would be reproduced. Studies in this field on the production of digital divides that would lead to an "information elite" or a "privileged hyper-connected minority" in the Global North (Genner, 2017, p. 198) on one, and uniformed masses on the other, side of the divide, have then further been developed by scholars integrating the category of gender and pointing to the "gender divide" (Hooda & Singh, 2011, p. 8). Furthermore, the gender divide has been analyzed in its intersection with class: "We suggest that these established roles, relationship and knowledges may be significantly different among working class families, and that in particular, gender plays into discourses around class and education to produce different experiences of technology" (Bird & Jorgenson, 2002, p. 256). On a global scale, scholars identify the existence of a global digital divide, arguing that power structures of the northern versus southern hemisphere are being reproduced (Wimmer, 2007, p. 141) and argue for an intersection of locality with gender as well (Wheeler, 2004, p. 138). It can be stated that this early literature investigating digital divides and its further differentiation is an expression of the need to "push against peculiarly narrow presumptions about the universality of digital experience" (Coleman, 2010, p. 489). Intersectional approaches in the study of digital divides that look at interlocking systems of oppression could be beneficial

9 Sociologist Marshall McLuhan has outlined some of the most important concepts for the discussion of the effects of new technologies until today in his examination of the profound societal changes introduced by the invention and propagation of the letterpress.

to demystifying and differentiating the empowerment approach by combining it with the scholarship on digital divides.

In 2011 in academic and media publics, the focus was being directed at digital media as a tool for protests and activism in light of the protests that started in Tunisia in December 2010 and were later referred to as the "Arab Spring".[10] The conception of modernization associated with the usage of technologies to get on the path of liberal democracies regained ground. The 'hype' of Tunisia's unrest followed here the dynamic of social media attention economies, which left aside, first, the dimension of 'dignity' that was demanded by a less connected class from the interior of the country and second, questions of how to actually tackle the structural problems that led to the uprisings in a post-revolutionary society. One respondent, B.L., states:

> *"The only thing I find is a bummer that there are many young people who are very competent, patriotic and aware, but who cannot become influent. Why? Because the media and the international community builds up only specific young people to become influent, be publicized and recognized" (B.L., Tunis, April 2014).*

Nevertheless, Facebook remains an important ubiquitous tool for activism, mainly because of a lack of alternatives. Campaigns that were in direct relation to the political process of institutional transformation were launched online. #Hell (open up!), for example, regrouped activists that successfully called for more transparency in parliamentary sessions and voting of the National Constituent Assembly. However, Amira Chebly remembers that political campaigning and constructive influence on the political process by the opposition needed to be organized by different groups as well. When in 2012, the clause of "complementarity" of women and men's roles in the family appeared in the first draft of the constitution, women's rights activist saw the danger of a potential backlash and successfully mobilized to overturn the article.[11] However, Chebly reprehends: "We have to stop counting on Facebook, where we share massively information or issues and then later? What is the efficiency? It's not Facebook that will save us but many mobilized associations" (Amira Chebly, Tunis, May 2013).

---

10 However, with the rise of ISIS, research investigating the manipulation and control of social media and many-to-many forms of communication by radical Islamist groups for recruitment and mobilization came into the focus of policy actors as well.

11 For a similar concern see the Iranian case illustrated by Mina Naeli in this volume.

The empowerment idea of social media has to be read critically with regards to the digital divides and the topics the young people address. National and international mass media may not get out of sight in their selective representations that cannot be challenged by creating publicness on ICTs alone.

4 Modernity in Transformation? Tunisia as a Case Study

4.1 Questioning "The Modern Tunisian Woman": "Not All Women Have the Same Interests"[12]

Investigating changing gender relations via a rights-based approach and gendering political institutions constituted two major access points for the analysis of the period after the uprisings of 2011 (Charrad & Zarrugh, 2014). Here, it has been shown how women's rights constitute an identity marker within a polarizing political scene between secular and religious elite forces (Gray, 2012 p. 285; Khalil, 2014, p. 196; Marks, 2013, p. 224).

I argue that women's and feminist movements in Tunisia are very much associated with a secular state project, until this day legitimizing dominant versions of feminism. The feminist and women's rights discourse remained anchored in a liberal pro-Western dictum that produces a "monolithic" image of women of a secular urban middle class background (Mestiri, 2016, p. 82). The Nidaa Tounes party could fruitfully exploit this legacy again by relying on a revitalization of Bourguibism incorporated by Béji Caid Essebsi, the party leader in the transformation period. They won the elections in 2014 and founded a coalition of national unity, the leftist party association Popular Front remaining the only parliamentary opposition.

Besides this centrality of gender in political campaigning, women remain marginalized at the representational dimension of the public sphere, i. e., as producers and subjects within the mass media system.[13] Lubna Skalli has argued that state and private media alike have "built-in mechanisms" that minimalize and neutralize

12 This quote is from a young unemployed activist who sometimes engages in a development organization in Sidi Bouzid. The argument about the importance of recognizing differences among women in order to actively shape policies that respond to different realities according to educational resources, economic situation and locality has been expressed many times in the interviews.

13 For a division of the public sphere into the structural, the representational and the interactional dimension, see Dahlgren, 2005, p. 148ff. For a critical revision of this model and an application in the Tunisian context, see Antonakis (2017).

women's voices (Skalli, 2006, p. 54). The uprisings did not change structurally the hegemonic inscription of gender in the representation of the mass media. Media activists Mahdhaoui and Silva argue: "Despite the apparent abundance of media spaces, Tunisian media continue to reproduce the same heteronormative and patriarchal patterns of domination" (Silva & Mahdhaoui, 2016, p. 98). Here I would add that patriarchy is manifested in the centrality of the media system that marginalizes women from different localities. The misrepresentation of women in the mass media has pushed young women to actively enter the media sector to initiate change after the uprisings. In this perspective, women who had been politicized and empowered during the uprisings would find their access to journalism through 'citizen journalism':[14] B.L. from the city ElKef, next to the Algerian border, who later migrated to Tunis and was active during the uprisings, argues:

> *"I wasn't at a journalistic school, I rather did professional formations, but it was the passion and the will to learn and to use the media as a support to enhance the opinions of people, to increase their sensibility of certain topics such as problems of the youth or women. You need a more powerful tool for this such as TV debates that can broadcast different voices. I try to act very efficiently in that perspective" (B.L., Tunis, April 2014).*

The importance of integrating women into the mass media system of different localities is discerned by Hayet Amami, who founded the association "Victory of the Rural Woman" in Sidi Bouzid in 2012: "We need media and we need media that go to the citizens, especially in the internal regions of the country. To convince citizens to take independent choices, especially women to take their own political choices" (Hayet Amami, Sidi Bouzid, April 2014).

Besides these voices pushing for change by changing representations of women and pointing to the political-educational dimension of mass media, feminist media projects online that "use journalistic and audio-visual knowledge and tools to create this new safer media space of expression and artistic and political development" (Silva & Mahdhaoui, 2016, p. 98) could take advantage of the liberalization policies starting already under the interim government in 2011. However, they need to be analyzed more closely with regards to the communication infrastructure they rely on within national and international ecologies. For instance, Sana Belaid, who comes from a village in the ElKef governorate, regards YouTube as the best choice for dissimulating "the realities" of the situation of peasant women and showing

14 It has been argued in my interviews as well that the emergence of citizen journalists was to curb the centralization of the media system at the Tunisian capital.

their struggles. The short documentary she produced with some help of an international NGOs, however, has so far generated only a few clicks. Her documentary cannot be watched in Tunisia for what seem to be copyright reasons for the music utilized in the movie.[15]

4.2 Modernity and Technology Optimism

Tunisia has a long history of showing to an international community its willingness to promote ICTs as a tool for modern development.[16] Since the late 1990s, official institutions such as the UNESCO or the Internet Society Forum have pointed to the Internet as a liberating tool to "present their autonomous voices in the service of their own culturally diverse and regionally specific forms of liberation" (Wheeler, 2004, p. 143). This call came in the context of a significant trend showing the bypassing of women in the Arab region by new technologies. The Arab Human Development Report urges for the need to provide easy Internet access to women since 2002; otherwise, the "progress of a society as a whole" would slow down (Wheeler, 2004, p. 142; Arab Human Development Report 2002, p. 76). In 2005 Tunisia hosted the World Summit on Information Society (WSIS): The digital divide and its gendered dimension was addressed and guidelines put forward to specifically improve women's access to the Internet. At the same time, however, the Tunisian government was labeled the "enemy of the Internet" by Reporters Without Borders in the same year (RSF, 2005). While it remains crucial to address the unequal distribution of resources and access to the Internet according to gender, it is also important to remark Ben Ali could coincidentally promote his authoritarian regime to the international community by instrumentalizing women's issues – specifically, by highlighting technological innovations and women's rights – while at the same time obfuscating the actual Internet censorship that was largely practiced.

Despite the rhetoric, the point of departure in Tunisia is a highly controlled public sphere affecting on- and offline communication via an elaborated and comprehensive censorship system. Civil society organizations and their offices, cafés, taxis and so on were highly controlled by the civil police before the uprisings. The classical me-

15 In Tunisia, the message that the copyright by Kontor New Media Music is violated appears. Find the movie *Amal* here: https://www.youtube.com/watch?v=sX0W7BhIU14.

16 The paradigm of modernization theory with its inherent development positivism was articulated in communication studies as well: Scholars argued that mass media that had developed rapidly in the 1950s and 1960s would help to bridge global divides between the North and the South and between the urban and rural areas (Schramm, 1964).

dia landscape was state-controlled, so that sources of valid critical communication were drained (de la Ferrière & Vallina-Rodriguez, 2014). The Tunisian government controlled new information and communication technologies via their Agency Association Tunisienne Internet (ATI), subordinated to the Ministry of Communication. The ATI was considered the "heart of censorship" of the Ben Ali regime.[17] However, it were not only the national state actors who held the means of controlling and delimiting the communication infrastructure for different groups in society. Ron Deibert warned already in 2005 that "pressures from security and commercial sectors to regulate and control the Internet are beginning to alter its basic material framework" (Deibert, 2008, p. 137). According to the Freedom House's Freedom on the Net country reports of 2015 and 2016, Tunisia's Internet is "partly free" now. While direct blockings and persecutions have certainly ceased, the Ministry of Communication "has sought greater cooperation with social media companies to take down content that incites violence or extremism" (Freedom House, 2015) in the frame of its anti-terrorism policies. These developments threaten indeed the freedom of expression and other rights and "boos[t] surveillance" (ibid.).[18]

5 Challenges in an International Digitalized Environment

In the following section, I will look at different examples of online feminist digital cultures whose developments were enabled by the political process in Tunisia, but are restricted and challenged by the infrastructure they are co-constituted by. I will analyze them with regards to the two theoretical lenses I have outlined above, the national-international nexus and intersectionality. I would like to point out the challenges accompanying digitalization and globalization of the communication environment from an intersectional perspective while emphasizing gender and locality.

17 In June 2013, the ATI opened its doors to national IT-specialists in order to guarantee more transparent access to their working methods. The ministry was renamed "Ministry of Technologies of Communication and Digital Economy".

18 For further presentations of intimidations and attacks against the opposition after 2011, see the Freedom on the Net country report Tunisia https://freedomhouse.org/report/freedom-net/2016/tunisia.

5.1 Practicability of Digital Security

The issue of digital security is of specific importance for feminist projects online. Feminist digital security scholar Jennifer Radloff understands the importance of digital security as a feminist practice and hereby broadens the scope of feminist ideas and practice and applies it to a digitalized environment. Creating feminist 'safe' spaces online poses several questions that might not be evident at first sight: Registering blogs and websites requires private information that can then be used to track the person and harass her in real life. At the same time, working together with webmasters is very important for keeping control over the content. Content management systems such as *wordpress* are vulnerable to hacking attacks, but constitute a cheap and easy access option for initiatives and networks with no funding. Another easy and cheap option is Facebook pages and groups.[19] Facebook pages are spaces that function within an untransparent technological setting. Becky Kazansky (2016) and others have argued that "implementing digital security strategies [...] requires substantial technological knowledge". Trainings for feminist networks and NGOs in digital security have thus increased over the last years. A respondent working in a feminist NGO complains that the methods demonstrated in digital security trainings are rarely employed in practice. She advances three arguments to illustrate this: first, when employing the tools, communication and access to information is slowed down; second, mistrust prevails whether the tool kit they learn to employ in trainings can be applied in their post-authoritarian contexts. Government surveillance is stronger and operates on different levels, especially those that affect the platforms for activists' socializing. Finally, trainers often come from Western countries and do not know the specificities of the national context and different socializations with state security practices. The NGOs still would participate in these trainings because they are deemed to be efficient by (Western) donors. This debate about digital security as a mere Western problem is not new to this particular scholarship and practice. There is awareness in the community that "tool usage and digital security practices by participants either dropped off some months after a training or were not successfully integrated into their working practices" (Tactical Technology Collective, 2016).

19 Two professors for information and communication science, Sami Zlitni and Zeineb Touati, give an overview of the numerous groups and Facebook pages dedicated to the issue of women's rights in Tunisia (Zlitni & Touati, 2012). The authors claim that most of these pages explicitly stated not to have any political affiliation but to simply offer a space for debate and the sharing of information.

Furthermore, effective digital security presumes that every member of their communication network would employ the same methods, making it as strong as its weakest chain (Radloff, 2013). In my interviews, most of the activists agreed that freedom of expression was one of the only positive and tangible outcomes of the 2011 uprisings. However, especially against the background of the anti-terrorism legislation, activists fear for a greater intervention of the state.

5.2 Dominance of Facebook and "Algorithmic Harms"

A second challenge that I would like to highlight is related to the vulnerability of the digital infrastructure used for the circulation of feminist content that comes with "algorithmic harms" identified by Zeynep Tufekci. Facebook often constitutes the cheapest and indeed, the only, means to communicate and connect. In my interviews, many pointed to the loss of credibility of Facebook as a platform: While it had been considered a main news source for obtaining information about the protests in the country (besides friends and family [Antonakis, 2012]), it was now considered a platform where pages had been "bought up" by political parties, false information could spread more easily, and the need to verify and contextualize information became even more important. Adding to that, the possibility of expression and participation in the public sphere now leads to a sort of information overkill.

K.R. is a human rights activist from Siliana, a structurally neglected city in the center of the country. She states that 'shares' on Facebook are very often based on appeals highlighting the emotional side of the information. Others have pointed as well to new pages and sites that have sprung up after the uprisings and fed into more polarizing discourses and the circulation of fake news. For K.R., Facebook is both a tool to work with as well as a tool that is used too much for entertainment: "First of all, I mistrust Facebook, but I use it in my manner (...) I'm not using Facebook like others. I use it as a tool for activities with young active citizens all over Tunisia" (K.R., Siliana, April 2014). Feminist digital rights scholar Kazansky (2016) coined the term of "forced reliance" to point to these interdependencies: "We call this a forced reliance because Facebook, as a networking platform, facilitates the maintenance of existing social ties and serves as a popular and dominant channel through which new relationships are created and sustained, and because there is no comparable replacement available" (p. 192).

Journalist and *globalvoices* contributor A.A. erased her Facebook account after the uprisings and now focuses on Twitter: "I think Facebook sucks when it comes to privacy. Also there are so many distractions, and I rather limit the number of platforms I use, to be able to work more productively. So the first reason is privacy concerns and the second reason is distractions. I use Twitter cause I feel it's more professional" (A.A., Tunis, April 2014).

Second, the censoring of photos of female bodies, i.e., naked nipples, has become a subject of discussion in feminist media communities (Wong, 2016). 'Hidden' moralities expressed by the all too familiar censoring of female bodies in the digitalized context are an important subject of actual feminist debates today.[20] In the case of the Facebook page "The uprising of Women in the Arab World", (UWAW) the photo of a young Syrian woman, 'Dana', with short hair, showing her ID photograph in which she is veiled, was censored in 2012 for around three weeks. Four feminists from Palestine, Egypt and Lebanon, created this network in the aftermath of 2011. Yalda Younes, who was "inspired by the use of the Internet in the revolutions of the Arab Spring" launched the UWAW Facebook group in October 2011 (Sadik, 2013). From a discussion platform it evolved into an action oriented 'group' that even transgressed the lines from the virtual to the real space and organized campaigns transregionally and regrouped women's rights activists from different countries. Henda Chennaoui can be considered as the Tunisian representative of the Uprisings of Women in the Arab World and has participated in its actions locally.[21] The group addressed the censorship issue openly and called for support to restore the image on Facebook. It sparked a debate on censorship and the transparency of decisions to erase content on Facebook beyond the MENA region (Salam, 2012). The Facebook page was offline for around three weeks. Henda Chennaoui remembers the incident: "It's the politics of Facebook, which is not really clear. We tried to understand its politics towards the movement. It's a sensibility that we cannot fully grasp" (Tunis, April 2013).

The case exemplifies how the "hidden influence of algorithmic gatekeeping", identified by Zeynep Tufekci as an algorithmic harm (2015, p. 207), impacts feminist counterpublic coalitions relying on Facebook. The co-founder of the Uprisings of Women in the Arab World, Sally Zohney, an Egyptian women's rights activist, explains that Facebook administrators told them that the picture was taken down because of too many reports that considered it "inappropriate". Additionally, they were told not to repost the picture on their private accounts. When they did, their private Facebook accounts were banned for up to two months. "This is when we realized that Facebook is not the best alternative to store all our work and our cam-

---

20 See, for instance, the regular discussion on the forum Gender IT by Datta (2014) and others.

21 She is a Tunis-based journalist for Nawaat, an online platform, where she investigates issues related to transitional and socio-economic justice, gender and environmental problems, and other marginalized topics.

paigns and to be free in deciding what should we add in terms of content. So we got many friends to help us to create our website, to store our pictures and document the campaigns" (Sally Zohney, via Skype, January 2017).

Most of the time, as it was in the case of 'Dana', it remains undisclosed whether the banning of the content from the public platform is caused by 'reporting' by a critical mass of other users or because of the internal moral standards inscribed into the algorithms of the US based social media companies themselves. Facebook appears to be an open platform but at the same time hides algorithmic gatekeeping and editing decisions (Tufekci, 2015, p. 209) that impact the representations of women. This exemplifies the issue of hidden moral hegemonies encapsulated in the untransparent algorithms acting within a local-global nexus.

5.3 Multifaceted visibilities

Entering a new era of social networks and ubiquitous connectivity in the web 2.0 era, as Radloff (2013) states, means that an equal number of threats as opportunities for women and human rights defenders have surfaced globally. She highlights that "Internet and digital tools and spaces have a profound impact on the magnitude of threats and have simultaneously broadened and increased the kinds of surveillance and harassment to which human rights defenders, both men and women, are being subjected" (p. 147). With the following analysis, I will attempt to present this dialectical relationship for feminist actors in Tunisia's transformation period.

The unblocking of the censorship led to increased visibility among marginalized communities.[22] Groups and chats on Facebook engaged with communities claiming more libertarian rights, bringing together queer or also regional communities, as illustrated by Facebook pages such as "Head up, you are in Sidi Bouzid", updating on (ongoing) protests and sharing solidarity with activists arrested by the police. However, S.L. from Sidi Bouzid scrutinizes the value of visibilities and new "voices" when there are no responses: "The only thing that has changed after the revolution is that I got courage and we speak up now. But what is it good for, if nobody listens?" (S.L., Sidi Bouzid, April 2014).

Violence against women remains central to feminist struggles and has – by contrast to subjects that are easily politically exploited in an ideological setting such as the (un)veiling of women's bodies – hardly been addressed in wider publics. Lina Ben Mhenni is a blogger and human rights activist and author of the book

22 For a discussion of visibilities in the context of an "Arab anarchist diaspora" see Almut Woller's contribution in this volume.

"A Tunisian Girl" that has been outspoken against persisting corruption in the country and continues to advocate for women and human rights. International publics took note of her when she was nominated for the Nobel Peace Prize in 2011.

> *"As a blogger, I always get testimonies from women, who tell me about their experience with sexual harassment or harassment of being told to go home because they are not veiled. (...) I talk about them and I publish them [anonymously]. But if it is about some serious violations I delegate them to the ATFD to take care of the case, because I don't have an association" (Lina Ben Mhenni, Tunis, April 2013).*

Ben Mhenni's account exemplifies the opportunities and limits of her visibility. As a famous blogger, she can function as an 'amplifier' of the voices of harassed women. Their testimonies are communicated to her beyond time and local constraints. At the same time, she is dependent on the national context to follow up on the cases by forwarding them to the feminist association ATFD, the Tunisian Association of Democratic Women,[23] and consequently took active part in the renegotiations of the structural dimension of public sphere.

The blog's visibility in public has on the one hand given her the opportunity to function like an amplifier of voices in order to speak out against violence against women. On the other hand, her visibility restricted her freedoms in a time of mounting pluralism: "Before, I could work freely, but now everybody knows my face and I have enemies and it gets dangerous, so I'm under the protection of the police, because I got death threats and all." Ironically, while before the uprisings the police constituted the clear opposition for her, the threats she is subjected to now remain of an unknown source and she is now being protected by a police agent in public.

Not only do the hyper visible subjects, but also women's rights NGOs and their members highlight problematic two-sided visibilities. The former president of the ATFD points out how Facebook facilitated attacks against them: "We were particularly attacked on Facebook: Defamation, moral attacks against each of our members, threats, deformation of the history of the ATFD, everything has been used" (Ahlem Bel Haj ATFD, Tunis 2013). While profiting from social media by engaging within the women's rights community, campaigning and raising awareness about gender

23 The ATFD can be considered one of the most influential women's rights organizations in Tunisia opposing patriarchy. During the constitutional process between 2011 and 2014, they brought in feminist positions and evolved into an influential actor participating in legislative drafting of the institutional level. Since its creation at the beginning of the 1990s, it provides legal and psychological assistance to women subjected to violence. For an analysis of the ATFD in the political transformation see Antonakis, 2015.

equality in a broader public, the activists have to come to terms with the fact that visibility does not come without its costs. Against this background, women's rights organizations and feminist networks have to develop specific media and communication strategies to respond to defamation online. One issue is then how to react to these threats, knowing about the social media economy that functions at an increased level of entertainment and rapid speed. The question whether to ignore or to react, take security measures or even try to file law suits, must be considered within the particular time and locality of the attacks. Responses require different resources, such as money, time and energy, which well-established NGOs may have, but leave non-institutionalized actors and networks often without protection. This again proves the importance of examining not only the national context in order to understand the dynamics of the conflict and to find answers within the specific situation, but also highlights the importance of an intersectional analysis to see the measures of protection that can be taken by different actors.

Last but not least, national and international visibilities of the situation of women in Tunisia can be harmful especially with regards to biased and superficial reporting that feeds into the polarized political environment. These processes can get exacerbated on social media: "Reading an article on the situation of women in Tunisia on CNN or another international media appears to me to be taken with consideration. They often exaggerate the actual situation." (B.L., Tunis, April 2014). O. J., who comes originally from a small village near Kairouan, argues:

> *"Media often concentrate on issues that are secondary, like salafism, the niqab... It is very important to talk about this as well but we have to keep track of the actual developments with regards to transitional justice, the regional development and equality between the regions, equality of chances of all citizens and so on."*

Their statements reveal how symbolic and 'catchy' subjects feeding the short-lived attention and entertainment economies of social media, nationally and internationally, marginalize discussions on feminist issues that intersect with demands of socio-economic justice.

6 Conclusion

This article's aim was to shed light on the dynamics between national and international communication infrastructures and the additional challenges women's rights activists face. I attempted to illustrate the long-term changes in gender activism with the example of Tunisia, and pointed to three challenges resulting from how digital media have shaped the social practices and the environment of the actors in what digital anthropologist Coleman has called the "prosaics of digital media" (Coleman, 2010, p. 488). While I claim that the difficult practicability of digital security, 'multifaceted visibilities' and Facebook censorship are certainly impacting feminist work globally, national particularities may not be overlooked. Especially in a state considered to be "exceptional" in the region and whose revolutionary process led to a new technological optimism, pointing out challenges can help to draw a more realistic picture.

The challenges highlighted here underline the importance of taking into consideration the very different consequences digitalization, globalization and monopolization of the communication infrastructure may bear for women who dispose of few or no resources needed to react to novel threats. It can be argued that the study of the distribution of these resources can either be situated on a global scale looking at the interdependencies of a post-colonial state, or it can be nationally-oriented, pointing out geographical and socio-economic disparities between the rural and urban areas, including unequal Internet access.

After the uprisings, Tunisia stands out again to address the digital gender gap. In 2015, along with Costa Rica, Sweden, Switzerland and the United States, as well as with UN Women, Microsoft, Mozilla and the Association for Progressive Communication in the framework of the World Summit of the Information Society, it engaged in an action plan addressing increasing digital divides (International Telecommunication Union and Partners, 2015). While addressing the digital gender divide on the global scale is desirable, it must be analyzed within the context of multi-layered transformations and not simply made to fit the modernizing paradigm of technology determinism. These international state-level commitments can only constitute an added dimension rather than a substitute for paying close attention to socio-economic structural change – otherwise, the initiatives run the risk of sustaining rather than reforming a system of "communicative capitalism" (Dean, 2007, p. 226).

References

Agre, P. (2002). Real-Time Politics: The Internet and the Political Process. *The Information Society, 18*(5), 311-331.

Antonakis, A. (2012). *Der Quellcode der „Tunesischen Revolution" 2011 – Partizipation an der Schnittstelle von Gegenöffentlichkeiten.* Vol. Working paper No. 5. Berlin: F. U. Middle East Institute. Retrieved from http://www.polsoz.fu-berlin.de/polwiss/forschung/international/vorderer-orient/publikation/WP_serie/WP5_info.html

Antonakis, A. (2015). Contested Transformation: Mobilized Publics in Tunisia between Compliance and Protest. *Mediterranean Politics, 21*(1), 128-149.

Antonakis, A. (2017). *In Transfromation? Renegotiating Gender and State Feminism in Tunisia between 2011 and 2014: Power, Positionalities and the Public Sphere* (Doctoral Dissertation). Freie Universität Berlin.

Arab Human Development Report (2002). *Creating Opportunities for Future Generations.* United Nations Development Program and Arab Fund for Economic and Social Development. Retrieved from http://www.arab-hdr.org/contents/index.aspx?rid=1

Bellin, E. R. (2002). *Stalled Democracy: Capital, Labor, and the Paradox of State-sponsored Development.* Ithaca, NY: Cornell University Press.

Bird, S. E. & Jorgenson, J. (2002). Extending the School Day: Gender, Class and the incooperation of Technology in Everyday Life. In M. Consalvo & S. Paasonen (Eds.), *Women and Everyday uses of the Internet: Agency and Identity* (p. 255-274). New York: Peter Lang.

Bond, P. (2012). Neoliberal Threats to North Africa. In F. Manji & S. Ekine (Eds.), *African Awakening: The Emerging Revolutions* (p. 252-272). Oxford: Pambazuka.

Borsali, N. (2012). *Tunisie: Le défi égalitaire – Ecrits féministes.* Tunis: Arabesques.

Brand, L. (1998). *Women, the state and political Liberalization.* New York: Columbia University Press.

Bueger, C. & Stockbruegger, J. (2017). Actor-Network Theory: Objects and Actants, Networks and Narratives. In D. McCarthy (Ed.), *Technology and World Politics: An Introduction* (p. 42-59). London: Routledge.

Carstensen, T. & Winker, G. (2007). E-Empowerment of Heterogeneous Feminist Networks. In I. E. Zors (Ed.), *Gender Designs IT – Construction and Deconstruction of Information Society Technology* (p. 109-120). Wiesbaden: VS Verlag.

Charrad, M. (2008). From Nationalism to Feminism – Family Law in Tunisia. In K. R. Yount (Ed.), *Family in the Middle East – Ideational Change in Rgypt, Iran, and Tunisia* (p. 111-125). London: Routledge.

Charrad, M. M. & Zarrugh, A. (2014). Equal or complementary? Women in the new Tunisian Constitution after the Arab Spring. *The Journal of North African Studies, 19*(2), 230-243.

Coleman, G. (2010). Ethnographic Approaches to Digital Media. *The Annual Review of Anthropology, 39*, 487–505.

Crenshaw, K. (1989). Demarginalizing the Intersection of Race and Sex: A Black Feminist Critique of Antidiscrimination Doctrine, Feminist Theory and Antiracist Politics. *The University of Chicago Legal Forum, 140.*

Dahlgren, P. (2005). The Internet, Public Spheres, and Political Communication: Dispersion and Deliberation. *Political Communication, 22*(2), 147–162.

Datta, B. (2014, September 16). Never mind the nipples: Sex, gender and social media. *GenderIT.org*. Retrieved from http://www.genderit.org/feminist-talk/never-mind-nipples-sex-gender-and-social-media

Dean, J. (2007). Feminism, Communicative Capitalism, and the Inadequacies of Radical Democracy. In R. E. Dahlberg (Ed.), *Radical Democracy and the Internet* (p. 226-245). New York: Palgrave McMillan.

Deibert, R. (2008). Black Code Redux: Censorship, Surveillance, and the Militarization of Cyberspace. In M. Boler (Ed.), *Digital Media and Democracy – Tactics in Hard Times* (p. 137-163). Cambridge: MIT Press.

de la Ferrière, A. & Vallina-Rodriguez, N. (2014). The scissors and the magnifying glass: Internet governance in the transitional Tunisian context. *The Journal of North African Studies, 19*(5), 639-655.

Freedom House (2015): *Freedom on the Net – Country Report Tunisia*. Retrieved from https://freedomhouse.org/report/freedom-net/2016/tunisia

Genner, S. (2017). *On-Off – Risks and Rewards of the Anytime-Anywhere Internet*. Zurich: VDF.

Gray, D. H. (2012). Tunisia after the Uprising: Islamist and Secular Quests for Women's Rights. *Mediterranean Politics, 17*(3), 285-302.

Hooda, B., & Singh, P. (2011). Does Developpment Communication foster Feminist Contemplation? *Global Media Journal – Indian Edition* , *2*(2), 1-17.

International Telecommunication Union and Partners (2015). *Action Plan to Close the Digital Gender Gap*. Retrieved from http://www.itu.int/net/pressoffice/press_releases/2015/CM21.aspx

Internet World Stats (2016). *www.internetworldstats.com*. Retrieved from http://www.internetworldstats.com/africa.htm

Jensen, H., sm Kee, J., Venkiteswaran, G. & Randhawa, S. (2012). Censorship, Surveillance, and the Body Politic(s) of Malaysia . In R. Deibert, J. Palfrey, R. Rohozinski & J. Zittrain (Eds.), *Access Contested – Security, identity and Resistance in Asian Cyberspace* (p. 65-83). Cambridge: MIT Press.

Kazansky, B. (2016). FCJ-195 Privacy, Responsibility, and Human Rights Activism. *The Fibreculture Journal, 26*, 189-207.

Khalil, A. (2014). Tunisia's Women: Partners in Revolution. *The Journal of North African Studies, 19*(2), 186-199.

Khiari, S. (2004). *Tunisie: le délitement de la cité : coercition, consentement, résistance*. Paris: Khartala.

Madrigal, A. (2011, January 24). The Inside Story of How Facebook Responded to Tunisian Hacks. *The Atlantic*.

Marks, M. (2013). Women's Rights before and after the Revolution. In N. Gana (Ed.), *The Making of the Tunisian Revolution: Contexts, Architects, Prospects* (p. 224-251). Edinburgh: Edinburgh University Press.

Marzouki, I. (1993). *Le Mouvement des Femmes en Tunisie au XXeme Siècle. Féminisme et Politique*. Tunis: Cérès.

McLuhan, M. (1962). *The Gutenberg galaxie the making of typographic man*. London: Routledge.

Mestiri, S. (2016). *Décoloniser le féminisme*. Paris: VRIN.

Oxfam (2017). *Just 8 men own same wealth as half the world* . Oxfam. https://www.oxfam.org/en/pressroom/pressreleases/2017-01-16/just-8-men-own-same-wealth-half-world.

Radloff, J. (2013). Digital security as feminist practice. *Feminist Africa, 18*, 145-155.

Ragan, S. (2011). Tunisian government harvesting usernames passwords. *The TechHerald*. Retrieved from http://thetechherald.com/articles/Tunisian-government-harvesting-usernames-and-passwords/12429/

Reporters Without Borders (2005, November 17). The 15 enemies of the Internet and other countries to watch. Retrieved from: https://rsf.org/en/news/15-enemies-internet-and-other-countries-watch

Richter, C., & Badr, H. (2016). *Communication Studies in Transformation – Self-reflections on an Evolving Discipline in Times of Change*. Arab-German Young Academy – Transformation Group Working Paper No. 2/2016.

Sadik, N. (2013, March 8). The Uprising of Women in the Arab World. *New Internationalist Blog – People, Ideas and Action for Global Justice*. Retrieved from http://newint.org/blog/2013/03/08/womens-rights-campaign-arab-world/

Salam, Y. (2012, November 13). The Uprising of Women in the Arab World censored by Facebook. *GenderIT.org*. Retrieved from http://www.genderit.org/feminist-talk/uprising-women-arab-world-censored-facebook

Schramm, W. (1964). *Mass Media and National Development – The role of information in developing countries*. Urbana: University of Illinois Press.

Schwab, K. E. (2007). *The Global Competitiveness Report 2006–2007*. World Economic Forum. New York: Palgrave Macmillan.

Silva, N. & Mahdhaoui, K. (2016). Human. In K. Lalor, E. Mills, A. S. Garcia & P. Haste (Eds.), *Gender, Sexuality and Social Justice: What's Law got to do with it?* (p. 98-102). Sussex: Institute of Development Studies, University of Sussex.

Skalli, L. H. (2006). Communicating Gender in the Public Sphere: Women and Information Technologies in the MENA. *Journal of Middle East Women's Studies, 2*(2), 35-59.

Smith, B. (1978). Toward a Black Feminist Criticism. In: G.T. Hull, P. B. Scott & B. Smith (Eds.), *All women are white, all blacks are male, but some of us are brave*. (p. 156-175). New York: The Feminist Press.

Tactical Technology Collective. (2016). *Executive Summary: Researching digital security training for human rights defenders*. Retrieved from https://secresearch.tacticaltech.org/summary

Tufekci, Z. (2015). Algorithmic Harms beyond Facebook and Google: Emergent Challenges of Computational Agency. *Journal on Telecommunications and High Technology Law, 13*(2), 203-218.

Walker, R. (1992). Becoming the Third Wave. *Ms. Magazine, 11*(2), 39–41.

Wheeler, D. L. (2004). Blessings and Curses: Women and the Internet Revolution in the Arab World. In N. Sakr (Ed.), *Women and Media in the Middle East – Power through Self-Expression* (p. 138-162). London and New York: I.B. Tauris.

Wimmer, J. (2007). *(Gegen-)Öffentlichkeit in der Mediengesellschaft Analyse eines medialen Spannungsverhältnisses*. Wiesbaden: VS Verlag.

Wong, J. C. (2016, September 9). Zuckerberg accused of censorship after Facebook deletes 'napalm girl'. *The Guardian*. Retrieved from https://www.theguardian.com/technology/2016/sep/08/facebook-mark-zuckerberg-napalm-girl-photo-vietnam-war

Zitrain, J. (2008). *The Future of the Internet and How to Stop it*. Yale: Yale University Press.

Social Movements and Social Media in a Post-Revolutionary Political Culture: Constitutional Debates in Egypt[1]

Hanan Badr

1 Introduction

After popular mobilizations successfully toppled the dictators in Tunisia, Egypt and Libya in 2011, a substantial amount of research focused on the role of the media in mobilizing popular dissent in the Arab uprisings. One strand of literature argued that the Internet expanded the public sphere, allowed more pluralism, and challenged the centralized political system. According to this argumentation, the new media enabled autonomous decentralized communication by challenging actors (Shirky, 2011; Khamis & Vaughn, 2011; Abdulla, 2011). The Internet and communication technologies raised interest in online public deliberations, with the World Wide Web perceived as incorporating the utopian democratic communication. The hypothesis postulated that the digital public sphere has more potential to empower citizens through access, to limit censorship and to enable deliberations to form an enlightened opinion. While the transformation years 2011-2013 in Egypt came with increased freedoms and lively contestations, the course of events showed, toppling Mubarak brought about a "change of regime without a regime change" (Wickham, 2013, p. 154). Scholars initially tried to adapt the transformation paradigm and interpret the events of the so-called Arab Spring as a fourth wave of democratization; however, the evolving regional dynamics replaced this hypothesis with the paradigm of resilient authoritarianism. The result was a mere transfer of power to a new political elite, yet with the same mechanisms of marginalization and repression dictating the political game.

1 This publication is based on a research project sponsored by the German Federal Ministry of Education and Research (BMBF) and realized at the Orient-Institut Beirut, Cairo Office.

C. Richter et al. (Hrsg.), *Digital Media and the Politics of Transformation in the Arab World and Asia*, Studies in International, Transnational and Global Communications, https://doi.org/10.1007/978-3-658-20700-7_8

Amid the rise of politicized debates during 2011-2013, the constitutional debates largely dominated deliberations in politics and media as they symbolized the future of the new republic. Various actors participated in these public deliberations, which intended to draft a new constitution. The process showed intense contestation and legal battles over the post-revolutionary rational-legal legitimacy. However, these constitutional deliberations also demonstrated parallels to the legal mechanisms in place before 2011.[2] Throughout his three decades in power, Mubarak opted for a rational-legal form of legitimacy to justify his rule. He often referred the political struggles to the judicial processes for the regime's own survival: to maintain order, to create the impression of the rule of law, and to shift responsibility for unpopular policies to other judicial institutions (Moustafa, 2007, p. 1ff.). Yet, sometimes the rulings of the relatively autonomous Supreme Constitutional Court (SCC) challenged the authoritarian regime, expanded freedom of expression, and shielded the civil society from executive domination. However, the judiciary never questioned the "core legal mechanisms" of the regime that maintained its power over the political life (Moustafa, 2007, p. 232). Eventually, the legal battles became sites of political contestation and at the same time a base for legitimacy. In addition to the legal measures, Mubarak's regime managed its survival through a strategy of limited pluralism to sustain the political process and lend it some credibility. The regime used two tactics: a) marginalization and exclusion of radical opponents, such as the followers of political Islam, and b) co-optation of actors who moderately challenged the official discourse (Lust-Okar, 2005). These tactics divided the structure of contestation and encouraged rivalries to prevent any possible alliance, which resulted in a weakened and fragmented opposition. These strategies – relying on the legal legitimacy and dividing the opposition – resulted in a polarized competition, non-strategic deliberations and volatile short-term alliances in the political landscape, which were unable to foster a soundly based, consensual and credible alternative for the public (Shukr, 2015, p. 11).

After the uprisings in 2011, Mubarak's collapse resulted in a new legitimacy crisis due to the power vacuum he left in the executive office. Usually, revolutions are a structural break from the norm, so they offer a "structural opportunity" (Collins, 2001, p. 177) for actors to challenge the basis of the regime. Therefore, Egypt's post-revolutionary period witnessed an urgent quest for re-gaining legitimacy that could secure the foundations of the new political rule. While the Supreme Council of the Armed Forces (SCAF) intervened to avoid more destabilization and an eventual state collapse, it also adopted legal mechanisms to establish a

2 Similarly, Anna Antonakis in this volume emphasizes the trajectories of hegemonic power relations after a regime change in Tunisia.

new legitimacy after the removal of the ailing autocrat from power. The SCAF channelled the transformation process into slow-paced legal channels, instead of initiating a quick and radical political change. Launching the transition period, the SCAF started by annulling the 1971 constitution along with its 2007 amendments, and organized the first referendum on the constitution on 19 March 2011. While a new constitution was not a high priority for the protesters, they wanted neither Mubarak nor his son to run for presidential elections in 2011. At the same time, in 2007 controversial constitution amendments took place that reinforced the presidential powers and the authoritarian character of the regime (Bernard-Maugiron, 2008, p.416). Against this background, a constitution replacing the old one would serve as a source of renewed rational-legal legitimacy for the post-revolutionary political order. Indeed, Egypt was on a turbulent legal and political path as the short period between 2011 and 2014 witnessed a "constitutional confusion" that included the initial amendments to the 1971 constitution, ten constitutional declarations, two constitutions, and one special communiqué issued by the SCAF on 3 July 2013 (Mady, 2013, p.45). These numerous drafts and declarations aimed at legitimizing the new power holders, whether these were the military or the Muslim Brotherhood (Leihs & Aly, 2016). The legal manoeuvres aimed at establishing and fostering legitimacy on rational-legal grounds (Brown & Mokhtar, 2013). Egypt's post-Mubarak transition and constitutional deliberations have been "anything but straightforward", because every step has been politically or legally challenged by one group or another (Democracy Reporting, 2013). Hence, the bitter and protracted constitutional debates emerged.

After the initial euphoric interpretations of what has been framed the "Arab Spring", few communication studies on Egypt tried to explain the deliberative processes that took place in the open phase from 2011-2013. The present article links the movement's constitutional debates to the concept of political culture and its specific characteristics in Egypt, in particular the role of the religious and nationalistic discourses in shaping public deliberations. Against this background, the focus of this article is to scrutinize the online deliberations of the social movements surrounding the 2012 constitution in a transformative context. This will show how political actors from a broad political spectrum used the digital media to articulate their claims in the constitutional debates. Empirically, this study focuses on deliberative processes of four selected social movements as shown in the online communication of their official Facebook pages. These are the April 6 Youth Movement, Revolutionary Socialists, Muslim Brotherhood and Salafyo Costa. After Mubarak's ouster, each movement promoted a political project with different ideological foundations. The selected movements represent four major ideological currents in Egypt: the social democratic, the socialist leftist, the political Islamist and the independent Salafist. In spite of their different histories and stages of development, the movements have the following characteristics in common: a) they primarily target youth, whether in their recruitment or rhetoric, however to a lesser degree the Muslim Brotherhood; b) they make intensive use of social media in their political communication; c) at some point, all of them have constituted an oppositional challenge to the political system, with the exception of the Muslim Brotherhood between June 2012 and July 2013 while the Brotherhood member Mohammed Morsi was president; and finally, d) all social movements were propelled into the foreground of the mainstream media after the revolution. Each of the selected social movements is briefly presented below.

2 Actors in Deliberation: The Selected Case Studies

The April 6 Youth Movement (hereinafter referred to as April 6) was officially formed in May 2008 by a group of youth, after they had successfully organized the April 6 strike in 2008. This "Facebook Strike" was a virtual campaign planned in solidarity with the Mahalla workers' protests who had challenged the privatization plans and sought their social and economic rights (Radsch, 2011, p. 63).[3] April 6 describes itself as an "Egyptian resistance movement".[4] It does not have a strict ideological philosophy, but in general, it supports social democratic policies, human rights and citizenship. Its principles include a call for a civilian and democratic state based on all rights for all people. The unprecedented opening up of the public sphere in 2011 gave the movement freedom to organize several successful public campaigns. This phase witnessed a rise in its membership, but at the same time, April 6 firmly refused to become a political party. It preferred to remain a pressure group, and to maintain its independence and maneuverability. Social media play a crucial role for April 6, as a "platform providing access for the ordinary citizens" (Gharib, 2015). Despite the growing restrictions imposed by the government, the April 6 coordinator maintained in personal conversation that Facebook continues to play a role for the movement. The posts focus on timely issues in politics, economics and society. Editors pick up controversial and unique stories with a sensational angle and attractive hashtags to gain visibility and secure increased viewership. The April

3 For more information on the role of April 6 in the strike see also the contribution of Merlyna Lim in this volume.

4 Official website of the April 6 Youth Movement in the Zaytoun district, https://www.facebook.com/6april.zaitoun?fref=ts.

6 main Facebook page has launched several successful hashtags that have publicly framed political events in recent years.

Established in the early 1990s, the *Revolutionary Socialists* have a strong ideological focus on the political economy. After the collapse of the Soviet Union in 1990/91, the Revolutionary Socialists aimed at rejuvenating the socialist thought by advancing the labor movement and taking a strong anti-capitalist position against the neoliberal market economy. In their view, only a full revolution and not reform would result in successful changes to society (Revolutionary Socialists, 2015). The movement has also witnessed a generational shift towards the youth, who spurred the revival of "street politics" in Egypt (El-Hamalawy, 2007).

The Revolutionary Socialists regard the media as an important tool to reach out to the public. Selected members from the political bureau are responsible for conceptualizing and implementing the movement's media strategies, including administrating the Facebook pages. While the language on Facebook is attractive – concise, clear, and visually appealing – the Revolutionary Socialists' website offers lengthy theoretical texts or longer explanations on certain political positions (Tallima, 2015).

The third movement, the *Muslim Brotherhood*, is the oldest social movement in the sample; Hassan El-Banna founded it in 1928 while Egypt was under British rule. Its main collective identity revolves around Islam and its principles. Throughout the years, the Muslim Brotherhood has adopted the conservative approach preached by its founder. Members believed in "religious determinism" (Kandil, 2015, p. 85), meaning that spreading a righteous way of living through *da'wa* (preaching the principles of Islam) would ultimately result in the desired Islamic state. Organizationally, the Muslim Brotherhood is hierarchical; at the top of the decision-making pyramid is the Supreme Guide, who presides over the 13-member Guidance Bureau (Tadros, 2012, p. 7f.). Throughout its long and complex history, the Muslim Brotherhood has included different generations that range from dogmatic to more liberal social conservatists (Radsch, 2014, p. 77f.).

The revolution undoubtedly catapulted the Muslim Brotherhood into the foreground of politics as the "most powerful civilian actor" (Wickham, 2013, p. 154). From 2011 until 2013, the Muslim Brotherhood obtained the majority of votes in all subsequent parliamentary and presidential elections, as well as in constitutional referenda. As Pioppi observes, "[a]fter the fall of Mubarak, the Muslim Brotherhood decided to act as a stabilizing force, to abandon the street and to lend democratic legitimacy to the political process designed by the army" (Pioppi, 2013, p. 51). In 2012, their position changed, for the first time in history, from that of challengers to incumbents. During the one year of Morsi's rule, however, the broad-based coalitions and popular support slowly waned because of the Muslim Brotherhood's mismanagement as well as due to the constitutional declaration that cost them valuable legitimacy from non-Muslim Brotherhood members. This eventually led to the build-up of a wide popular dissent mobilized by secular opponents and counter-revolutionary forces against the Muslim Brotherhood. The Muslim Brotherhood's sudden and abrupt exclusion from the political scene prompted them to return to their particularistic discourse based on victimization, sacrifice and isolation from society. At the same time, disagreement between the proponents of the old guard and the proponents of the new rules borne out of the political climate since 2013 persists (Fahmi, 2015). While the Muslim Brotherhood had managed to voice their demands in a few oppositional newspapers under Mubarak, the Internet offered a remarkable new opportunity. This was reflected in a vibrant Islamist blogosphere (Richter, 2011; Radsch, 2014, p. 80). Between 2011 and 2013, unprecedented freedoms resulted in a rise, diversity, and visibility of Islamist media ranging from the Salafist-oriented Muslim Brotherhood groups to the more liberal social conservatives. Social media in particular offered a platform to committed youth for creative and cost-effective methods of communication. Because the Muslim Brotherhood includes a wide base of diverse members in terms of socio-economic, political, and religious views, the decentralized social media also reflected views that ranged from the loosely sympathetic, to the strictly dogmatic and ideological.

The fourth and youngest movement in this study is ***Salafyo Costa***. Formed in March 2011, the movement integrates identity elements by combining the corporate name of the global coffeehouse chain, Costa Coffee, with Salafism. Salafyo Costa operates independently of the traditional Salafist sheikhs, although some religious scholars remain a source of religious and moral inspiration. It wants to express a message of modernity, tolerance, and above all co-existence. Salafyo Costa tried to establish a common ground for Islamists and liberals that transcends mutual stereotypes. Since the movement's members lack common religious and ideological ground, it prefers to work on common social issues, like poverty and development (Tolba, 2012). Salafyo Costa builds its collective identity as a revolutionary group that adheres to the principles of democracy, freedom, and social justice.[5] The highest values for the group are inclusion and tolerance. Yet, since the violent dispersal of Raba'a al-Adawiya Square[6] and the killing of one of its founding members, the

5 For a discussion on the role of collective identity in social movement formation and the problems arising through the mediation in social media see the contribution of Mina Naeli and Abir Kopty in this volume.

6 During the one year of Morsi's rule, popular support slowly waned. Eventually, a campaign called Tamarod (Rebel) mobilized wide popular dissent against President Morsi. After a short three-day ultimatum, he was ousted by then Defense Minister Abdelfattah El-Sisi on 3 July 2013. A new political road map was declared. The Muslim Brotherhood reacted

movement has chosen to avoid any political discourses because of internal divisions and external restrictions (Tolba, 2015). Nowadays, Salafyo Costa has shifted its focus entirely to charity work. In 2014, it obtained a license as a non-governmental organization that organizes regular activities in the fields of development.

The social media have been crucial for the Salafyo Costa movement from the start: "Facebook is our only window to the public, because we own no other media outlets" (Antoun, 2015). In order to preserve the ideal of tolerance, the movement follows a rigid moral code in moderating its Facebook group. Five so-called elected "watchers of principles" monitor the group page for violations, along with four additional committee facilitators. They deliberate in a secret group for founding members only to decide on the posts to be published. Publishing guidelines include the following: highlighting statements and activities of the members, no incitement to hatred or racism, and no involvement in petty conflicts with other political actors (Antoun, 2015). In addition, the groups forbids celebrating rituals of any religion as well as sarcasm (Tolba, 2015). The administrators monitor posts regularly and delete inappropriate public member contributions.

3 Theoretical Framework

3.1 Deliberation, Social Movements and Social media in a Transformative Context

Deliberative processes became highly relevant in the post-Mubarak political setting from 2011 until 2013. After the 25 January 2011, the increasing politicization of the public sphere and growing freedoms encouraged political and social actors to deliberate on a new social contract. Indeed, various contesting actors, both secular and religious social movements, outlined new future prospects for Egypt. Deliberation is "a process in which participants exchange arguments and counter-arguments and thereby become informed of the views of one another" (Wiklund, 2005, p. 251). It can serve as a tool to reach consensus and create solutions to matters of common interest, in which the actors negotiate their own particular interests and take into

by creating the so-called Anti-Coup Alliance (ACA) or National Alliance Supporting Legitimacy (NASL) that organized sit-ins at Raba'a al-Adawiya and Al-Nahda squares, intending to defend the legitimacy of Morsi's presidency. The confrontation ended in a massacre in Raba'a al-Adawiya and Al-Nahda Squares after a raid by the Egyptian security forces.

account the views of other actors. Here, reason and argumentative persuasion as opposed to tradition and coercion function as a source of validating arguments (Dahlberg, 2005, p. 112). While deliberation seeks a consensus, the process does not mean eliminating the radical ideological groups that hold strongly to their positions and do not readily agree to consensus (Dahlberg, 2005, p. 127). The ideal rests on the assumptions that collective decisions produce "better" decisions than unilateral or exclusive approaches (Connelly, 2009, p. 185). Ideally, rational deliberations use public reason to overcome differences and divisions by showing willingness to compromise and adapt. At the same time, societies need convergence; otherwise, decisions cannot be common and binding for the population, if only conflict and hegemony characterize the mode of communication. Public deliberation processes enable "social learning through rational argumentation to produce democratically legitimate outcomes" (Wiklund, 2005, p. 252). In particular, the theory of liberal democratic citizenship aims to minimize the differences and to provide access for all citizens to the public sphere and to encourage an egalitarian spirit among them to put aside their particularities. In the post-modern world, however, a dilemma arises if the consensus ignores the particularities that might constitute the core of people's identities, such as their beliefs, political affiliations, gender, and religion. Maintaining particular interests while at the same time trying to bridge the differences through generalizable arguments for the common good might seem to be irreconcilable goals (Gencoglu-Onbasi, 2011, p. 435ff.).

Therefore, the discursive principle of the public sphere emphasizes the transparent rational and critical discussions necessary to reach either consensus or an argumentatively developed majority. Ultimately, this enhances the legitimacy of decision-making and community building among participants in the communicative and discursive practices (Jarren & Donges, 2011, p. 100ff.). Ideally, public discourses are always in the process of formation, because the contestation of positions on social and political issues is constantly developing to accommodate rational legitimacy and the force of a better argument. The more complex an issue, the more time the public deliberations will take until diverse actors reach a minimum consensus. Dialectically, the resulting consensus will be a starting point for further deliberations, and so on. In an open political system, the Internet can function as a deliberative forum by adding pluralistic voices to the public deliberations, thus strengthening the otherwise marginalized actors.[7] The decision-making process can incorporate the inputs into the official cycle, and hence respond to the critical voices and strengthen itself from within.

---

7 For a critical review of this perspective see the contribution of Anna Antonakis in this volume.

These assumptions are particularly relevant to the role of the media after the Arab uprisings. Since the protests revealed the prominent role of online discourses in destabilizing the political structure, a massive research wave has focused on the liberating role of the Internet and communication technology in the Arab uprisings (Herrera, 2011; Diamond, 2010; Dutton, 2013; Badr, 2015). However, mere access to open and free communication does not progress the arguments among participants; other core values such as mutual recognition and responsiveness are crucial to building overlapping consensus through deliberation (Rawls, 1987). While political developments after the so-called Arab Spring raise questions about the potentials and limits of social media as an online forum, thus far little research has investigated the online deliberative processes in the Egyptian context after 2011. There are two opposing lines of argumentations, with evidence for both: The first one acknowledges the potential of Facebook as a forum of collective deliberation, which can prioritize issues and expectations. Social media can provide a channel for pluralistic political debate, especially if they connect to traditional forms of media and civil society (Iskander, 2011, p. 14). Therefore, social media can function as a tool for national debate, shaping public opinion, supporting massive political and grassroots organizations, and becoming a primary source of news (Sabry, 2013). The other line of argumentation sees that badly facilitated negotiations can reproduce hegemony and aggravate conflict in divided societies. Due to Egypt's long history of having a "monolithic and restrictive media environment" (Khamis, 2011, p. 1160), citizens have limited experience in negotiating pluralistic interests. Even studies in established Western democracies demonstrated that increased access does not necessarily mean higher deliberative quality (Jarren & Donges, 2011, p. 112). While social media can trigger informational cascades in tightly controlled media environments, they have little effect on the ultimate outcomes of the real political power struggles. On the contrary, social media activism is likely to generate greater repression over time that targets both the alternative and mainstream media spheres (Faris, 2013, p. 182ff.). This study will reflect on both views connecting the role of the social media in Egypt to the concept of political culture.

3.2 Nationalist and Religious Discourses in Egypt's Radically Polarized Political Culture

Political culture explains the setting in which the deliberation processes took place in Egypt. The concept refers to the sum of attitudes towards the political system and its components, as well as attitudes to one's own role as a citizen in this system (Fuchs, 2010, p. 221). In this sense, the concept comprises attitudes towards the political order in general (polity), the decision-making system (politics), and the result in actual politics (policies). As a learned process, political culture can change over time, but is mostly stable. Political and social institutions, economic structures, personal and collective experiences, historical events, as well as the practices of the political elite shape the political culture.

In Egypt, the political culture is radically polarized, where lines of divisions do not derive from ethnic or religious backgrounds, but from ideological sources. Distinct dichotomies in social and political narratives show a high level of contestation among actors. The polarized pluralism reflects a broad political spectrum in which citizens and actors tend to take clear ideological positions. This differs from the moderate pluralism, where the ideological differences are not so sharp, and actors tend to be located more towards the centre and are more willing to accept the essence of the political order (Hallin & Mancini, 2004, p. 60). In addition, Egyptian political culture is characterized by an illiberalism that has limited the capacity for negotiating social and political issues. The political centre has the capacity to shape the mainstream political culture as well as to foster certain illiberal attitudes through classic socialization practices, such as education and media. In the Mubarak era, scholars spoke of the "persistence of authoritarianism as a source of radicalization" (Storm, 2009, p. 997) as well as of a "decline of pluralism" (Brownlee, 2002, p. 6).

The present article operationalizes political culture as the attitudes towards the collective self-perceived identity.[8] Displaying a high national pride, two sources of cultural power shape the Egyptian political culture. Discourses of national patriotism and religious sentiments influence the public sphere and constitute powerful cultural access points for the political actors. While the official narratives of national patriotism remain largely uncontested, the religious discourses put forward by competing actors display a deeper divide.

The national patriotic discourse in Egypt "represents the post-independence national narratives that were constructed by the state elite, as well as reconfigured to serve the goals of the regime consolidation and maintenance" (Brand, 2014, p. 1). Since the overthrow of King Farouk in 1952, the official foundational narrative has focused on the successful anti-colonial revolution, national liberation, and the establishment of the Republic of Egypt (Brand, 2014, p. 6-67). Promises to alleviate the socio-economic grievances attempt to discursively build the legitimacy of the ruler. The Weberian state is "an authoritative set of institutions with sovereignty over a territory and the legitimate use of force" (Sika, 2014, p. 76). It monopolizes

8 Although attitudes towards the political system and society, including their various components, as well as attitudes towards international actors and powers constitute an important part of political culture, they go beyond the scope of this article.

the official narrative through the sectors of education, culture, and security, which uphold, continually reproduce, and adapt the narrative to the changing contextual variables. Immediately after Mubarak's removal, public attitudes towards the political actors favored the SCAF as the governing authority to peacefully lead the transition to democracy and hand over power to an elected civilian president (DEDI, 2015, p. 22). Egypt's military embodied the official narrative of nationalism and patriotism. Until now, the SCAF publicly has built its legacy on nationalism, competence and sacrifice for the nation. Choosing to oust Mubarak in response to the protests bolstered its credibility – as the prominent Tahrir slogan in 2011, "The people and the army are one hand", showed.

Religious discourses often have influenced debates in the Egyptian public sphere. Religion is a source of traditional legitimacy in Weberian social theory and functions as a source of cultural power in Habermas' terms. Even in secular countries, employing religious arguments has an advantage in public deliberations, especially on morally contested issues, because it provides a discursive opportunity structure to the social actors who use it, as in the issue of abortion (Ferree et al., 2002, p. 84). In recent decades, Egypt's political culture has shown increasing indicators of Islamization from below. Publicly neglecting or challenging religious norms and practices has become increasingly difficult (Flores, 2012, p. 6). Public opinion polls show that the majority of the population support a form of democracy that is consistent with religious edicts, even if the respective ideologies are different (Hafez, 2010, p. 60).

The role of religious discourses in public deliberations raises two main questions. First, which authority should set the tone of the religious discourse, interpret religious texts, and shape the deliberative processes by means of religiously compelling arguments. In the absence of a hierarchical clerical system in Sunni Islam, a plurality of voices exists. In Egypt, different representatives of Islam compete for power over interpretation of texts and for popularity among religious Muslims. They include Al-Azhar, the Salafists and the Muslim Brotherhood. These religious actors vary in their loyalties, pragmatism, and flexibility. Since the days of President Nasser, Al-Azhar, the widely acknowledged traditional mosque and university, has been weakened through its co-optation by the regime and financial dependence on the state; thus, much of its independence has been compromised (Sika, 2014, p. 80). While – mostly Saudi-financed – Salafists were newcomers to the political scene and added complexity to it, they have become more inclined to adopt a pragmatic and practical discourse (Al-Anani & Mallik, 2013, p. 57).

The second question on the influence of religion is its capacity to form consensus. Religion is binary in essence, as it differentiates between believers and non-believers. In Egypt, political actors have used conservative religious discourse to delegitimize the opposition from the liberal and leftist camps as well as believers from other confessions. The phase from February 2011 until mid-2013 witnessed a "marathon of national elections and referenda", which stressed only religious particularities and aggravated the polarization of society (Maghraoui, 2014). Mixing religion with politics stifled the ability of the secular powers to state open political criticisms to Islamist actors, who had debunked them as infidels (Hamzawy, 2014, p. 406), and resulted in a binary worldview that channelled political communication in a non-reciprocal pattern. The logic of polarized dichotomies dictated the public deliberations, which led to heavily contested and fragmented discourses, aggravated by external media pluralism and an obvious parallelism between the press and political positions. This influenced the constitution-writing process.

4 Method and Sample

This article analyzes the online political discourses by four social movements in the controversial constitution debates of 2011–2013. The selected social media are the official Facebook pages of April 6, Revolutionary Socialists and Salafyo Costa, and the Muslim Brotherhood's Facebook page *IkhwanOnline*. Empirically, the paper applies qualitative content analysis to all Facebook posts related to the issue of the draft constitution within the period of 13 February 2011 to 10 April 2013. This phase started with suspension of the 1971 constitution by the SCAF in February 2011 (yet it was officially voided in March 2011 after the referendum), and ended with the decision of the Supreme Committee for Elections to postpone the parliamentary elections announced for April-May 2013 (which took place two years later in November 2015 due to the interruption of the transformation process). Figure 1 illustrates in detail the timeline and the polarized climate of the drafting process of the 2012 constitution, which the military later annulled in 2013.

The total material consisted of 487 posts. April 6 had published 168 posts on its Facebook page about the constitution, the Revolutionary Socialists had published 151, the Muslim Brotherhood 154 and Salafyo Costa 14 posts. The study applied qualitative content analysis through the inductive category development technique (Mayring, 2010) and reduced the textual material into central statements that describe the type and content of argumentation. Varying in length and complexity, the posts contained 965 central statements. The analysis yielded two broad categories: procedural arguments deliberating the constitution drafting process itself; and arguments related to the constitution text itself (for more details see Badr & Ghali, 2016).

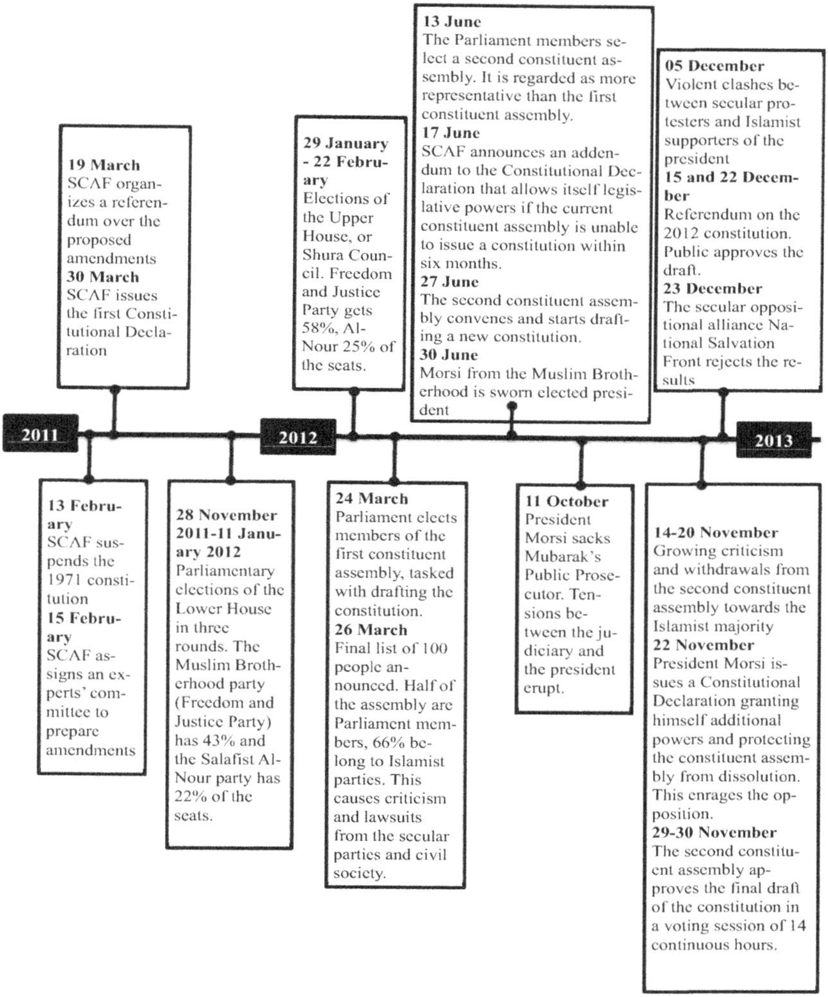

Fig. 1 Timeline of major milestones in the drafting process of the 2012 constitution in Egypt (Based on Aly & Leihs, 2016, visualized by author)

5 Polarized Online Deliberations: From "Egypt's Most Glorious Constitution" to Egypt's "Constitution of Shame"

The four social movements engaged in an intensive contestation either to legitimize or to de-legitimize the constitution drafting process and its text. The constitutional debates had a procedural and a content-related strand of arguments. On the procedural level, deliberations contested the a) representativeness and diversity of the constituent assemblies, b) the quality of the constitutional deliberations, and c) the desired outcome of the constitutional debates, consensus versus particular interests. On the level of the constitution's content, the movements contested the identity of the state in the envisaged text. In each aspect, claims reflected the collective identity of each social movement, and connected the arguments to the nationalistic and religious discourses as cultural access points in the Egyptian political culture.

5.1 Criteria of Representativeness and Diversity of the Constituent Assemblies

A remarkable number of posts discussed who writes the constitution and deliberated the formation criteria of the first and second constituent assemblies. Fairness of representation, degree of diversity, and the qualifications of the assembly members were central values. April 6 and the Revolutionary Socialists expressed skepticism towards both successive constituent assemblies and mostly delegitimized them, except during short phases of national reconciliation in summer 2012. The April 6 movement completely rejected the first constituent assembly, calling it unrepresentative because it did not represent the Egyptian people justly (April 6 Facebook page on 28 March 2012). In the early days of the second constituent assembly, the April 6 Facebook page praised the cooperation among the members and the strenuous efforts to collect the suggestions of people from all lifestyles, provinces and syndicates to ensure pluralism. Yet with growing illiberal and exclusionary practices of the Islamist members, conflicts erupted and the Coptic, secular, and young members gradually withdrew (see Figure 1). This prompted April 6 members to withdraw eventually on the basis that the second assembly was not inclusive as it lacked representation of women, youth, and Copts: "Old men are messing with our future and the future of our children" (April 6, 30 November 2012). The movement then expressed its skepticism towards the efficiency and credibility of the second constituent assembly rushing into the voting process over the draft in November 2012. The Revolutionary Socialists firmly rejected the first constituent assembly as it reflected political loyalism, while the Parliament neglected legal expertise. In the second constituent assembly, the Revolutionary Socialists participated in a hearing where they called for radical reform of the political system: "A revolution means all power and wealth to the people. The constitution simply should reflect that." (Revolutionary Socialists, 22 July 2012).

The Muslim Brotherhood, with its member Mohammed Morsi holding the presidential office, maintained that neither of the two constituent assemblies lacked legitimate foundation because they both reflected the electoral majority. Therefore, the popular will shall ensure fair representation. The Muslim Brotherhood also proclaimed that other weak oppositional movements and parties should not complain about their lack of representation, as they lacked the mobilization power and public trust because they are elitist and isolated. The Muslim Brotherhood described the first constituent assembly as efficient, patriotic, and loyal.[9] In the face of growing criticism towards the second constituent assembly, the Muslim Brotherhood highlighted the progress achieved by assembly members who worked hard despite the negative polarized atmosphere (IkhwanOnline, 31 July 2012).

The degree of diversity vs. Islamist domination in drafting the constitution was debated heavily by the different actors. The secular movements, namely April 6 and the Revolutionary Socialists persistently criticized the Muslim Brotherhood's dominance in the constitution drafting process. Both movements argued that the constituent assembly reflected the Islamic current that already combined legislative and executive powers. The secular movements maintained that the majority should not write the constitution all alone because the document will build the state foundation for generations to come: "A constitution belongs to all people and should be written by consensus" (The April 6, 20 March 2012). Sharper in tone, the Revolutionary Socialists absolutely rejected the first constituent assembly because an "arrogant and power-hungry gang" controlled it (Revolutionary Socialists, 2 April 2012).

However, at the opposite end of the spectrum, the Muslim Brotherhood maintained that the constituent assembly ensured the representation of all population segments, which guaranteed the desired consensual approach. The movement accused the secular powers of sabotaging the democratic process (IkhwanOnline, 29 March 2012).

As Salafyo Costa gave a statement in the hearing session in the second constituent assembly, it framed its participation as a positive role towards rebuilding Egypt. Salafyo Costa confirmed their identity as a pro-revolutionary movement

9 Statement by the Islamist legal scholar and public figure, Tarek El-Bishry, posted on IkhwanOnline, 27 March 2012.

that seeks co-existence and mutual understanding. As defined by their goal, the movement wanted to prove that co-existence was possible by solving conflicts constructively, and that reform was possible from within the official bodies. Giving recommendations and suggestions for the draft constitution was seen to be for the benefit of the country.

5.2 Quality of the Constitutional Deliberations: Transparency and Speed of the Drafting Process

A substantial part of the procedural arguments within the constitutional debates reflected on the quality of the constitutional debates themselves. For April 6, transparency was a high ideal. It was realized though awareness campaigns. The movement argued that the constitution is public property, so it is the people's right to participate in the process. Under the slogan, "Write your constitution", the movement engaged in a deliberative discussion with the Facebook page members, empowering them with information and collecting their suggestions. The movement coordinator undertook the task of delivering all suggestions to the constituent assembly. For the Muslim Brotherhood, TV live coverage of the constitutional deliberations and hearing sessions established transparency. Salafyo Costa defined the constitution as a "social contract" that regulates the relationship between the state and its citizens (Salafyo Costa, 5 July 2012). As a group of heterogeneous non-politicized Egyptians, the page tried to spread awareness and to encourage deliberations among its members, and asked them to share their aspirations for the new republic. In a lengthy post, Salafyo Costa explained the importance of the constitution in shaping competencies. It aimed at building a cross-ideological identity highlighting the ideals of citizenship and the common good. It engaged Facebook users: "what would you like to see in my constitution, in your constitution, in our constitution?" (Salafyo Costa, 5 July 2012).

In terms of the speed of the deliberative processes, the Muslim Brotherhood Facebook page asserted that the constitution drafting should be swift in order to reach the desired political stability quickly. The ruling Muslim Brotherhood focused on the benefits of a speedy process to stimulate economic prosperity. At the same time, they mentioned that the deliberations over the draft constitution took weeks, and were not limited to the final sessions alone (IkhwanOnline, 20 December 2012). On the other hand, while April 6 cautiously agreed on the need for stability, it also argued that it did not come with "half-baked texts"; issuing a non-consensual constitution would only deepen the rifts in the Egyptian public opinion (April 6, 25 November 2012). April 6 was critical of the "race against time" to push through the constitution drafting process. As Figure 1 shows, the SCAF set a deadline in June 2012 that the constituent assembly should finish the constitution within six months of its selection. Therefore, April 6 criticized the pressure put by the SCAF to coerce the political powers into choosing either to establish a consensus on a new constitution, or to reinstate the old 1971 constitution (April 6, 1 December 2012). Both April 6 and the Revolutionary Socialists agreed that the SCAF was the true power holder in post-Mubarak Egypt, as it dictated the transformation path by setting goals and deadlines, which prevented deliberations from developing naturally in their own time.

5.3 Desired Outcome of the Constitutional Debates: Consensus vs. Particular Claims

All movements agreed that consensual deliberation on the constitution will establish the desired national unity, yet the argumentation about this varied according to the political positions of each movement. April 6 repeated the slogan, "everything can be done by contest, but the constitution should be reached through consensus" (April 6, 10 April 2012). The movement initiated an awareness campaign, discussing the individual paragraphs of the then proposed constitution. It maintained that Egyptians should create consensus by deliberations, not by a numerical majority, because the constitution belonged to all Egyptians (April 6, 20 April 2012). Shortly before the referendum in mid-December 2012, April 6 lamented that the Muslim Brotherhood had wasted a real opportunity to build a post-revolutionary consensus on the constitution by arguing in a religious discourse not a democratic one (April 6, 22 December 2012), as will be shown in the discussion over the debate on Egypt's identity. The Revolutionary Socialists were highly critical of the non-consensual approach of the Muslim Brotherhood, which neglected the voices of oppositional minorities.

The Muslim Brotherhood maintained that consensus resulted from the referendum on the constitution. Since the constitution belonged to the people, and not to the rivaling political elites, the Muslim Brotherhood argued that it was entitled to speak on behalf of the people because it had the electoral majority (IkhwanOnline, 17 July 2012). The Muslim Brotherhood maintained that the consensus inside the second constituent assembly exceeded 90 percent (IkhwanOnline, 31 October 2012). The Muslim Brotherhood Facebook page described the opposition as obstructing the dialogue and only wanting to reach a political deadlock without offering a real alternative. Salafyo Costa criticized all parties, religious and secular, for being unable to co-exist and to deliberate constructively. Summing up, the analysis showed that all movements agreed on establishing consensus, yet the instruments to reach it varied from one movement to another depending on its power and political position. While for the Muslim Brotherhood, consensus equaled the electoral majority, the Revolutionary Socialists and April 6 saw that only negotiations and inclusion of the opposition established the needed consensus.

5.4 Constitutional Debates on the Identity of the Egyptian State

On the content level, the social movements discursively engaged in a fierce contest over the identity of the state. In line with Egypt's divided political culture, the Facebook pages reflected opposed political views in Egypt over the role and visibility of religion as well as over the nationalistic role of the military in the state. Regarding the role of religion in the constitution, April 6 blamed the Islamist voices, especially the Salafists, of over-emphasizing the issue of religion and Islamic identity to establish their hegemony on moral grounds. April 6 further criticized the strong focus on religion in the constitution articles 2, 4 and 219.[10] These three articles, respectively, defined the identity of the state as Islamic, described the role of Al-Azhar in interpreting the Shari'a, and named the sources of Islamic jurisprudence. Therefore, April 6 accused the Islamist powers of using a "constructed danger, because Islam was in no real threat in Egypt" (April 6, 25 November 2012). Similarly, the leftist Revolutionary Socialists saw that the constitution reflected the visions of narrow-minded Islamists who misused the religious rhetoric in politics in order to manipulate the people and to transform Egyptian identity into a "Wahhabi-inspired culture" (Revolutionary Socialists, 22 March 2012).

On the other hand, the Muslim Brotherhood accused the secular opposition of seeking to destroy Egypt's Islamic identity, since the constitution derived from the Shari'a and Islamic heritage. As long as the opposition threatened Egypt's identity, the Muslim Brotherhood was determined to protect it. The movement launched a campaign called "a constitution that resembles us" (IkhwanOnline, 31 October 2012).

Because of its Salafist ideological roots, the role of religion was important to Salafyo Costa. Yet, diverse and independent as the movement is, it offered a unique point of view in the constitutional debates. While the movement criticized some articles for not conforming to the Shari'a, at the same time it tried to interpret citizenship in light of religious principles. Salafyo Costa wrote that the efforts to

10 It should be noted that the 1971 constitution also included references to the Islamic Shari'a in article 2.

pass the constitution would ultimately fail: "If the legal text did not reflect pluralist Egypt as it was, then it would not last long" (Salafyo Costa, 29 March 2012).

In a limited number of posts, the social movements debated the role of the military in the 2012 constitution. Both April 6 and Revolutionary Socialists criticized what they called the "militarization of the 2012 constitution". This referred to the privileged status of the military in the political and economic system. The April 6 movement rejected to bring civilians before martial courts, fearing its unjust use would stifle the political opposition or journalists (April 6, 19 November 2012). The Revolutionary Socialists were by far the most critical about the role of the military in the constitutional drafting process. They argued that the SCAF used the conflicts among the civil society while silently leading a counter-revolution to secure its own political power and survival (Revolutionary Socialists, 15 April 2012.). In its Facebook page, the Muslim Brotherhood denied that the constitution favored the military. It maintained that it was Egypt's best constitution in history as it secured the civil rights and freedoms. Finally, the Salafyo Costa movement rejected certain articles that privileged the political role of the military in public life. They said that the constitution lacked checks and balances for the military budget. The establishment of a National Defense Council with a military majority and a guardianship role lacked control by civilian institutions (Salafyo Costa, 20 November 2012).

The results show clearly that the social movements adopted different positions towards the 2012 draft constitution. April 6 and the Revolutionary Socialists refused the constitution and vehemently mobilized the public for a no-vote. April 6 derided the constitution with many negative labels that reflected its inadequacy and domination by the Islamists. On their Facebook page it repeatedly called the draft "the one faction constitution", "the deformed constitution", "the corrupt constitution" and "the Muslim Brotherhood's constitution" (11 December 2012). In addition, the movement organized nation-wide campaigns and protests under the slogan: "Your constitution does not represent us". The Revolutionary Socialists firmly opposed the draft constitution as well. They escalated their confrontational style against the Muslim Brotherhood after the Ittihadeya presidential palace clashes on 5 December 2012, only ten days before the referendum. "The constitution shall only pass over our dead bodies", the Revolutionary Socialists wrote (8 December 2012). In the clashes, Islamist militias beat up and tortured secular protesters, including prominent members of the Revolutionary Socialists. In their posts, the movement labeled the constitution "the constitution of shame" and "the exclusionary constitution" and their page covered the anti-constitution activities and campaigns (13 December 2012).

The Muslim Brotherhood called the public for a yes-vote. Their Facebook page framed it as the "most glorious constitution for Egyptians", a constitution that would bring dignity and prosperity to Egyptian citizens. It highlighted the political gains as well as the stability that would benefit the country's economy. The Muslim Brotherhood's Facebook page repeatedly highlighted the president's efforts to open a national dialogue (IkhwanOnline, 25 December 2012). Finally, the discourse of Salafyo Costa was not as critical of the constitution as that of the two other movements. Highlighting co-existence, the movement wanted to offer a pragmatic solution beyond polarization and towards independent thinking. However, they strongly opposed the boycott as a political option: "Go out and say what you think, but do not boycott!" the page urged (Salafyo Costa, 3 December 2012). At the same time, unlike other Islamists, Salafyo Costa defended the protests and mobilization against the draft constitution, as criticism of the constitution was said to improve it.

6 The Social Movements and the Evolving Constitutional Debates

This article analyzed the constitutional debates in post-revolutionary Egypt in order to understand the transformative processes within a radically polarized political culture between 2011 and 2013. In the debates, social movements contested both the procedures and the text of the constitutional draft. Both the religious and the nationalistic discourses shaped the Egyptian constitutional debates over the new social contract. The evolution of the online discourses pointed to the tension between the particularistic and the universal claims of the social movements. While the radically polarized political culture did not prevent the moment of unity of mobilization in Tahrir Square, this did not guarantee success in the subsequent political bargaining processes over power. The analysis of the constitutional debates does not support the euphoric hypothesis of technological determinism because the results give reason to doubt the deliberative capacity of the social media alone to reach minimal consensus through rationalized deliberation processes. Throughout the conflict-laden transitional period, the particularistic agenda of most social movements dominated the foreground, allowing little room for universal argumentation to create a degree of overlapping consensus through public reasoning. Deliberative processes alternated between polarization and consensus, depending on the political position and degree of pragmatism of each social movement. Indeed, the constitutional debates showed a brief episodic reconciling dialogue among the different actors, when social movements temporarily attempted to form a broad consensus in summer 2012.

The contestation over the constitutional debates changed over time according to the political position of the social movement in particular political moments. For example, April 6, the Revolutionary Socialists, and Salafyo Costa were optimistic about the second constituent assembly formed in June 2012 and initially participated in the hearings. Yet, with increasing Islamist domination and exclusionary practices during the constitutional drafting process, the April 6 movement coordinator withdrew from the second constituent assembly and strongly delegitimized it. The Revolutionary Socialists and Salafyo Costa also changed their deliberative style. When the more powerful Muslim Brotherhood initiated inclusion mechanisms, the weaker opposition followed a less confrontational argumentation and worked on forming a consensus, adopting a less antagonistic argumentation towards the Muslim Brotherhood. This pattern shows that exclusion of political competitors radicalizes the opposition. The more stakeholders and political actors are genuinely involved in the deliberation, the less conflictual their position and argumentation will be. One concludes that the inclusion of challengers in the decision-making process moderates their position and communicative tone. On the other hand, discrediting the political actors for their binary religious discourses, or ridiculing their mobilization capacities or secular ideological world-views radicalized the social movements' discourses. A degree of responsiveness and social learning can take place. At times of inclusion, the radical, polarized actors respond to deliberation. Evolving positions and discourses are not a sign of weakness, but signal adaptation. They prove a movement's desire to balance its particular claims with the shared universal goals of the larger society.

When contrasting the social movements, the findings show that the argumentation differed with the degree of homogeneity and dogmatism of each movement. Forging a collective identity for members in cross-ideological movements, such as April 6 and Salafyo Costa, was more challenging than in ideologically homogeneous social movements, such as the Revolutionary Socialists and the Muslim Brotherhood. The heterogeneous social movements showed a higher degree of internal deliberative processes that intended to convince their followers and members through sound argumentation and transparency. In this sense, both April 6 and Salafyo Costa were "deliberative democrats", as the consensus-building deliberative processes were more important than the (political) objective at which they are aiming (Dahlberg, 2005, p. 128). Throughout the constitutional debates, the positions and discourses of April 6 and Salafyo Costa showed a higher degree of openness and responsiveness towards the surrounding systems compared to the other two ideological social movements. Their discourses encouraged members to participate and contribute.

In particular, Salafyo Costa's discourse reflected efforts to reach a common good and national consensus, as well as co-existence. Even amid growing criticism of the constitution, the heterogeneous composition of Salafyo Costa made its position more inclusive and non-condemning. The Revolutionary Socialists and the Muslim Brotherhood, on the other hand, adopted centralized organizational models in their political communication. Neither movement used Facebook pages as an online platform to openly deliberate or negotiate their positions, since the deliberations had already taken place inside the movement's ideological organization. They used social media to publicly announce and mobilize the public for their final decisions, not to openly deliberate them.[11]

After Mubarak, the social movements' constitutional debates reflected the fundamental quest for a new source of legitimacy in times of transition. Two cultural access points in Egypt's political culture shaped the constitutional debates. Based on the nationalistic discourses, its popularity boost, and high credibility, the SCAF successfully presented itself as the only institutional guaranty for overseeing the building processes of the new political order. The Muslim Brotherhood, a longtime challenger of the Egyptian regime, posed itself in as early as March 2011 as a strong player, using credible religious rhetoric in the political field. Both sources of legitimacy, nationalism and religion, rendered the SCAF and the Muslim Brotherhood the most powerful players in the transition phase from 2011-2013.

Against this background, the results indicate that the social movements struggled over the right to represent the Egyptian people based on their self-perceived power position. In particular, the procedural components of the constitutional debates revolved around the question of entitlement to representing the popular will. While Islamists favored the principle of electoral legitimacy, the secular social movements claimed the same right based on revolutionary legitimacy. This relied on public protests and demonstrations to embody popular dissent and to achieve diversity, pluralism, and representation of the marginalized people.[12] In the delicate transition phase, the Muslim Brotherhood prioritized the electoral outcome instead of the inclusion of the extra-institutional opposition. When the movement evolved from an oppositional actor to an elected party, dominating the parliament and the presidency, it changed its discourse to a stabilizing tone to secure its power.

11 This finding corresponds with the results of Mina Naeli's study in this volume on the usage of different Internet-mediated communication channels for internal deliberation by women's rights movements in Iran.

12 In the Egyptian public discourse, the media dubbed this as a struggle between "electoral legitimacy" and "revolutionary legitimacy". The latter term, in its radical form, delegitimized the political process altogether, because it was claimed it would rely on manipulation and power imbalances.

At the same time, its position within the political system was more powerful than the other three social movements, which remained as oppositional challengers from outside the system. This explains why the Muslim Brotherhood regarded the electoral majority, their main asset, as the most important source of legitimacy and public acceptance. On the other hand, the secular social movements favored revolutionary legitimacy, in particular the Revolutionary Socialists, April 6, and to a certain extent Salafyo Costa. They lamented the exclusionary measures, lack of diversity of the constituent assemblies.

While the first post-Mubarak transformative phase in Egypt is over, the constitutional debates bear lessons for future negotiation processes in a radically polarized political culture. The failure of the actors to achieve consensus over the fundamental legal text led to the turbulence and the abrupt ending of the democratization process in mid-2013. Currently, the social movements are not publicly as active as in the open phase from 2011-2013. Yet, if the system opens up again in the future, they have the potential to reemerge as strong political actors in the public deliberations.

References

Abdulla, R. (2011). The Revolution will be Tweeted. *Cairo Review of Global Affairs, 3*, 41-49.

Al-Anani, K. & Malik, M. (2013). Pious Way to Politics: The Rise of Political Salafism in Post-Mubarak Egypt. *Digest of Middle East Studies, 22*(1), 57–73.

Aly, H. & Leihs, N. (2016). Egyptian Constitution Timeline, 13 February 2011 to 31 January 2014. *Orient Institut Studies, 4*. Retrieved from http://www.perspectivia.net/publikationen/orient-institut-studies/4-2016/aly-leihs_timeline

Antoun, M. (2015, May 15), *Interview with administrator of the Facebook page of Salafyo Costa*.

Badr, H. (2015). Limitations of social media euphoria in communication research. *Égypte/Monde arabe, 12*. Retrieved from http://ema.revues.org/3451

Badr, H. & Ghali, M. (2016). Social movements, constitution debates and online deliberations in the post-Mubarak Egyptian public sphere. *Orient Institut Studies, 4*. Retrieved from http://www.perspectivia.net/publikationen/orient-institut-studies/4-2016/badr-ghali_movements

Bernard-Maugiron, N. (2008). The 2007 Constitutional Amendments in Egypt, and Their Implications on the Balance of Power. *Arab Law Quarterly, 22*(4), 397-417.

Brand, L. A. (2014). *Official Stories: Politics and National Narratives in Egypt and Algeria*. Stanford, CA: Stanford University Press.

Brown, N. & Mokhtar, A. (2013). Egypt's judiciary between a tea ceremony and the WWE. *Foreign Policy*. Retrieved from http://foreignpolicy.com/2013/05/14/egypts-judiciary-between-a-tea-ceremony-and-the-wwe/

Brownlee, J. (2002). The decline of pluralism in Mubarak's Egypt. *Journal of Democracy, 13*(4), 6-14.

Collins, R. (2001). Weber and the Sociology of Revolution. *Journal of Classical Sociology, 1*(2), 171-194.
Connelly, S. (2009). Deliberation in the face of power: Stakeholder planning in Egypt. *Policy and Society, 28*(3), 185-195.
Cross, R. & Snow, D. A. (2012). Social Movements. In G. Ritzer (Ed.), *The Wiley-Blackwell Companion to Sociology* (p. 522-44). Malden, MA: Blackwell Publishing.
Dahlberg, L. (2005). The Habermasian Public Sphere: Taking Difference Seriously? *Theory and Society, 34*(2), 111-136.
DEDI The Danish Egyptian Dialogue Institute (2015). *The Future of Egypt's Democracy – The Voice of the Egyptian Voter.* Cairo.
Democracy Reporting (2013). Egypt's elections. More legal roadblocks. An assessment of Egypt's framework for parliamentary elections under the new constitution. *Briefing Paper, 36.* Retrieved from http://democracy-reporting.org/files/bp_36_more_roadblocks_1.pdf
Diamond, L. (2010). Liberation Technology. *Journal of Democracy, 21*(3), 69-83.
Dutton, W. (2013). The Internet and the Democratic Accountability: The Rise of the Fifth Estate. In F. Lee, L. Leung, J. L. Qiu & D. Chu (Eds.), *Frontiers in New Media Research* (p. 39-55). New York: Routledge.
El-Hamalawy, H. (2007). Comrades and Brothers. *Middle East Research and Information Project, 242.* Retrieved from http://www.merip.org/mer/mer242/comrades-brothers
Fahmi, G. (2015). The struggle for the leadership of Egypt's Muslim Brotherhood. *Carnegie Middle East Centre.* Retrieved from http://carnegie-mec.org/2015/07/14/struggle-for-leadership-of-egypt-s-muslim-brotherhood/idbr
Faris, D. (2013). *Dissent and revolution in a digital age: Social media, blogging and activism in Egypt.* London: I.B. Tauris.
Ferree, M. M., Gamson, W. A., Gerhards, J. & Rucht, D. (2002). *Shaping Abortion discourse: Democracy and the Public Sphere in Germany and the United States.* Cambridge, MA: Cambridge University Press.
Flores, A. (2012). *Säkularismus und Islam in Ägypten. Die Debatte der 1980er Jahre.* Münster: LIT.
Fuchs, D. (2010). Politische Kultur. In D. Fuchs & E. Roller (Eds.), *Lexikon Politik: Hundert Grundbegriffe* (p. 220-224). Stuttgart: Reclam.
Gencoglu-Onbasi, F. (2011). Democracy, pluralism and the idea of public reason: Rawls and Habermas in comparative perspective. *CEU Political Science Journal, 6*(3), 433-457.
Gharib, S. (2015, October 10). *Interview with a media coordinator and administrator of several April 6 movement Facebook pages.*
Hafez, K. (2010). *Radicalism and political reform in the Islamic and Western Worlds.* Cambridge, MA: Cambridge University Press.
Hallin, D. & Mancini, P. (2004). *Comparing media systems.* Cambridge: Cambridge University Press.
Hamzawy, A. (2014). On religion, politics and democratic legitimacy in Egypt, January 2011-June 2013. *Philosophy and Social Criticism, 40*(4-5), 401-406.
Hellyer, H. A. & Brown, N. (2015). Authorities in crisis: Sunni Islamic institutions. *Carnegie Endowment,* Retrieved from http://carnegieendowment.org/files/Hellyer_and_Brown_Extended_Version.pdf
Herrera, L. (2011). Egypt's Revolution 2.0: The Facebook Factor. *Jaddaliya.* Retrieved from http://www.jadaliyya.com/pages/index/612/egypts-revolution-2.0_the-facebook-factor

Iskander, E. (2011). Connecting the national and the virtual: can Facebook activism remain relevant after Egypt's January 25 uprising? *International Journal of Communication, 5*, 1225–1237.

Jarren, O. & Donges, P. (2011). *Politische Kommunikation in der Mediengesellschaft: Eine Einführung*. Wiesbaden: Springer VS.

Kandil, H. (2015). *Inside the Brotherhood*. Cambridge: John Wiley & Sons.

Khamis, S. & Vaughn, K. (2011). Cyberactivism in the Egyptian Revolution: How civic engagement and citizen journalism tilted the balance. *Arab Media & Society, 14*. Retrieved from http://www.arabmediasociety.com/?article=769

Leihs, N. & Aly, H. (2016). Public Debate or Power Play? Reflections on Egypt's 2012 constitution in the transitional period. *Orient Institut Studies, 4*. Retrieved from http://www.perspectivia.net/publikationen/orient-institut-studies/4-2016/leihs-aly_debate

Lust-Okar, E. (2005). *Structuring Conflict in the Arab World: Incumbents, Opponents, and Institutions*. New York and Cambridge, MA: Cambridge University Press.

Mady, A.-F. (2013). Popular discontent, revolution and democratization in Egypt in a globalizing world. *Indiana Journal of Global Legal Studies, 20*(1). Retrieved from http://www.repository.law.indiana.edu/ijgls/vol20/iss1/11

Maghraoui, A. (2014). Egypt's failed transition to democracy: Was political culture a major factor? *E-International Relations*. Retrieved from http://www.e-ir.info/2014/04/29/egypts-failed-transition-to-democracy-was-political-culture-a-major-factor/

Mayring, P. (2010). *Qualitative Inhaltsanalyse. Grundlagen und Techniken*. Weinheim: Beltz Verlag.

Moustafa, T. (2007). *The Struggle for Constitutional Power: Law, Politics, and Economic Development in Egypt*. Cambridge: Cambridge University Press.

Pegorim, E. (2011). Soziale Bewegungen und das Social Web: Klimawandelkampagnen auf Facebook. In M. Elsler (Ed.), *Die Aneignung der Medienkultur: Rezipienten, politische Akteure und Medienakteure* (p. 137-54). Wiesbaden: Springer VS.

Pioppi, D. (2013). Playing with fire. The Muslim Brotherhood and the Egyptian leviathan. *The International Spectator: Italian Journal of International Affairs, 48*(4), 51-68.

Povey, T. (2015). *Social movements in Egypt and Iran*. London and New York: Palgrave Macmillan.

Radsch, C. (2011). Arab Bloggers as Citizen Journalists. In J. Downing (ed.), *Encyclopedia of Social Movement Media* (p. 61-64). Thousand Oaks, CA: Sage Publications.

Radsch, C. (2014). From Brotherhood to Blogosphere: Dynamics of cyberactivism and identity in the Egyptian Ikhwan In L. Hudson, A. Iskandar & M. Kirk (Eds.), *Media Evolution on the Eve of the Arab Spring* (p. 75-99). London and New York: Palgrave Macmillan.

Rawls, J. (1987). The Idea of an overlapping consensus. *Oxford Journal of Legal Studies, 7*(1), 1-25.

Richter, C. (2011). *Medienstrategien ägyptischer Islamisten im Kontext von Demokratisierung*. Berlin: Frank &Timme.

Revolutionary Socialists. (2015) *On Socialism*. Retrieved from http://revsoc.me/revolutionary-socialists/

Sabry, B. (2013). Bassem Sabry on Social Media in Egypt. *Jaddaliya*, April 2013. Retrieved from http://www.jadaliyya.com/pages/index/11299/bassem-sabry-on-social-media-in-egypt

Shehata, D. (2011). *Youth Mobilization in Egypt: New Trends and Opportunities*. Beirut: Issam Fares Institute for Public Policy and International Affairs & American University of Beirut. Retrieved from https://www.aub.edu.lb/ifi/public_policy/arab_youth/Docu-

ments/background_paper/20121114ifi_youth%20mobilization%20in%20egypt_background_paper_Shehata_final.pdf
Shirky, C. (2011). The political power of social media: Technology, the public sphere and political change. *Foreign Affairs, 20*(2). Retrieved from https://www.foreignaffairs.com/articles/2010-12-20/political-power-social-media
Shukr, A. G. (2015). The political alliances post-January 25. *Al Malaf Al Masry, 2*(14), 9-13.
Sika, N. (2012). Dynamics of a stagnant religious discourse and the rise of new secular movements in Egypt. In B. Korany & R. El-Mahdi (Eds.), *Arab Spring in Egypt* (p. 63-81). Cairo: The American University in Cairo Press.
Sika, N. (2014). The Arab State and Social Contestation. In M. Kamrava (Ed.), *Beyond the Arab Spring: The Evolving Ruling Bargain in the Middle East* (p. 73-98). London: Oxford University Press.
Storm, L. (2009). The persistence of authoritarianism as a source of radicalization in North Africa. *International Affairs, 85*(5), 997-1013.
Tadros, M. (2012). *The Muslim Brotherhood in Contemporary Egypt: Democracy Redefined or Confined*. London and New York: Routledge.
Tallima, H. (2015, May 7). *Interview with a member of the political bureau of the Revolutionary Socialists.*
Tilly, C. (2006). *Regimes and Repertoires*. Chicago: University of Chicago Press.
Tolba, M. (2012, May 20). *Interview co-founder and former head of Salafyo Costa.*
Tolba, M. (2015, June 8). *Interview co-founder and former head of Salafyo Costa.*
Wickham, C. R. (2013). *The Muslim Brotherhood: Evolution of an Islamist Movement.* Princeton, NJ and Oxford: University Press Group Ltd.
Wiklund, H. (2005). A Habermasian analysis of the deliberative democratic potential of ICT-enabled services in Swedish municipalities. *New Media & Society, 7*(2), 247-70.

About the Authors and Editors

Anna Antonakis, Dr. phil., is a post-doctoral researcher based in Berlin. She holds an M.A and a PhD in political science from Freie Universität. She engages with Intersectional (gender) theory and theories of public and counterpublic spheres and is interested in the creation of different networks of solidarity in a digitalized world. From 2013 to 2016, she was granted a fellowship in the project "Elite Change and New Social Mobilization in the Arab World" at the Institute for Foreign and Security Studies (SWP) in Berlin.

Hanan Badr, Dr. phil., is a post-doctoral researcher at the Department for Political and Social Sciences at Freie Universität Berlin and Cairo University. She is involved in the DFG-project "Media functions in transition". Until 2015, she was group leader at the BMBF-funded Orient-Institut Beirut project "Media, Culture and Transformation". Her research fields include political communication, comparative media systems and journalism with a focus on North Africa and Europe.

Andrea Hamm, BA, is a Master's candidate in Media and Political Communication at Freie Universität Berlin. Her research foci are political communication in social media as well as media transformation in Tunisia. She currently writes her Master thesis on social bots and their communication patterns during the French legislative elections in 2017.

C. Richter et al. (Hrsg.), *Digital Media and the Politics of Transformation in the Arab World and Asia*, Studies in International, Transnational and Global Communications, https://doi.org/10.1007/978-3-658-20700-7

Cilja Harders, Dr. phil., is the director of the Centre for Middle Eastern and North African Politics at Freie Universität Berlin. Her research interests include "politics from below", local governance and the tranformation of statehood in the Maghreb, Mashreq and Gulf.

Abir Kopty, MA, is a PhD candidate at the Institute for Media and Communication Studies, Freie Universität Berlin. Her research interests include the power dynamics in online communities and the use of social media networks for social and political activism.

Merlyna Lim, PhD, is Canada Research Chair in Digital Media and Global Network Society with the School of Journalism and Communication, Carleton University, in Ottawa, Canada. Her research and teaching interests revolve around socio-political implications of media and technology, in relations to social movements, citizen participation, and social change. Prior to joining Carleton University, Lim has held positions in Princeton University, Arizona State University, and the University of Southern California, among others.

Zihao Lin, BA, finished his Bachelor in Communication at Sun Yat-sen University, China and is currently a Master's candidate at Freie Universität Berlin. His research interests include contemporary Chinese media system, cultural politics and deaf identity in the making.

Mina Naeli, MSc., is a PhD candidate at the Institute for Media and Communication Studies at Freie Universität Berlin. She holds a BSc in Management and Information Systems from the London School of Economics and Political Sciences (LSE), and a MSc in Management and Information Systems for Development from the University of Manchester. Her research interests include social aspects of information technology, e-participation, and human factors in information systems development.

Susanne Reinhardt, BA, is a Master's candidate in Media and Political Communication at Freie Universität Berlin. Her research focus is political communication in online social networks with an emphasis on normalization and democratization. She currently drafts her Master thesis on network gatekeeping on Twitter during the German national elections 2017.

Carola Richter, Dr. phil., is professor for international communication at Freie Universität Berlin. Her research interests include media systems, foreign news and protest communication, in particular in the Middle East and North Africa. She is a founding member of AREACORE – The Arab-European Association for Media and Communication Researchers and a member of the Arab-German Young Academy for Sciences and the Humanities (AGYA).

Almut Woller, MA, focuses on contemporary anarchism in Arab countries in her ongoing dissertation. She is interested academically and otherwise in the works of Karl Marx, especially from the perspective of value-criticism, as well as in anarchist theory and practice. She is co-editing a book on "care revolution" between aspirations and reality in the leftist and alternative milieu.

Made in the USA
Monee, IL
12 September 2026

62973752R00108